My White Clouds

D. G. Bacas

ISBN: 1493771620
ISBN 13: 978-1493771622

Library of Congress Control Number: 2013909371
My White Clouds
Palm Harbor, FL

Cover: Watercolor by K. Raymond Eifert 1930, commissioned by A. D. Louvis in 1929 and
painted from a panoramic photo of Bordonia,

To my parents who lived the story . . . my husband who fostered it . . . and our children and grandchildren, who will read it and pass it on.

Contents

Introduction

The day I finished the last chapter of *My White Clouds*, I happily discussed the next step—publishing the book—with my editor. To my dismay, she reminded me that I had not yet written an introduction. Introduction? Who reads an introduction, anyway, since the book itself makes the author's intentions clear. I turned to a few famous authors to learn what they had written.

The Introduction to my edition of Plutarch's *Parallel Lives* is 32 pages—much more than I would need; a collection of Shakespeare's plays begins with an overly long discussion of quartos and folios; favorite Samuel Butler translations of *The Iliad* and *The Odyssey* might not work either since they are weighed down with words such as "perforce" and "sanguinary."

I was, at last, relieved to learn that Miguel Cervantes, in 1610, also was puzzled about what to write in an obligatory introduction to *Don Quixote*.

Thanks to Cervantes, I found the courage to introduce *My White Clouds* in a straightforward manner. A disclaimer is needed here: Citing the above-mentioned sages is not meant to place this writer in their realm, but merely to call upon them as old friends—thanks to Eleni Louvis. *My White Clouds* is her story, of a girl born in a village in Greece at the beginning of the twentieth century. Eleni was my mother, who first taught me to read, and who continued to encourage my love of books. Whenever white clouds floated west above her village, they signaled fair weather and a better life to be found across the ocean. Her descriptions of silkworms as a cottage industry in her home near Sparta; of harvesting wheat and olives the old-fashioned way; of playing the mandolin with schoolmates in Ohio; and later, of her life as a mother and housewife in Washington, DC, remind us of a past that is ancient history. Eleni's story is based on her youthful journal, and she presents it with a twinkle in her eye.

Acknowledgments

My thanks to my daughter, Anne Burke, and to Mary Glerum, and Donna Bacas, who, when faced with over 200 pages of the rough draft, actually read them and made invaluable suggestions; and to Nancy Dimitry, who prepared the manuscript for the publisher.

Anne, Derek, and their household—Thomas, Stephen, and Val—as well as my son Jim and his wife Nancy—and Jessica, Casey, and Peter, each in his or her own way—helped me continue writing. Without the encouragement of my sister, Athena Davies, and my brother, Solon Bacas, I might have left our parents' memoirs on a shelf.

I am grateful to Mary Mastoris for the travels we shared with our husbands, her infinite wisdom about food and antiques, and our sessions on recipes and Greek proverbs, and grateful too to friends and readers Marie Combias, Rene Christus, and Lilyan Shepardson. Many thanks to Despina Sideridis, teacher of Greek studies, for her advice about Greek history, language, and customs.

I also would like to thank Barbara Schloss, my editor. Without her encouragement, insights, and skill, *My White Clouds* would not have been brought to fruition.

Prologue

In the year 1901, a girl was born in a village in Greece. Every day she traversed the deep ravines swirling with eerie mists, to fetch water for her family. She overcame her fear of the ghostly woods on her way to the spring by watching the clouds and dreaming that one day she would follow their path to America. Her name was Eleni, and she prayed that one of her brothers, who resided in that distant land across the sea, would send for her.

In time, her prayers were answered, and she began to write of her experiences. She named her journal *My White Clouds,* and it is the basis of this book by the same name. Eleni Louvis was my mother. Her lifetime spanned the twentieth century: as a girl in rural Greece; the wife of a veteran of World War I; the mother of a son who served in World War II; and a grandmother and great-grandmother.

I remember her as a stylish and pretty woman, with green eyes and light brown hair. As a child, I thought she had a nice life because, occasionally, she had her hair marcelled into waves at the beauty parlor, and she went to dances with my handsome father. As time went on, I realized that not only could she bake the best apple pies but also whatever she cooked was the best— except for calves liver! She raised fragrant red, pink, and yellow roses in her garden in Washington, DC, lined us up to learn whether we liked butter by placing a buttercup under our chins, showed us how much it hurt to be snapped by a snapdragon, and in spring, fed us young dandelion greens that, using her trowel and a bag, she dug up and brought home from a nearby field.

She filled our home with vases of forsythia, dogwood, roses, zinnias and marigolds, each in its season, from her garden. She was a loving mother to her four active children—although I had my doubts when she insisted that I practice the piano for half an hour every day—for which I later forgave her and thanked her.

Both parents were born in Greece, and both had left their villages while still in elementary school. By the fourth grade, most Greek children were familiar with the exploits of Odysseus, and the axioms of Plato and Aristotle. As much as they respected and loved what America stood for—once they had children—my parents began to fear that our Greek heritage would be tainted if we learned everything in English. So, they sent us to after-school classes to study, in Greek, the great thinkers of their native land.

Without television and *Sesame Street* to show what fun learning could be, many students lost interest in the old stories of Homer and Sophocles. To them, the Trojan Horse and the Cyclops were from the Dark Ages, and the Riddle of the Sphinx was old hat, and so they dropped out of Greek School. Now, however, most of these children are grandparents who take vacations in Greece and sponsor organizations that support Greek education and the preservation of the environment and the antiquities of Greece.

All episodes concerning her immediate family that Eleni described happened as she remembered them. The chorus of women, including *Theia* Despina and her family, represent the stories of people she had known.

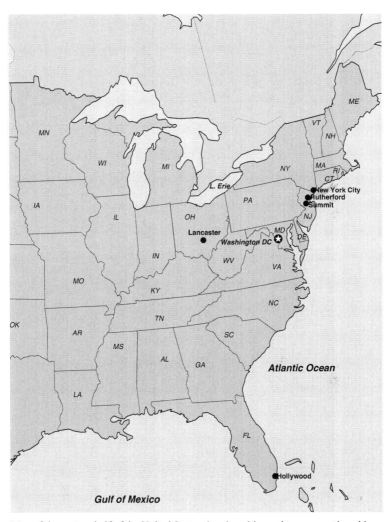

Map of the eastern half of the United States showing cities and towns mentioned in the book.

Source: The National Atlas of the United States of America

Map of Greece showing locations of cities and villages mentioned in the book.
Image credit: ⌐a href= 'http://www.123rf.com/photo_10818570_political-map-of-greece-with-the-several-states-where-south-aegean-is-highlighted.html'>schwabenblitz / 123RF Stock Photo⌐/a>

CHAPTER 1

The Family

I arche einai to imisi tou pantos.
The beginning is half of every action.
— PYTHAGORAS, 530 BC

The day of my birth has long since been forgotten, but the small village where I was born still perches, secluded, un–changing, against the foothills of snow-capped Mount Taigetus. Our town is Bordonia, in the county of Kastania, province of Lacedaemon, not far from historic Sparta.

The way to my father's house is rock-strewn and dusty. Dirt paths and worn stone steps lead villagers from one level to another, as they follow their sheep and goats to the grazing fields, while they collect firewood, as they have done for centu-ries. Today's visitors must pass the post office with the tele-phone, and the general store and coffee shop in the center of the village. Just beyond the last pole that carries modern electricity, the path turns toward my childhood home.

Now, as I am writing about a recent visit, my sister Ourania lives there alone and seems content tending to her chickens, a donkey to carry home kindling for the fire, and a goat to supply milk and to breed for market each year. In winter, she still pulls her woolen shawl tight against the rain and cold and goes out to the olive grove to gather olives that will be pressed into oil at the mill. "I have always used the oil from my olive trees, Eleni," she maintains, "and I will continue to do so until Charon ferries me across the River Styx to Hades."

Our house was similar to the others in Bordonia, built of native gray stone with a roof of orange terracotta tiles. The street gate led into our courtyard, where the goats and the pack animals were brought in from the fields and fed and the bundles of brushwood unloaded from their backs. A porch, the *hayati,* extended along one side of the house and commanded a sweeping view of the valley below. Underneath, where the hill sloped down into the kitchen garden, was a door to the *katoyi,* the underground area, where the animals were sheltered in winter. Deep in the *katoyi* were the barrels of wine and a set of stairs to the ledge where wheels of cheese and crocks of pickled meats were stored.

From the *hayati*, we entered the kitchen where we cooked, ate, and slept in winter. A fire always glowed in the hearth during cold winter days. Next to the kitchen was a larger room called the *heimoniatiko,* the winter-room. A plain pine table and chairs provided a place to receive visitors. The walls were lined with low wooden bins, *apothikes,* where wheat and corn and dried beans were stored for winter. The tops of the bins were padded with woolen blankets and served as seating and as our beds. The loom stood in one corner, and either my mother or my eldest sister Arista kept a steady pace throughout the winter, weaving woolen fabric from our sheep to be sewn into clothing, blankets, and rugs for the family. Ourania and I were not old enough to work the loom, but we were taught to sew, mend, and crochet from an early age.

A stone wall without windows sheltered the north side of the house from Boreas, the North Wind, notorious for the frigid winds of winter. The site of our house was also planned in relation to another mighty force of nature. Hovering in the background was majestic Mount Taigetus, which divided the Aegean Sea from the Ionian Sea. In Greece, physical features of the terrain have always been personified, and Taigetus was referred to as a mighty masculine presence. He soared eight thousand feet at the highest point near the village of Xirocambi, the tallest rib stretching a hundred miles from the northern Peloponnesus down into the sea at Cape Taenarus, the southernmost point of the Greek mainland. It was here that mythical Charon, with his thousand-eyed dog Cerberus, waited to ferry passengers over the River Styx into the dark entrance to Hades.

It was from the icy streams of Taigetus that we obtained water for drinking, cooking, washing, and irrigating our fields. In summer, the sun melted most of the snow near the peaks, but the deep ravines of that gray eminence were etched in white year round. In winter, Taigetus was a forbidding glacier with winds shrieking around the narrow passes and chilling travelers to the bone. The inhabitants of the area were in the habit of saying, "Taigetus had much snow last night, and he won't let anyone through today" or "Taigetus was shrouded in fog, yet he grudgingly permitted me to find my way home." Fortunately, summers in Greece were long, and it was then that Taigetus flaunted his many charms. The skies were a deep blue and the fat clouds floated lazily over crags enhanced by the ever-changing colors of fragrant blossoms. People followed steep mountain footpaths by choice to breathe in the fresh air.

Taigetus, that magnificent, inhospitable yet protective mass of rock, influenced the route out of the village. By mule and by foot, through remote hamlets on the mountain, villagers made the treacherous journey through the ravines and slopes that led first to Sparta, then to the port of Kalamata on the Messenian Gulf, and finally to Athens. From there they made their way to America. By the year 1901—when I was born, according to my family's estimates, since female births were not usually recorded—boys had been exiting their impoverished villages for decades. A depression following the uprising against the Ottoman Turks, who had ruled Greece for 400 years, contributed to sending my father first—and later in succession, seven of my brothers—to the fabled land across the sea. My father returned after a year. But the boys spent their childhood in Sparta, running errands to earn a few coins a day, barely enough to eat. In about four years, they would have eked out the few drachmas they needed to pay for steerage class on the crowded steamships that would take them to America. Before I was born, two of my brothers, Spiros and Andonis, had left Bordonia for Sparta, and then for America. Each brother followed: Yiannis (who joined the Greek army to seek his fortune), Georgios, Theophanis, Peter, Stavros, and Soterios.

The more my brothers' letters extolled the wonders of this land so far way, the more I dreamed about going too. I never tired of telling Ourania and my younger brother Leonidas about America, and the streets paved with gold, and the money that hung from trees. Sometimes when I was alone, I walked high into the hills, then sat and studied the clouds gliding over Taigetus, envying the biggest, whitest ones on their way to America.

It was raining hard one morning when Ourania, Leonidas, and I sat down to our breakfast of *trahana*, hot wheat gruel. By seven-thirty, we were running to school, wrapped in woolen capes to keep ourselves dry, as well as the brushwood we carried for the pot-bellied stove. Classes from the first grade to the fifth grade were taught in the same room, but when it was time for gym class, which was compulsory three times a day, boys and girls went separately to the *gymnasterion;* this was a small, unheated shed used only in bad weather, but we much preferred calisthenics and foot races outdoors, even in the snow—Spartans that we were! Differing with *Kyrios* Tagas, our teacher, however, earned us the hard slap of a ruler on an outstretched hand.

In Greek history class we studied not only ancient Greece, but also learned about the suppression of the Greek language and of Christianity under the Turkish Occupation—which had lasted from 1453 to 1821—and about children under cover of night attending secret schools. To perpetuate the Greek language and religion, the children met with teachers or priests in abandoned buildings safe from detection. While grateful for what our forefathers had fought and died for, I envied those long-ago children. I pictured their teachers as kindly old priests, who sent them home after a few hours of night school, so that they had all day to play, although I knew that life could not have been easy for people dominated by foreigners. My days were spent in what seemed like many hours in school, then home to help mother; finally, around sunset, with no time to play after a light supper, I started my homework. I would take my books and sit wherever the last light of the day fell, and do my lessons aloud.

Kyrios Tagas informed us that he walked past our houses every night and was aware of those who were not studying. We had no way of knowing, of course, whether or not he really did this, but I always studied near an open window or door, so that he could hear me recite my lessons. I was not the only pupil to believe him. People strolling along village lanes after supper reported hearing childish voices floating out into the twilight, multiplying "5 × 5 is 25," "6 × 6 is 36." Or rather, the multiplication tables, as recited in Greek with a somewhat poetic lilt: "5, 5, 25—*pente, pente, eikosi-pente;* 6, 6, 36—*exi, exi, trianta-exi.*" Spelling was another bane. Competitions were announced at the last minute, and the good students learned to practice often, pay attention in class, and be quick in responding to questions.

Thus, we felt tortured in preparing for final examinations, the dreaded *exetasis*. On those fateful mornings, I could barely swallow a glass of water, as I kept repeating, 9, 5, 45—*ennea, pente, saranta-pente;* 9, 6, 54—*ennea, exi, peninta-tessera*—wailing that I would not be able to remember anything when *Kyrios* Tagas called on me. My mother and Ourania, and sometimes my father, would leave work that morning—as did the families of my classmates—and troop into the schoolhouse. First, the priest led us in prayer, and then everyone raised their voices to sing the stirring Greek national anthem, *Ymnos tis Eleutherias,* "The Hymn to Liberty," written in 1829 by our poet laureate, Dionysius Solomos.

> *Se gnoriso apo tin kopsi*
> *Tou spathiou tin tromeri.*
> *Se gnoriso apo tin opsi*
> *Pou me via metrai tin yi.*

Ap'ta kokala vyalmeni
Ton Ellinon to iera
Kai san prota, andriomenni
Haire, oh haire, Eleutheria!

English version by Rudyard Kipling:

We knew thee of old,
Oh, divinely restored,
By the lights of thine eyes,
And the might of thy sword.

From the graves of our slain,
Shall thy valor prevail,
As we greet thee again,   ,
Hail, Liberty! Hail!

We took our seats and it was time for exams to begin. *Kyrios* Tagas stepped to the front of the room and called us, one by one—the youngest first. Exams were oral, and we were expected to answer very quickly and accurately, as we had practiced many times in class. *Kyrios* Tagas told us that the children who had attended the secret schools did not have books at home. That was the reason they had to memorize all their studies. Memorizing for the *exetasis,* where I had to recite in front of my classmates and our parents, was such an upsetting experience for me that I no longer envied those early children. On the way home from my examinations that day, Ourania said, "If you married young, you wouldn't have to go to school anymore."

"But I cannot marry until I am at least fifteen. That would be in five or six years, Ourania."

"You could always hide on a boat and go to America! Our brothers would keep you. They would not want to send you back." We laughed as we planned my escape from the village.

"Why don't I go first to France?" "No, their grapevines went bad once." By the time we were home, we had decided that I was too young to go anyplace—yet.

Spring nights were chilly, and the wind still had a bite when the first peddler, the *pragmateuthis,* made his way up the steep hills to our village, carrying his marvelous satchel on his back. When he set it down near the *caffenio,* the coffee shop in the central square, I strained my neck to see what it contained: Sharp needles, spools of fine thread, and new shoelaces were among the packages deep inside the bag. Mother pointed out a small box, opened it, studied its contents, and then paid the peddler. When we returned home, Ourania, Leonidas, and I stood at her side while she opened the box on the table. It contained silkworm eggs. Raising silkworms had become a cottage industry for the women of our village a few seasons earlier. Mother verified for the second time that the eggs were fresh and clean. The spores were small, like caraway seeds, and it usually fell to me to be the first incubator, keeping them warm until the larvae hatched. I would curl up on one of the straw mattresses that was laid out on the kitchen floor, and kept the little box close to my body. It was fun at first, but after a few hours of inactivity, I coaxed Ourania or Leonidas to take a turn at keeping the eggs warm.

Those of us not serving as incubators went out to gather the tender young leaves of white mulberry trees. It was a beautiful time of year in Bordonia. The blue flax bloomed everywhere along with the *paparounes*, red poppies that brightened the countryside. Mother chopped the mulberry leaves into small bits, and my sister, brother, and I would drop these bits into the large, flat baskets that father had suspended from the ceiling in the winter room.

Mother always seemed to know the right time to open the box of silkworms. We pressed around her as she placed the open box of tiny eggs on the table and put a small piece of mulberry leaf into the box. When a silkworm hatched it crawled onto the leaf, and mother immediately set the leaf into one of the suspended baskets filled with the shredded leaves.

The larvae hatched quickly, and then our work began in earnest. It was a continual task to gather enough mulberry leaves and chop them fine to feed the insatiable silkworms. Fortunately, they grew so quickly that soon the leaves no longer had to be cut up. Once the silkworms were the diameter of a woman's index finger, they "graduated" to consuming whole mulberry leaves, and we then cut entire branches of leaves, and placed them in the suspended baskets. This saved us the task of multiple feedings of these voracious creatures.

The only unpleasant aspect of their culture was that, if a silkworm escaped from its basket and fell on the floor, it could be stepped on by accident. It left a pungent, unpleasant odor—so we learned to walk very carefully while the silkworms were in the house. At night when it was quiet, we could hear them ingesting their food—a quiet murmuring—mmmmm. As they matured, they became iridescent; this was so alluring to me that I would take two or three of the silkworms and drape them on one shoulder or on my collar and strut around the room as though I were wearing precious jewelry. Their opalescence originated from two glands, one on each side of their bodies, which distend with the viscous fluid that eventually becomes silk thread.

When they were fat and nearly transparent, the silkworms started to spin their cocoons. By this time, they had depleted our supply of mulberry leaves. Now, we gathered armloads of sweet-smelling purple heather named *reekie*, which blooms in the hills at this time of the year, and laid the *reekie* on top of the larvae. Without hesitation, they climbed onto the heather and began moving their heads, busily exuding a glutinous, transparent substance which became a fine, single thread that wrapped around each body. This they did for three days until the larvae were totally enveloped by the thread that constituted a tight, waterproof cocoon.

The finest silk is manufactured by unraveling each cocoon in a continuous thread, which sometimes is hundreds of yards long. However, within the cocoon, the larva is transformed into a moth, whose chief function is to burst through the cocoon and fly away to mate. If the moth breaks the filament, the threads are then carded, like wool and cotton, and used to make a rougher fabric called "raw silk."

In Bordonia, after most of the silkworms were encased in their snug cocoons, we invited friends and relatives to help us separate the cocoons from the branches of heather. We had fewer than three weeks to gather and bag them, and for my father to take the bags to the factory in Sparta. He had to deliver them before the moths broke through their cocoons.

At the factory in Sparta, nature would be tampered with. The cocoons were processed carefully by applying heat, usually a warm water bath that killed the moths but did not harm the silk. Then, the unbroken thread would be painstakingly wound on spools.

For two thousand years, silkworm culture was a closely guarded secret, practiced only in China. It is said that two monks visiting China in the sixth century learned how this process was carried out, and at great personal risk, carried some seeds to Emperor Justinian I in Constantinople. From the Byzantine Empire, the manufacture of silk spread throughout Europe.

Gathering the cocoons and bagging them brought our neighbors and relatives to help and to visit. My sister, cousins, and I took our places at the table where the heather was heaped; as other women gathered around the table, there was much talk, and finally, it was not surprising to hear my aunt announce proudly what she had told mother that morning—that Nikitas Tagas, our teacher, had asked for Sophia's hand in marriage.

Plucking a cocoon off the *reekie* and dropping it into the burlap bag at her side, *Theia* Despina added, "I do not see anything wrong with his being close to forty years of age, do you, Magdalene? He is a teacher, and as his wife, Sophia will be respected for the rest of her life."

I glanced at my cousin. She was too pretty to marry that gloomy man. My heart sank at the thought. Sophia gently pulled a cocoon from the heather and looked up at me and winked. She was like another sister to me, and listened to my criticism of my teacher as patiently as she did to my prattling about going to America. I was certain that she agreed with me on everything, and I could not believe that she would give up our dream and stay in Bordonia to marry *Kyrios* Tagas. He was not only stern, but also stout, and his eyes were too big. He was not the kind of man I envisioned for Sophia, and I was relieved when she whispered to me, "I cannot abide him, Eleni, and I will have nothing to do with any matchmaking with *Kyrios* Tagas, no matter what my mother says."

Her mother complained to her friends, "I do not know why Sophia disagrees with me. If she waits much longer to marry, she will lose her youth and good looks, and then no one will want her. What do you say, Magdalene?" My mother said quietly, "Sophia is sensible and knows what she wants. She has time. I would not worry if I were you, Despina."

Theia Xenia, our elderly neighbor, who was like a grandmother to my sisters and me, murmured agreement. *Theia* before a name means "aunt" and is used not only to address women who are related, but also as a title of respect to an older woman. *Kyria* means "Mrs." or "lady" and is more formal than *theia*. Men are addressed as *theios*, "uncle," or as *Kyrios* "Mr." or "sir."

Kyria Stamata, who lived on the road from Sparta, had three married daughters, and she knew everything about matchmaking. She shook her head vigorously, "Both your aunt and Xenia are wrong, Sophia. Your mother is right! Do you see the man my daughter Evlavia married? She refused Apostolos, the tinker, who made a very good living, and turned down Takis, the shepherd, after his second wife died. She waited, and finally when she was seventeen, she fell in love with this Stavros from Cosmas. All he had is what she brought him in her dowry. She is lucky that he takes the time to tend her vineyard and the four olive trees. Otherwise, they would have nothing. You know, time passes. You cannot be choosy. You already are sixteen."

Olga Hatzakos nodded agreement. She was a meek person, thin almost bony, and had moved to our village a year ago with her single daughter Eugenia. Quiet as Olga was, I thought she did not always think before she spoke. Now she said, shyly but firmly, "It is your duty, Sophia, to marry a good prospect. It is not every man that will want to marry into your family."

I looked at Eva. She was speaking to another girl, and apparently did not hear Olga's remarks as she continued. "If you accept *Kyrios* Tagas, you will set your father's mind at ease, since it will be difficult to find a husband for your sister, given her affliction." My eyes sought my mother's. In the family, Eva was like everybody else. We never thought of her as different. Yet, here was this woman, who had lived in Bordonia such a short time, openly talking about my cousin, as though she had something wrong with her. There was a silence as each woman concentrated on a cocoon. Then *Theia* Xenia broke the silence impatiently, "There is nothing wrong with Eva. For heaven's sake, Olga! The child was born with six fingers on one hand, and we don't talk about it because there is nothing to say. It is the way it is. What is the difference? Six or five fingers on one hand? As for Sophia, my own feeling is that she should not marry *Kyrios* Tagas. There are one or two young men in this very village with good prospects who would be more suitable for her."

Kyria Stamata chuckled, "There's always the shoemaker, Elias Andamas."

"Don't be funny, Stamata," *Theia* Xenia objected, "Sophia is too young to take care of two children." She smiled. "In a way, you are right, Stamata. Elias needs a wife. *Kyria* Olga, why do you not speak to the *proxenitis,* the matchmaker, about your daughter and Elias? He needs somebody to take care of his children, and Eugenia appears to be just the woman who could do it. She likes children, and from what I have seen of her, she is a good cook and housekeeper."

Olga's eyes filled momentarily with hope, but she lowered her head and murmured, "You do not know how I pray for such a thing, *Kyria* Xenia. But, we have nothing. I have no dowry for Eugenia. When my husband died, everything went to his brother and sister—according to the law. I am glad that my son, thank the Lord, found a job with my cousin in Alexandria. The small house Eugenia and I live in is all that my brother-in-law gave us. It is ours until I die—so that, as his brother's widow, I do not disgrace him—and then it will go back to his family."

"Eh, well, that is too bad," said *Kyria* Stamata. "The one they should marry off soon is Roula, the Danzos' youngest daughter. She is very forward with the young workers who come from out of town."

"She was walking up to the cemetery with one of them just yesterday," Theia Xenia shook her head,

"It was probably the mason from over in Corinth," *Theia* Despina said. "He flirts with all the girls."

Stamata nodded. "That can mean trouble. Those Corinthian boys have a bad reputation."

Aliki Theros, who lived next to the church, offered her opinion. "I think Roula Danzos is really after Petros Kanaris, the shepherd's youngest son. I hear she meets him after dark behind the church. The shepherd has his hands full with that boy."

Before we could be sent away, Sophia challenged me and our sisters to a game of *pentovolo,* a form of jacks. With Eva and Ourania we all sat down on the floor at one end of the room. Each took her turn throwing five small stones on the floor in front of her; and then as she tossed a larger stone up in the air with her right hand, she had to scoop up as many of the little stones with the same hand, before the bigger stone fell. We giggled as we whispered about *Kyria* Hatzakos calling attention to Eva's six fingers. "People are curious about something different," Eva sighed. "I suppose a finger looms as big as an eye in the middle of the forehead like the Cyclops!" We studied her left hand, as we had done often before. Next to her little finger, she had a finger one-half its size; as usual, we speculated on how nature created such variations, but not arriving at any solution, we went on with our game.

The first shrill peeps from the birds' nests alerted us to the arrival of spring: the ewe gave birth to her lamb and the baby goats came in twos. Pink and yellow flowers softened the prickly cactus while the waxy white petals of the orange blossoms exuded their sweet fragrance and the tiny white buds on the olive trees preened themselves for their big job ahead. While the days were still cold, for reasons that will become clear later, the cotton and woolen material that mother and Arista had woven during the winter had to be bleached of impurities, and I was glad that this was done only once a year.

Arista, like Ourania a few years later, had gone to school long enough to learn how to read and write, and then had her wish to stay home and help mother with the younger children, and with the cooking and the cleaning. She went to America one spring to help our brother Andonis, in Ohio, and I was left with Ourania and Leonidas to learn more about life on a farm than I wanted to know. Mother and Arista had woven lengths of cotton and wool cloth in a variety of weights, some to be fashioned into shirts and blouses, and the heavier cloth into jackets, blankets, and rugs. Before the fabric could be sewn, it had to be bleached with our natural, organic method—manure from horses or cattle. Since we did not have a supply of that particular compost— sparse foliage and brambles would not sustain such livestock— father loaded a supply of his unfermented *mizithra* cheese on the mule cart, and set out for the fertile Laconian plain, where he bartered the cheese for an adequate supply of manure. He dumped it into an old cauldron near the pig sty, far from the house, and filled the cauldron with water. As the mixture aged, father moved it around with a pole used only for that purpose, until days later when it was mashed and pulpy enough for mother and me to drop yards of heavy cloth into the cauldron. We used long poles to push the material deep until it was completely immersed in the rank liquid.

For days, the cloth soaked in the liquid manure until mother decided that it had been bleached to her satisfaction. After long exposure to the elements, this old-fashioned bleaching solution had lost much of its fetid odor. Since it fell to me to help with the rinsing and stretching that had to take place, I was glad for it. On the appointed day, father heaved the wet fabric out of the caul- dron onto a makeshift colander, and diluted the liquid left in the cauldron to spread over the garden as seasoned fertilizer. He thoroughly cleaned out the cauldron and the other equipment used for the bleaching, while mother and I rinsed the material and stretched it out over rocks and bushes to dry.

The next day, when the sun promised to be bright and hot, my mother and I filled two large baskets with the lengths of newly-woven and bleached cloth, and strapped them to each side of the donkey. Too large for the tubs we had at home, these goods would be transported to the nearby village of Horia, where the *loutrobeio,* the public washhouse, was located. There the heavy cotton and woolen fabric would be steamed, washed, and stretched to dry. The women of our village had a certain day designated for our use of the washhouse, and mother and I fell in step with *Theia* Despina and her daughters. Others were already ahead of us at the small building, isolated in a field near a stream, and we waited our turn. Each woman counted out her items for the manager to process, and then found a copse of trees where we sat on blankets until the fabric was ready to be dried.

Kyria Stamata dropped heavily onto the blanket, and as soon as she saw my aunt, exclaimed, "So, Despina! Will we hear wedding bells soon?"

Sophia had not sat with the women, and before we could hear her mother's reply, she walked away with Eva and me. As soon as we were out of the women's hearing, I asked her the same question. "You are not going to marry that mean teacher of ours, are you, Sophia?"

"No, Eleni," she smiled. "My mother was disappointed that I turned down an educated man, but my father agreed with me, and told *Kyrios* Paladinos, the matchmaker, when he came to our house on Sunday, that he did not approve of the match."

"What reason could he give, Sophia?" I was ten years old at the time. When grandmothers were not available to baby-sit, children sat in corners playing or sewing, privy to family discussions and opinions. "Your father could not tell him that *Kyrios* Tagas was too fat or too old for you."

Sophia laughed. "I think papa told him that I was not ready for marriage. *Kyrios* Paladinos is intelligent, and I know he understood what papa was saying." Eva had picked up a stick and had drawn a large rectangle in the dirt, then made some squares inside it, for the game of *koutsonilios*, hopscotch. For a time, until my aunt called us, we took turns throwing a stone into a square and hopping on one foot up and down the little track.

Then we helped our mothers carry the long pieces of material to the field, where we could stretch them in the sun to dry.

When we had finished, we sat down on a circle of blankets and opened our woolen bags filled with lunch. Slices of *mizithra* and dark bread were typical fare. Sophia's mother had her pass around a bowl of olives, and *Kyria* Aliki shared her store of dried figs and dates. Eva and I made several trips to the spring and brought back carafes of water.

"And now what do we have?" *Kyria* Aliki shrugged. "Sophia will not marry the teacher, and Elias Andamas is already taken."

"What's that you say?" *Kyria* Stamata was startled. She often was first to pass on any village gossip, and it annoyed her that Aliki, who claimed to be psychic, had the news first.

Elias Andamas took over as the village shoemaker when his father died. Everyone loved the kindly older man, and they hoped that Elias, an unsociable youth, would change and become like his father, but he did not. When he was nearly thirty-five and still unmarried, an elderly neighbor offered him two farms and a vineyard if Elias would marry his daughter. Xanthe, tall and clumsy, was a kindly girl of twenty-five and made a good wife for Elias. They had two children, and after Xanthe's father died, he left even more property to Elias, who was by now a prosperous landowner. When his wife died in childbirth, Elias took over the care of his children and kept working at his trade. By the age of forty-one he had become a cold, self-centered braggart. All his customers disliked him, but because of his wealth, the mothers of the village wanted their daughters to marry him.

"What do you mean, what is new about Elias Andamas?" *Kyria* Olga Hatzakos asked softly.

"Come, Olga!" *Kyria* Aliki beamed. "Everyone knows that *Kyrios* Danzos has gone to visit Elias with the matchmaker for his daughter, Roula."

"Maybe after he marries again, he will change into a kinder person," *Theia* Xenia observed.

Kyria Aliki laughed. "You may be right! They say he acts every bit the lovestruck youth."

"Poor man, he's making a spectacle of himself."

"It is no wonder, Xenia, the way he struts around boasting of his forthcoming marriage to the beguiling sixteen year-old." Aliki was indignant.

"So, that is the reason he has been passing my house every day," Stamata exclaimed. "He goes to the Danzos, hoping to see his betrothed, Roula."

"And later he appears at the coffee shop to sing the praises of his beloved." Aliki narrowed her eyes at Stamata. "One thing I know: that wedding will never come to pass. The silly girl thinks that life with Elias is all new dresses and pastries."

"Everybody knows the truth of that!" *Kyria* Stamata said dismissively. "If this village ever had a miser, it is Elias. As soon as Roula understands this, who knows what she will do!" As the cloth dried, the women gathered it up and folded it, and we made our way home in the late afternoon—both task and gossip accomplished.

One morning, I was awakened by the clatter of father leading Leonidas and my mother around the house beating on pots and pans with wooden spoons and singing—as he did every year on the first of March. Looking for any excuse to celebrate, Ourania and I took up kettles and spoons and joined the cacophonous parade.

> *Exo, psiloi, pontiki!*
> Out, you fleas and mice!
> *Mesa, Martis, kai hara!*
> In with March and happiness!

This playful jingle heralded our annual spring house-cleaning. For the next few days, mother put us to work beating carpets, cleaning out cupboards, airing out clothing and bedding, and scrubbing floors, so that everything would be clean by Easter. In the midst of this activity, my aunt sent word that the first leaves were emerging on their grapevines, and it was time for

beetle-picking. That night, mother handed me a lantern, caution-
ing me to keep it away from the jars of kerosene that Ourania
and Leonidas would be carrying. We met our cousins and other
young people in the village, and walked into the countryside
until we came to the first vineyard, the one that belonged to
Theios Yiannis. Grapevines are prone to attack by numerous
pests and diseases, so the growers must be alert. At the earliest
stage of their growth, the tender shoots are eagerly consumed by
what is known as the grapevine beetle, *pelidnota.* The fragility
of the vines that attracted these overwintering predators also
prohibited the use of toxic insecticides. If he did not want to lose
his crop of grapes, my uncle had to handpick the beetles from
the entire vineyard as soon as they appeared. After the leaves
unfurled, he would be able to spray the vines with bluestone, an
effective insecticide against the next invaders, but for now, he
needed our help. Despite the nature of the task, picking beetles
was a social event. When the need for pickers was announced,
all the young people flocked together to help in each others'
vineyards.

Roula Danzos appeared with her brothers soon after we
arrived at my uncle's vineyard. She was Sophia's age, and
because she lived in another part of the village, I did not know
her well. She had not touched one leaf when she sidled next to
Sophia and whispered, "Did you ever see anyone as handsome
as Mihalis, the stonemason from Corinth?"

I was on the other side of my cousin, picking beetles from a
row of vines and saw her drop some beetles into her jar of kerosene before she answered, "Don't engage in dangerous games,
Roula. You don't know anything about these boys who come
from out of town to work here. They usually go home to their
girlfriends and wives."

Roula frowned. "You're so serious, Sophia! I'm just passing
the time—having some fun with him." She tossed her head and
looked around at Kostas Zacharias, who was in the row behind
us. The handsome son of the *horofilakas*, chief of the rural
police, had been taking courses at the agricultural school in

Sparta, and had recently returned home to put his education to use on the family property. Roula crossed to where Kostas stood. She made a face at the jar he held and announced, "You carry the kerosene, Kosta, and I will drop the little bugs in it." A short while later, as we trooped along the moonlit road to the neighboring vineyard, Roula edged away from Kostas, who had not responded to her playful manner, and she moved ahead to join a group that was reciting and singing, and included Petros Kanaris, the son of the shepherd. Petros placed an arm over Roula's shoulders in welcome. Kostas was not offended that she had left his side, and Sophia and I did not mind it when he raised his voice close to us, as we all recited the patriotic nursery rhyme addressed to the moonlight. This was the ode of the children attending the secret schools during the Ottoman Occupation:

> *Fengaraki mou lambro,*
> *Fengeh mou na perpato*
> *Na piyeno sto scholio*
> *Na mathaino grammata,*
> *Tou Theou ta pragmata.*
>
> Bright little moon,
> Shine on my footsteps
> That I may go to school
> To learn to read and write,
> And the teachings of God.

Our last vineyard that night on the march against the scourge of the vineyards was *Theia* Xenia's vineyard. She invited everyone into her house for refreshments before we returned home. As we helped ourselves to dried figs, dates, and walnuts, Kostas and Sophia had much to say to each other, and Ourania, who observed everything, commented to me that she thought Kostas liked Sophia.

A few days later, as I set out to fetch fresh water from the springs at the chapel of *Ayios Yiannis* (Ayiannis), I met Sophia. I was glad to have company, because it was more than a half-hour's walk from the house, and no matter how familiar I was with it, the narrow trail through the dark woods always frightened me. Ourania saw us and called to Eva, and the four of us, each holding a water jug, started on the path. Ourania and Eva raced ahead. Sophia did not have much to say at first, then she looked at me. "Did your mother talk to Arista about marriage every chance she could before she left for America?"

"I don't think so," I replied.

"Well, mine is driving all of us crazy, lately: All she thinks of is what to serve at the weddings she will have for Eva and me!"

"Doesn't she know that you are going to America with me?" I asked her.

"Eleni," she laughed. "America must be a wonderful place, but the more I think of it, the more I know I could not leave my country."

"My brothers and Angela are there to take care of us," I assured her. She started to say something, but stopped in midsentence. Her cheeks turned pink as she watched two young men walking toward us. Kostas Zaharias and his brother Georgios approached from the spring at Ayiannis, their donkey carrying two large water jugs. "*Yiasas!* Hello!" Kostas greeted us, his eyes not leaving Sophia's face. "On your way to Ayiannis?" My cousin nodded, and Kostas said, "It is crowded today. Everyone is trying to get home before the rain." When they had passed us, he called back. "Do not tarry, Sophia. There's a storm coming."

"Thank you. We need only fill our flasks and return home."

The two youths continued on their way, and Sophia and I glanced uneasily at the sky and hurried to the spring. Ourania and Eva had gone ahead; each had filled her *veeka*, a narrow-necked, terracotta jug. We greeted friends, then headed home. Before we had gotten very far, large drops of rain splashed the road and then our shoulders and we started to run. I am not certain whether Kostas Zaharias had waited for my cousin or whether he walked slowly, but there he was—just ahead of us. His brother and their jug-laden donkey were not in evidence. Kostas held a cloak over Sophia's head, mumbling something about the rest of us coming under its protection, but Ourania refused him laughing. She grabbed my hand with her free hand, urging Eva and me to run home with her. It was well after we had reached our house, soaked, and had dried ourselves that Sophia arrived. Eva waited to walk home with her sister from our house, and I was relieved that their mother had gone home, and was not there to speculate about the meaning of Sophia's encounter with Kostas.

That spring, in 1910, a form of hysteria swept over the region. An unfamiliar celestial object was becoming brighter than any other body in the night sky. We were told that *Komeetees,* the long-haired comet, was approaching the earth, and a quiet panic seized our village and the rest of Europe wherever it was visible. For weeks the topic of discussion was *Komeetees.* At that time, when the world had no electricity, people tended to sit outdoors on a pleasant night and enjoy the night skies as an ever-changing, star-lit stage. From an early age, we had come to know the constellations and planets. So it was no wonder that this comet, appearing out of nowhere and taking a position in our sky, where it did not belong, caused such widespread fear.

Kyria Olga Hatzakos and *Theia* Xenia were visiting mother one day, when *Kyria* Olga asked, "Did you see *Komeetees* last night? He is coming closer to Bordonia. I think he will land in the Delouris's cornfield.

"Where did you hear that?" *Theia* Xenia asked with slight disapproval. "My son Heracles told me this morning that *Komeetees* is turning away from Sparta and moving out toward Patras."

Kyria Olga wrung her hands. "Oh, my poor cousin lives in Patras! What's to become of him and his wife and children!"

Komeetees loomed in everyone's mind: What is he like? "A big fireball," some said. "If he falls on the village, we'll all be burned to a crisp." Menis Zacharias, the fifteen-year old brother of Kostas, raced to the *caffenio* one afternoon holding a black stone. Even though it was not warm enough to spend much time seated outdoors in the village square yet, the tables and chairs had been moved outside for fear that a direct hit by *Komeetees* would bring the roof down on the patrons who were drinking coffee and discussing politics. Menis was holding a dark stone. "Look!" He showed it around. "This was on the path as I was coming home. It doesn't match any of the other stones that were near it."

"You've picked up a piece of *Komeetees*!" Elias Andamas, the shoemaker, declared.

"*Ohi,* no," the mayor scoffed. "It would burn your hand if it were *Komeetees.*"

"But it cooled off during the night," the boy maintained. "Look how it sparkles: as though it has passed through the sky and near the stars."

Elias Andamas stood up, as if to remedy the situation, "You see! *Komeetees* is beginning to break apart. Any day now the rest of him will crash down on top of us."

When night came, people in villages and cities where the comet was visible spread blankets in their yards and slept outdoors, fearing that their houses would collapse upon them if *Komeetees* fell during the night. I remember seeing the comet— a very bright, unfamiliar object in the sky, where there had been no star or planet before. I later read that this particular comet, at one point in its orbit, had a tail that streaked across two-thirds of the sky from the horizon to the zenith, but I do not recall this phenomenon, and remember only that it was larger and brighter than any other star in the heavens.

The menace was over, at last, when we were told that *Komeetees* had landed elsewhere, perhaps in the sea, as some said. The comet that had caused widespread fear in May of 1910, to those ignorant of astronomy—not only in Greece but all over Europe—was Halley's Comet. Instead of being terrorized, we should instead have considered ourselves fortunate to have seen this particular comet, which even Halley, the English astronomer for whom it was named, never did see. He had correctly calculated that the comet that kept reappearing throughout recorded history was the same comet that had been sighted in

240 BC and about every seventy-seven years thereafter. It was portrayed in the French Bayeux Tapestry commemorating the Battle of Hastings in 1066—William the Conqueror's victory over the Anglo-Saxons. Halley died in 1742 but had accurately foretold the comet's reappearance in 1759. In 1986, Halley's Comet was once again visible in the northern hemisphere. I was visiting my family in New Jersey, but on this, my second sighting, it was barely visible to any of us; and it was nothing like the blazing light that I had seen in May 1910.

CHAPTER 2

Home and Church

Ola kala, kai to meli kalo.
All is well, and the honey
is good, too.
                        — GREEK PROVERB

Even if I dared to pretend that I was asleep, mother's quiet voice would make my eyes fly open and my bare feet hit the floor. "Eleni," she woke me one morning, before the sun had lit the skies and it was still dark. "Papa has men helping him with the plowing at the farm, the *Lefko,* today. We are out of flour and I have to make bread to send with their lunch." I rubbed my eyes, splashed water over my face and dressed as fast as I could. In the kitchen, I swallowed a glass of fresh goat's milk, and with a slice of yesterday's bread, I ran out. Mother was already in the courtyard with a bag of wheat she had taken from one of the bins in the winter room. Quickly securing the sack to the side of the donkey, she said, "Now, hurry to the mill and hurry back!"

I took hold of our donkey's bridle and led it toward the flour mill in Orahos, the neighboring village. With its slow, measured steps, the donkey seemed half asleep, and no amount of prodding could hurry the slow-moving animal. When we reached the mill at last, it was my turn to dally.

I had never seen the huge wheels at work and became so engrossed in watching the massive millstones as they crushed and ground the kernels of wheat that I soon lost all track of time, forgetting that mother needed the flour immediately. I walked

23

around in awe, taking everything in, and only when the miller's daughter Polizoi asked me to play our version of jacks with her, did I remember the urgency of my errand. "I can't stay and play *pentavolo*!" I wailed. "I've already been here too long."

I tapped the donkey with a stick all the way home, as though it had been at fault. I knew that I was in for it. Mother needed to mix the flour with the yeast and let it rise in time to bake a proper loaf of bread. With my tardiness, however, it would not be ready to take to the men at our farm with their midday meal. Mother did not spank hard, but nettle plants sting, and I did not need the pain of those sharp thorns on my bare legs to remind me not to waste her time again. Watching her careworn, gentle features as she hurried to fry the tasteless corn meal cakes she would have to substitute for the thick loaves of *psomi,* bread, that father and his workers were expecting, was punishment enough. It was a lesson I would not forget quickly, since I could not sit down comfortably for several days.

As soon as the meal was ready, I humbly followed Ourania, and we carried the food, a savory vegetable stew, to the men at the *Lefko*. When they saw us arrive, they assembled quickly. I avoided father's eyes as he peered into the bread basket and frowned at the corn meal substitutes. Every culture has its essential foods, without which a meal is incomplete. To the Greeks, *psomi* is a mainstay of the table, and it was an embarrassment to father that he had to serve mealy biscuits to his helpers instead of thick slabs of wheat bread.

While the men ate, father poured out cups of homemade wine for them, and Leonidas came up to me and tugged at my hand. "Come on, Eleni, Ourania! The chicks are hatching!" We followed him to the enclosure where the laying hens watched us as we carefully approached the eggs that Leonidas had set aside for hatching. Some of the smooth, white ovals rolled a little and then began to crack from the mysterious force within them. After we watched a few of the wet, scrawny chicks emerge, we lost interest in this phase of their lives, and turned to the bright yellow chicks that had hatched a few days earlier. They fluttered around and made thin peeping sounds and kept us amused. I chose the one I thought was the fluffiest and smartest little chick and adopted her. I named her "Eleni" after me. I fed her special tidbits of grain as she grew, and I talked to her like a friend. That summer, Eleni followed me everywhere I went—from morning, when I called to her—until night. My father did not seem to mind my spoiling her, because when she was old enough, she faithfully produced an egg every day. Chickens were everywhere in the homes and in the village; in the winter, at night, we kept ours in a fenced area near the goats and sheep in the basement; in summer, they roosted outside the house in the bushes.

Eleni would waddle beside me as I helped tend the rest of our farm family—the donkey, the mule, the goats, occasionally a few sheep, and a pig. Each animal was chosen with care, since we did not have money to buy feed for many voracious creatures, nor did we own much arable land. The donkey subsisted on leaves that we collected from the nearby fields. Sometimes he seemed to live on nothing. At least one goat was a necessity because she supplied us with milk, and luckily ate virtually everything without demanding a delicate diet. When we had more goats, we sold their milk to the shepherd, who made cheese from it. Every year, the goat would be bred, and we would sell both of her kids.

Ourania, Leonidas, and I would have liked to live in the relaxed, easy conditions at the *Lefko*, if our parents had allowed it. The shelter at the farm was a simple structure of four stone walls with a thatched roof and a hard-packed, dirt floor. When the weather was bad, the animals were corralled in one half of this cabin, and those family members who tended them stored their provisions and slept in the other half. Most of the time, father let us sleep on blankets outdoors, but this time, only Leonidas stayed, and Ourania and I returned home.

The next morning, after Ourania had left with the goats, mother and I filled two baskets with clothes to be washed. We carried them down the hill to the stream that ran along the back of my uncle's property. It was not as crowded as the larger washing area on the other side of town, and mother came here when she did not have a heavy load. We had arranged the clothing— shirts, blouses, pants, and underthings—on a flat rock, when *Theia* Despina took a seat beside mother.

"Did you hear about Petros Kanaris and Roula Danzos?"

"Girls," my mother turned around. "Find us some brush-wood, please."

Our mothers needed a few minutes to themselves, just as we needed to hear about Roula's escapades from the older girls. Roula did not interest me as much as anything that might involve Petros Kanaris. He had curly black hair and laughing eyes, and his scrapes never failed to attract the attention of even the youngest girls.

"What is this about Petros?" I asked Sophia as we left our mothers.

Picking up dry sticks as we strolled along, my cousin shook her head in dismay."He has really done it this time!" She paused. "Do you remember *Kyria* Aliki telling everybody that Roula has been meeting boys in secret? She finally got herself so entangled that she cannot get out of it without marrying Petros Kanaris. The two of them ran off to the mountain last night!"

"They didn't!"

"Now he has to marry Roula," Eva said. "It is her fault. She was so eager to be with him that she would try anything."

"As silly as she is, I think Roula knows better than that, Eva," Sophia replied. "It is Petros who does not look before he leaps. He likes to joke with his friends, and boast about his con-quests. From what Kostas has told me about him, I believe that he persuaded Roula to go to the mountain shelter with him with-out considering the consequences."

Eva nodded. "And this time he is committed, isn't he? *Kyrios* Danzos will not let his daughter be disgraced, so they will have a wedding."

Sophia agreed. "And *Kyrios* Danzos will have a new employee!"

When we returned, our mothers had completed the washing, and we helped lift the clothes from the stream, squeeze out the water, and stretch and drape them over the bushes. At lunch, everyone talked about Roula and Petros and the effect their elopement would have on Roula's betrothed, the shoemaker, Elias Andamas.

"She has not been behaving like a decent girl lately," *Kyria* Aliki pronounced. "How many times have I seen her walking through the village by herself. I can't even count them on my two hands. That girl was bound to be in trouble some day."

That night, no one went to sleep early. *Theia* Despina came to visit with her husband, *Theios* Yiannis, and Sophia and Eva. Their brothers, Nikos and Stratis, played outside with Leonidas. My father brought chairs out for the parents and sliced oranges to pass around to the rest of us as we sat on mats in the courtyard. When Ourania overheard our parents discussing the elopement of Petros and Roula, she shushed us, and we turned our attention toward the talk of our elders.

Theia Despina was saying, "Magdalene, every time something like this happens, it takes me back to the day that Demetrios persuaded your friend Kaleroi to talk you into picking flowers in the field."

My mother sighed, "Fifteen is too young for a girl to leave her father's house."

Theios Yiannis, a cousin of my father who had married my mother's sister, defended himself. "Demetrios did not confide to any of us that he intended to elope with you, Magdalene, or we surely would have found a way to stop him. You were much too young."

"He was a rash young man," mother sighed and smiled wearily."

"Take it from me," *Theia* Despina chuckled, "From what I know of the Louvis men, they never grow old."

My father moved closer to mother and said, "It was fate, Magdalene. I could not resist those blue eyes of yours when I saw you in the village that year. Something came over me, and I could not get you out of my mind. You had always been a skinny little girl with bony arms and legs when you came to visit your sister. But that year, I could think of nothing but you, and how much I wanted you for my wife."

With a tone she reserved only when speaking about her marriage, mother answered, "You might have waited until my father gave you permission to marry me. What does a fifteen-year-old know of life?"

"That *Kyrios* Andonis Pantazopoulos, your father—may God rest his soul—was so stubborn!" It was papa's turn to assume a resentful tone. "I went to him like a gentleman. Wore my good suit and spent an hour away from the fields just to ask for your hand."

"But you did not behave like a gentleman after that," mother said accusingly.

"I listened to him politely, Magdalene. But then he told me that I wasn't good enough for his daughter—that all I wanted to do was go hunting rabbits, and that I did not like to work—and if I came back a year or two later, he would still say no. What was I to do? I loved you so."

"Yes. And you went straight to the *caffenio*, where you filled up on *tsipouro*!"

We had heard this story before. I glanced at father because I liked to see him smile and the corners of his eyes crinkle. "It was *retsina,* not *tsipouro*." (*Retsina* is a table wine flavored with resin; and *tsipouro* is a strong distilled liquor.)

Mother, a quiet, uncomplaining person, aired her customary grievance. "Whatever it was, why did you want me? There were other girls you could have had. And yet, you persuaded my friend Kaleroi to invite me to come and pick flowers with her in that field far from the village. And you suddenly appeared, like Hades abducting Persephone, and you took me into the hills against my will. You knew that my reputation would be ruined, whether or not anything happened, and I would have to marry you."

"As you well know, I did not take further advantage of you until the priest married us, Magdalene, and I am not sorry for what I did." He always asserted this as he walked away.

Although Greece had declared and fought for its independence from the Ottoman Empire in 1821, it was nearly a decade before the new nation had a stable government. Young men released from duty in the revolutionary army, as well as refugees from territories still under Turkish dominion, roamed the countryside looking for work. Having spent the war years in daring exploits against the enemy, these heroic veterans were not constrained by the usual customs and taboos. To protect young women who lived or worked on isolated farms, a law was passed requiring marriage if a man took a girl by force. By imposing marriage, it was hoped that the men would think twice, and that women would have more protection from abduction. However, when this law began to be abused by men who could not win the girls they wanted by following the traditional methods, it was rescinded.

Tales of elopement and morality were a part of our childhood. Such cautionary tales taught us the facts of life as much as did the task of leading a nanny goat to a ram to be bred. I was on the way one day, with our goat and having quite a struggle with her. Goats eat anything that strikes their fancy, so I had to choose my path carefully. I did not lead her near trees because she stripped the bark off, munching it as contentedly as if it were tender mulberry leaves. Nor did I go near a yard with another goat or one with chickens because the other animals leapt out at us to start fights with our goat. As we passed the *fourno*, the bakery, I saw Sophia. We greeted each other, but she was very quiet. She pointed to a large pan filled with vegetables for stew that the baker was shoving into his cavernous oven. They must be having company for dinner, I thought. She did not explain, but said, instead, "I'll walk with you, Eleni. Your *katsika,* goat, may give you trouble."

Sophia and her mother had been preoccupied with other activities lately, so I was surprised that she took the time to walk with me. At the breeder's, it took both of us to lead the goat into the stall. Billy goats are large, intractable creatures with long beards that give them an autocratic appearance, and our goat had balked at the sight of her new mate. I had to spank her gently, as I had seen Ourania do, to make her settle down. On the way home, Sophia walked slowly, then turned to me and said, "Éleni, I hope that you will not be too disappointed that I have decided not to go to America."

"Mother has not made plans for me to go yet. If you cannot decide to go with us on our trip, you could come later, couldn't you?"

"No," she shook her head. "I do not think that life in Bordonia is so bad, and I believe that I would be just as happy marrying someone from right here in the village."

I studied her face, with its dreamy look, to be certain that she was not teasing me. We parted at my gate. I was too young to reflect on Sophia's decision for long. All thoughts of her defection in not accompanying me to America flew out of my mind when I arrived home and mother suggested that I visit *Theia* Aseemo, my father's sister. I did not see her often because she lived in Soustianous, a village two hours away. I always enjoyed my solitary walks to her house. *Theia* Aseemo was a widow with no children, and even though I had a godmother who was very nice, I thought of this aunt as my fairy godmother. She treated me like a special guest whenever she invited me to her house, and she talked to me as though I were a good friend.

On the day chosen for my visit, mother handed me a parcel for *Theia* Aseemo that contained dried figs, a well-wrapped piece of *mizithra,* a white, unfermented cheese made from our goats' milk—and a loaf of bread. I took a detour off the main path to chat with a friend and admire some cherry trees that were in bloom, so it was dusk by the time I reached the chapel just outside of *Theia* Aseemo's village. This *erimoklisaki,* a secluded little church, had been built by a shepherd years ago. His son, John, was very sick, and the distraught father had come to this solitary place to pray to *Ayios* Yiannis—Saint John—for his son's recovery. He vowed that if his son's condition improved, he would build a shrine in this place, dedicated to the saint. When his son recovered, the shepherd kept his word. It took him three years, but he finished the chapel. On January 7, the name day of Saint John, the Baptist, the village of Soustianous held church services here. The remainder of the year, the chapel was empty although a small oil lamp near the altar was attended by a devout woman in the village who kept it lit, and the door always was unlocked for anyone to enter for prayer. Many small memorial chapels such as this one are tucked away in rural areas throughout Greece.

The white-washed walls embraced me as I entered *Ayios Yiannis* this darkening afternoon. I proceeded to light my candle, comforted by the scent of the oil and the resinated frankincense. When I reached into my pocket for a coin to place in the collection box, I hesitated. No one was there to see me. I could light the candle and keep my coin, and no one would be the wiser. But I believed that some form of punishment would befall me, so instead, I dropped my coin into the box, lighted my candle, and left.

I had the secure feeling that I was protected and safe as I stepped out of the shrine into the shadows of early evening. Before I had gone far, however, I noticed a leather pouch on the road, and picked it up. It contained some gold pieces, valuable currency. I had never held so much money in my hands before, and I ran the rest of the way to my aunt's house, excited to show her my discovery. Although the money impressed her, she was more enthusiastic in welcoming me. She hugged me warmly and asked about my parents and the rest of the family. She gave me extra kisses, she said, for the wonderful bread, cheese, and fruit from home. Then she set me down on a stool by the hearth and handed me supper of bread and cheese, and placed a square tin box on the table. When I had finished, she opened the tin box, so I could see it contained butter cookies covered with powdered sugar. Very carefully, so as not to spill its precious powdery coating, she placed one of the delicate cookies, a *kourambie,* in my hands. Then, she stood smiling, with her arms folded across her chest, as I ate it.

While we washed and put away the dishes and utensils, I told her again how I had gone into the chapel, and when I came out, how I found the pouch lying on the ground. She was a good listener and wanted to please me. She promised that she would ask the priest if he knew of anyone who had lost money. She advised me to tell only my mother about this and not boast to my friends. After a few weeks had passed, and no one claimed the money, mother said it was ours, and she put it away for me. I do not think she saved it for my trip to America, but long before that, had spent it on necessities for our family and something for *Theia* Aseemo.

Always on the breakfast menu at *Theia* Aseemo's was *hirino*. I would awaken, at first unsure where I was. Then, the tantalizing fragrance of ham preserved in spices sizzling in a frying pan would bring me to my senses. In the serene atmosphere of my aunt's home, I felt that I could speak to her frankly, and I introduced one of the subjects on my mind. "Do you think a girl should marry before she is seventeen?"

My aunt stopped smiling and looked at me sternly. Her dark hair was parted in the middle and pulled tightly back into a neat bun, and when she frowned, the skin at her temples stretched tightly. "Shame on you, Eleni! You are much too young to think of marriage. You wait until your mama and papa choose the right boy for you, when you are older."

I laughed, "It is not for me that I am asking, but for Sophia."

Her expression changed and she asked, "What do you know about Sophia?"

"Well, the other day we were walking, and she said that she did not think she wanted to go to America, the way everyone else does. I wanted to ask her if Kostas Zacharias was the reason, but I decided I would do so another time. Sophia used to tell me everything, and now she is like a stranger."

Theia Aseemo was a big woman with a hearty laugh. "Eleni, she is a few years older than you are. She is a woman, ready to marry, and if Sophia seems different to you, it is because she is trying to decide if this is the right young man for her to settle down with to start her family."

"So, you do not think she is too young?"

"She is old enough if her mama and papa think so."

"There is one thing that worries me very much, *Theia.*"

"What is it, my child?"

"Sophia's parents are right now choosing the right kind of man for her to marry, aren't they?"

"Well, yes—probably. We hope so. She is such a beautiful girl that I am certain they will find the right man."

"Then, how in the world will my parents find the right husband for me if I am here, and he is in America?"

She made a chopping motion with her hand as though she was about to paddle me. "You make fun of your aunt, eh?" She started for the door. "Come, let us milk the goat. Then we will take a little walk to the village and learn the latest news."

I returned home that afternoon, sad to leave my aunt, but knowing I was not expected to stay longer. Overnight visits were limited at the time. I assumed it was because there was so much to do at home, but sometimes I wished that I could be away on trips all the time. I wondered how other families got along without many sons and daughters.

My objections did not stop mother from making plans for me. She would not give in easily, even when my father asked her. "No, Eleni," she shook her head, a few days later, as I tried to follow my sister out of the house. "You may not go to the fields today." Ourania had gathered our four fidgety goats on the lane by our house, and was preparing to lead them to a pasture away from the village.

On his way out, my father noticed my disappointment. "Magdalene, let Eleni go this time."

I stood quietly by, hoping papa would prevail. Rarely did I have the privilege of spending the day with my sister and the other shepherdesses who took the animals to graze. Once out of the village, all they had to do was make sure that their flocks did not stray onto private property, where they were not permitted to graze. The girls planned where to meet, and then they would sit on hillsides and gossip. But mother did not think this was a good example for me. She was resolute. "Ourania can bake and sew little stitches and knows how to cook a chicken. Today, Eleni will help me bake bread."

Father had placed dried sticks from the grape arbor into the outdoor oven that had been built against the hill, halfway to the lower yard. Lighting the fire, he placed two bricks inside the oven, added larger sticks on top of the kindling, and covered the opening. Then he left to spend the day in the fields, as he did every day. While in the kitchen, mother heaped a quantity of corn meal, whole wheat flour, water, and yeast on the trestle table. She rarely made bread with only corn meal; it was less expensive, but it produced a loaf that in one day became so hard that it had to be dipped in water to be eaten. Bread made solely of whole wheat flour, on the other hand, was dark and dry, and did not keep well.

The yeast starter was similar to the culture used to make sourdough bread. It was kept moist in a ceramic crock, and each week a portion of starter was saved for the next breadmaking. Mother mixed all the ingredients together and then began to knead and pound the dough. Stepping aside, she motioned to me to take over. My forearms became white with flour as I pressed the heels of my hands into the warm, yielding mass. I was just beginning to appreciate the feel of the dough when my mother sighed and shook her head as she watched my skinny fingers struggle to punch down the heavy dough. She gently shoved me aside. "We will never get done today if I leave this to your inexperienced hands, Eleni."

Grasping the dough, she slapped it on the table, and flipped and kneaded it many more times until it became a smooth, tan mound. When it was ready, she covered it with a towel and let it rise at one end of the long, wooden table. I followed her into the kitchen, where we chopped onions, and prepared them with green beans and tomatoes for dinner. We rarely ate meat. The sheep and goats were raised for their milk and their wool, so that lamb was roasted only on special occasions. The same was true of the pig. Chickens did not need much care, and although their meat was tough and stringy compared to today's chicken meat, it was a treat. My father had killed a chicken that morning, and mother cleaned it and cut it up ready for our large roasting pan. She added the vegetables, salt, oregano, and poured olive oil over everything. As long as we were heating the oven, the food would cook along with the loaves of bread.

While the dough rose, mother sent me to walk—just as I did several times a day—to the fresh water spring at Ayiannis. Never comfortable walking the route through the woods, I filled the terracotta jug and hastened homeward. I would have to return later that day, but Ourania or Leonidas usually were with me then. In the garden, mother mixed a quantity of mud that she would use to seal the oven. Most of our meals and the weekly loaves of bread were baked there. A large pot of soup or stew hung over the fireplace in the kitchen on winter days, when soup was required and it was difficult to use the outside oven. On special occasions that demanded larger quantities of food and extra bread, we splurged by engaging the village baker's large oven. When the dough had expanded to twice its original size, mother punched it down, turned it over, and shaped it into ten round loaves, which she set aside to rise again.

We scrubbed the table and washed the kitchen floor. By the time we had finished, the loaves had risen, so that each was almost a foot in diameter. Mother carried the loaves, and I followed her to the outdoor oven, carrying a bucket of water and a mop. She touched the wet mop to the bricks and when they sizzled, she knew the oven was ready for baking. With a shovel, she moved aside the bricks and the ashes left by the kindling, and ran the wet mop over the bottom of the oven to wipe away the soot. The oven hissed and steamed, and the mop became a blackened mess; then it was rinsed clean and the floor of the oven was primed for baking. Mother shoved the loaves into the oven with the wooden paddle, and then slid in the roasting pan with the chicken and vegetables, where it would cook next to the loaves of bread. She then covered the opening with a metal sheet, which she secured with the mud she had prepared earlier, sealing the cover all around and trapping the heat inside.

As we were washing our hands in the kitchen, I ventured to ask her the question that was so often on my mind. "When do you think I will go to America, Mama?"

"If you went to America now, Eleni, what could you do there? You cannot help your brothers, since a girl your age would be in the way more than she would be of any use. You will have to stay here until you can go to America with Ourania and Leonidas." She put her arms around me, something she rarely did—parents were not demonstrative at that time—and drew me close to her. "You have many years before you, so do not attempt to grow up too soon. You will be a woman and living in America before you know it." So—as my children and my children's children have done—I listened to my mother even though I did not like the idea of having many years ahead of me before my dreams could come true.

The following week, on the regular washday, I helped mother fill a large basket with clothes. We shivered in two layers of sweaters when we left the house, but by the time we had walked to the far end of the village, the sun had warmed us. Balancing the basket on one side of the donkey and a copper kettle, a *harani,* on the other side, we proceeded to level ground by the creek, where there was room for most of the women of the neighborhood. Mother found three large, smooth, flat rocks and placed them in a triangle, while I gathered wood for the fire. As soon as the blaze started, we placed the cumbersome kettle on the stones and filled it with water from the creek.

Sophia, Eva, and their mother were already there. As our mothers rubbed the garments with large, uneven pieces of yellow, homemade soap, my cousins and I slapped at the heavier clothing with flat paddles. By lunch time the soapy clothes had soaked in the boiling water, had been rinsed in the creek and were wrung out and stretched out to dry over rocks and shrubs.

Elderly *Theia* Xenia related the latest details about Elias Andamas and his troubles. It was finally over with him and his foolish ways, she informed everyone, as we unpacked our noon meal. After Roula eloped with Petros—practically in front of Elias' eyes—he changed. He had been an overconfident blusterer, but now he played the part of the rejected swain. Reports circulated in the village that he spent his days until late in the evening at the *taverna,* the pub. As a distant relative, Xenia helped care for his house. His neighbors—Olga Hatzakos and her daughter Eugenia—saw that his children went to school on time and ate their meals.

"After a few weeks of this," *Theia* Xenia said with disapproval, "I decided it was time to take steps. I went looking for Elias, hoping he would come to his senses. I found him one day moping at the *taverna* over his glass of *tsipouro*—in the morning! 'Look here, Elias,' I said. 'I am an old woman, and I cannot sweep your house as well as my own every day.' He stared at me. Then he asked, in surprise, 'You are doing that for me, *Theia*?'

'You should be ashamed of the way your neighbors are obliged to take care of your children,' I said to him. 'My children?' Again, he appeared surprised. 'Are they not all right?' By this time, I knew that he had lost touch with reality. 'Children have to eat, Elias. Where do you think they find food? You have let the house and everything go. *Kyria* Olga and her daughter Eugenia take the children to their house every day and give them dinner, and later, before you return home from the *taverna*, they hear their lessons and feed them supper.' After that day, after staggering home, he began to cook for his children and watch out for them."

Theia Xenia spoke softly, but everyone near the creek could hear her when she bragged, "But the best part is that Elias liked the pastries and casseroles Eugenia has been bringing him. Yesterday, when her mother could not go to church because her back hurt, Elias walked Eugenia home. And do you know what he said to her? He said this to Eugenia: 'I think it would be good if you married me some time soon, so that you and your mother can take care of my house and my children all the time!'"

"What!" Ourania exclaimed. She had taken her goats home after their early outing, and had run across town to join us. My sister was not one to tolerate unkindness, and she could not refrain from expressing herself. We sat together with Sophia and Eva in rapt attention.

"He should say things like that to the matchmaker, not to Eugenia's face!" *Theia* Despina was indignant.

Again Ourania was moved to declare, "How mean of him to propose marriage to Eugenia like that."

"It was cruel. That is true. But that is not the worst," *Theia* Xenia went on as the women gathered around her. "He told Eugenia that because she was not young, she should not expect romance or any gifts from him. He told her that since it was his second marriage, there was no need to spend money on a fancy wedding."

Several voices exclaimed loudly, "Shame!"

"How could he say that to Eugenia! Such a dear girl—even if she is 24!"

"He should talk! He's already past 35!"

"Did she walk away crying?" Eva was touched.

"So, what happened?" My sister asked. "Did she tell him off?"

Mother gave Ourania a look of warning to indicate that her questions were unwelcome, but my sister could not always help herself. *Theia* Xenia smiled and responded, "You will be happy to know that Eugenia went at once to her mother and told her what Elias Andamas had said to her. Olga talked it over with Eugenia, and they decided that day to tell the matchmaker that she would accept Elias's proposal."

No one spoke for a moment. After condemnation of this man came female acquiescence. As *Theia* Xenia observed, "Without marriage, what kind of a life would it be for Eugenia? When her mother dies, she would have no place to live, since the house is theirs only until that sad day; after that, she would become someone's servant. If she is settled with a man of means—Elias is a boor, but not a bad man—she would be better off."

This news rocked the village. Elias had gone from sad widower to delirious, annoying swain to a despondent drunk in only a few months. Now, he suddenly had announced his engagement to spinster Eugenia. He told Eugenia to make plans for the wedding right away, but his wishes had to take a back seat to the dictates of his religion. Lent was about to begin, and weddings were not allowed in the weeks before Easter. Elias complained to everyone that *Pater* Georgios was being unfair to him, and that he had heard that others had been given permission to marry during Lent, so why could he not have his way too?

"It is wrong, and I will not permit it!" *Pater* Georgios insisted.

Elias grumbled. Aleko, the tinker reported that the noise of pounding on leather shoes was louder than ever these days whenever he came by the shoemaker's shop. Eugenia and her mother sewed and cooked from morning to night. Mother said that they were very religious, and they did not care what Elias said—they would obey the priest. Only after they had made their preparations for the Holy Days of Easter, would they attend to plans for the wedding.

Christian life is a purposeful procession throughout the year. It marks in word and in song the Birth, Ministry, Death, Resurrection, and Ascension of the Lord, Jesus Christ. The celebration of The Resurrection of Christ on Easter Sunday was one of the most sacred moments in our lives. We prepared for it with reverence and respect. For forty days we observed a fast from meat and dairy products. But, on the day before the start of *sarakosti*, the forty days of praying and fasting before Easter Sunday, we observed *apokries*, which foretold the "absence of meat" and was a day of revelry.

That Monday of *apokries* was a national holiday; work was suspended, special foods were served, costumes were created, and parents prepared for the festivities and the masquerade as much as the children did—some more than others. Mother might tie a light blue scarf around her neck and my father might wear a colorful sash around his waist. One year, Ourania and I found a piece of red cloth that we draped to mimic a *syntagmatarchi's,* a colonel's, cape over Leonidas's shoulders; he acted the part by barking orders at our goat and waving a sword-like stick at her. We turned ourselves into princesses in long trailing skirts of pieces of sheer material we had found in mother's *baoulo,* trunk, and wearing tiaras made of grape vines decorated with twigs of basil and mint. When Leonidas was seven, he wanted a simple ghost costume, a tablecloth over his head, so that he could run after his friends and frighten them. Spare clothing, and even scraps of fabric were scarce, but we made do. Women owned only a couple of blouses, sweaters, outer jackets, and skirts to work in during the week, as well as several underskirts to layer according to the weather. They also had an outfit that was worn on Sundays, holidays, and to be buried in. It was the same for men. Children usually wore clothing that had worn out and was cut down for them. So, to find colorful fabric scraps for our masquerade outfits was a challenge; yet as families strolled in the town square, the day before Lent began, they were treated to original interpretations of clowns and kings with exaggerated noses, large eyes, and moustaches drawn with the juice of berries and charcoal. Marie Antoinettes wore large, white hairpieces amassed from sheep's wool. We paraded in our finery and admired each other's costumes, and tried to guess who was behind the masks that some wore.

We always had *makaronada*, macaroni, for dinner on this holiday. Mixing flour, water, salt, and oil mother would form a small ball of dough in her left hand, and roll it out very thin between the thumb and fingers of her right hand—letting one long rope of dough drop into the kettle of boiling water. Once the macaroni was cooked, she lifted it into a colander to drain. Macaroni was tossed with grated cheese, usually *mizithra*.

After dinner, everyone met at the *horostasio*, the paved area in front of the church, where tables were set up for snacks and drinks and for dancing into the night. The musicians arrived, only a flutist in the smaller villages, and sometimes a *bouzouki*, a type of guitar, and we sang and joined hands as we performed the traditional line dances of Greece. Sophia was a good dancer and was always passed to the front of the line as leader. Some leaders not only took the head of the line but also performed intricate solos, consisting of twists, dips, and heel slaps. The second person in line held a handkerchief taut with the leader as he executed deep knee bends. Only the men engaged in such athletic performances, while the women usually were more graceful and sedate, like Sophia. However, on this night, she did not dance as much as usual. Holding my left hand, dancing next to me, Eva whispered, "Do you see Kostas Zaharias? He likes my sister a lot." We observed them for a while, but I lost interest when Eva offered to teach me a new step. Later on, Ourania said that, whenever she saw Sophia that night, Kostas was next to her.

One afternoon, Eva and I had gone together to the spring to fetch water. Some of the older women were laughing and talking, when the black-robed figure of the priest appeared, surprising us as he called out, "Ladies! Ladies! No one has announced, to my knowledge, that Great Lent is over. Beware too much merriment during this period of sobriety and fasting! There is time enough after Easter to laugh and carry on." He emphatically bobbed his head at my cousin and me. "During this period of meditation, we need to set a good example for the young."

"Please, *Pater,*" *Kyria* Aliki extended a cup of water to him, "will you have some water?"

"No, no, thank you, Aliki; I am late already. I have promised Elias to help him decide the date of his wedding."

"I heard they wish to be married soon—before Easter," *Kyria* Stamata rasped in her deep voice.

The priest opened his eyes wide. "*Apayorevete!* Elias knows it is prohibited to have a wedding during Lent!"

"Well, I was married during Lent," *Kyria* Stamata stated brashly. "My husband had to go off to fight in the war, so *Pater* Papanicolaos married us."

The priest closed his eyes. "Papanicolaos was a very old man. He should not have done this, my dear."

"But doesn't the church give special dispensation in times of war, *Pater*?" Stamata continued doggedly.

"Eh, does that mean that you are not really married, Stamata?" *Kyria* Aliki cackled. "Maybe now you can rid yourself of your old man. You have a good excuse—after all these years of complaining about him."

Someone let out a whoop of laughter; after that, the three other women could not hold back and began to laugh without restraint. The priest shook his head as he turned away, leaving them to enjoy their joke without him.

"You've made him mad, Stamata," *Kyria* Aliki scolded, as she wiped her eyes.

The other woman nodded smugly. "Well, *Pater* thinks he knows everything, but this time he was wrong, and I thought someone should tell him so."

"*Panayia mou*! Mother of God!" *Theia* Aliki made the sign of the cross on her chest. "You should not talk about our priest like that, Stamata, or you will have bad luck!"

Church was the center of village life. Everyone was expected to attend the village church, *Ayios* Georgios. We could not be born, plant seeds, harvest, travel, celebrate, marry and die without a religious ceremony. On Sundays from daybreak until noon, we attended Liturgy; and we went to church often in the middle of the week on Holy Days. Working on Sunday and on a Saint's Day was not acceptable. Bathing on Saturday nights to be ready for worship services the next day was customary. In summer, we soaped and swam in the creek, but during the cold weather, we sponged ourselves with soap and rinsed in a large tub screened off in the kitchen. Mother always took her bath last. In the privacy of her kitchen, after the sun had set and everyone was asleep or nearly so, we could hear the quiet splashing of water on the nights that she bathed and then changed into a long, freshly washed nightgown. The next morning, she donned her clean, white, woolen, long-sleeved shirt with buttons to the neck, and her long petticoats of the same fabric—no matter what the season.

I rarely saw my mother without a dark kerchief, *mantili,* covering her hair. She would take the fabric, fold it in half to form a triangle and then stretch it smoothly over her brow, pull the ends down past her ears, crossing them at the back of her neck, then pulling them up and tying them neatly on top of her head. It was customary for widows to wear a black *mantili*; this custom was adopted by most women, but not girls.

One Sunday, in church, I noticed that Sophia had positioned herself close to the front of the balcony, and was not standing near the center in her accustomed place next to her mother and her sister. Twice, she turned her head and looked down and to the right. I craned my neck to see what had attracted her. Kostas Zaharias was looking up at her; blushing, she turned away from his gaze to stare piously at the priest at the altar. After that Sunday, Kostas would appear after church and walk Sophia home as far as her gate.

A few days later, all of the schoolchildren were called to church to participate in the Sacrament of Confession, *exomologia*. The boys wriggled and squirmed; the worst offenders were *Pater* Georgios's two sons. Even though they were altar boys, they teased and pulled the girls' hair minutes after dismissal from services, and I did not think *Pater* would get the truth from them at Confession. I had enough to worry about myself and what I would tell the priest—revealing my most serious offenses. We waited in the back of the church with our teacher until *Pater* Georgios, standing at one side of the altar, beckoned us to him, one by one. I knew I could hide nothing from my priest, and I quaked as I approached him when it was my turn.

He asked, "Do you look at boys, Eleni?"

"Sometimes, *Pater*," I answered meekly.

"Well, you must always be modest. That is good behavior. Now then, did you ever steal anything?"

This was it. "No." My heart was beating faster.

He fixed his eyes on me and repeated, "Did you ever take what was not yours?"

I must have been trembling. I knew I had to tell him. I swallowed hard and admitted, "Whenever I walk by *Kyrios* Andamas's fig tree when it's covered with ripe figs, is it a sin if I take one—sometimes maybe two little figs?"

Father coughed and turned his face away. "Well, ahem, Eleni, that is not right."

He sent me to the icon of the *Theotokos*, the God-bearing Virgin Mary, at the front of the nave, to kneel three times, each time requiring a full recitation of the prayer, *Pater Ymon,* Our Father. I felt lucky to have gotten off so easily.

Our normal diet was so basic that there seemed to be nothing left to eat during our fasting period. We ate bread, walnuts, raisins, dried apricots, and dried figs. *Octopodi*, octopus, squid, even snails, were allowed on the Lenten menu. Lentil soup was a staple, since this and other beans grew well in our soil and were plentiful and nutritious. *Fasolia nerovrasta*—beans steamed with onions, tomatoes, and herbs, without olive oil— also were permitted. Spaghetti was not a Lenten dish, because we ate it with grated cheese, and dairy products were not allowed, nor was salad dressed with olive oil, since olive oil was transported from the *elaiotrivio*, the oil press, in the skins of animals and, therefore was prohibited.

Throughout *Megali Evdomada*, Great and Holy Week before Easter Sunday, we presented ourselves for prayers at church during the day and at *esperinos,* vespers, just before sundown. As the days progressed through to *Megali Paraskevi,* Great and Holy Friday, a somber tone pervaded the village. A strict fast was observed; some ate nothing. It was a day of mourning, with everyone attending three church services: the Reading of the Royal Hours in the morning; the Descent from the Cross in the afternoon; and in the evening, Matins of Lamentation. No work was done. Neither cooking nor cleaning nor sewing was permitted—although the animals were cared for and fed, as usual. Weeks earlier, mother had dyed black all of the clothes we would wear to church on Good Friday, because even the children, like the adults, dressed in mourning. All through the day, from morning until night, the bells of *Ayios* Yiannis pealed dolefully their slow, drawn out diiing-dohhng, diiing-dohhng. We could hear their mournful knell echoing in the hills, accompanied by tolling of bells of other churches in the vicinity.

Each hamlet prided itself on the unique resonance of its church bells. When we were at a distance from our village, and bells were heard signaling an event, we recognized them as the bells of Bordonia, or whichever town it happened to be. There were bells for Sunday liturgy, for Holy Days, and the jubilant bells that signified weddings, Christmas, and Easter. Those signaling Good Friday were the same woeful notes that announced a tragedy, death, or a funeral.

On the morning of Good Friday, my sister, cousins, and I rushed out to the fields with the other girls of the village and filled our arms with wild herbs and flowers. We took them to church, where our mothers were draping each of the icons with black fabric. When we arrived with our bouquets, the women arranged them around the *epitaphios,* a sacred representation of the body of Christ on a pallet before His burial.

The evening service was concluded with the flower-decked *epitaphios* carried on the shoulders of four leading citizens around the village square. Quietly and reverently, carrying lighted tapers, the priest, the chanters, and the congregation followed. They accompanied the procession with songs of lamentation, such as this typical elegy:

"O, my clear Springtime, my sweet Child, whither hath thy comeliness disappeared?"

"The heifer mourned, beholding the Calf elevated on a tree."

With the refrain: "*Erranon ton tafon, ai myrroforoi, myrrhi.*"

"They sprinkled the Tomb, the myrrh-bearers, with myrrh."

The next day, *Megalo Sabato,* Great and Holy Saturday, after early morning church services, final preparations were made at home for the Easter feast. Mother prepared *mageritsa,* an egg-lemon soup, for our return from midnight services, when we would break our fast. *Mageritsa* was made with chopped tripe and other organs of the lamb that father would not be grilling on the spit the next day. These portions were washed and rinsed inside and out several times before they were chopped into small pieces and cooked with onion and made into a tangy soup, flavored with fresh dill. The *koulourakia*, twisted butter cookies, were ready. The eggs had been boiled, dyed red, and placed in a basket; round loaves of sweetened yeast bread, *tsoureki,* waited with a red egg in the center. Red symbolized happiness and the egg's shape, eternity.

Families saved all year to have new, finer clothes for Easter, and we spent hours on Holy Saturday—bathing, combing our hair, and arranging our clothes for that special day. Clad in our best, we arrived at church one hour before midnight on Holy Saturday. At this spiritual service, on the stroke of midnight, all candles and vigil lights were extinguished and the interior of the church was in total darkness. A hush fell over the congregation. Suddenly, a light emerged from the inner sanctum, and the priest appeared with a lighted taper, singing "*Defte lavete fos*! Come ye, take light! Take from the Light that never wanes. Come glorify the Christ, risen from the dead."

In our village church, Telemachus Kanaris, the lame son of Takis, the shepherd, was carried to the altar by two men, and throughout his lifetime, always was the first person to take light from the priest's candle. Then, the chanters and congregants in the front row touched their candles to the lighted one that Telemachus held; then slowly, those with lighted candles turned to light the candles of those behind them. Row by row, the church was illuminated—all the way to the women and children in the balcony.

The Resurrection was proclaimed by the priest, followed by the congregation singing the Resurrection Hymn:

> *Christos Anesti, ek nekron, thanato thanaton patisas,*
> *kai tis en tis mnimosin, zoi harisamenos.*

Christ is risen from the dead, by death trampling death,
and to those in memory, granting joy and happiness.

The church bells pealed everywhere—rejoicing. With the priest carrying aloft the Banner of the Resurrection, all worshippers followed him and the chanters into the street, with candles raised high, walking and singing around the square. Returning to the church, we settled in for Sunday matins and the Divine Liturgy. Once again, we sang *Christos Anesti!* At the conclusion of services, we filed to the altar, where the priest handed each congregant an egg, dyed red.

At home, we broke our fast with bowls of the *mayeritsa*; then exhausted, we went to bed. We awakened late on Easter morning to the aroma of lamb roasting on the spit in our lower garden and a large pot of macaroni bubbling on the hearth. Ourania washed the tender, bitter greens that were part of our menu on Easter, and my sister, brother, and I danced around father, trying to coax him to give us a browned piece of the roast before the rest of the lamb was fully roasted. Father and *Theios* Yiannis took turns turning the handle of the spit, because his family always came to our house for Easter.

At the table, father passed the basket of boiled eggs dyed red, so that everyone was holding an egg. Then, he held up his egg to mother, who was seated next to him. He tapped his egg with hers, and her egg cracked. Then, father proceeded to tap the egg of the next person at the table. As each one hit another's egg, he proclaimed, "*Christos Anesti!*" (Christ has Risen) and the other responded, "*Alithos Anesti!*" (Truly He has Risen). Each person had a turn at cracking his neighbor's egg, until there was only one egg, or one end of an egg, that had not been broken. The owner of the intact egg was the winner. Father sliced the *tsoureki* and mother served the bitter greens with olive oil and lemon juice. We sated ourselves on roast lamb and macaroni.

After midday naps, it was time once again to dress in our Easter finery for church for the *Agape* service. It was a celebration of Love and Forgiveness. If there had been a misunderstanding between two people, good luck would come to the one who was first to apologize that day. After church, people kissed each other on the cheek and danced to the music of the fiddler until late into the night.

CHAPTER 3

The Stranger

Ta matia sou tessera.
Beware! Use your eyes as
though you have four.
— GREEK PROVERB

The following Sunday, in the morning, a stranger arrived in Bordonia. Even before he dismounted from his horse, the entire village knew about his arrival. Aliki Pontos, whose daughter lived on the road that led into town, learned about the visitor when her grandson, Phillipas, brought her the news. "A *xenos*, a stranger, is coming. He is rich and he has a horse and a boy to help him dismount!"

Kyria Aliki left immediately for church, stopping at our house to spread the word. "The man is well-dressed, Magdalene. Phillipas says he is a *geros*, an old man, with white hair and dark skin with many wrinkles. He stopped and asked *Kyrios* Zacharias, who was walking through the square, to take him to see the mayor. And he said that he was going to church and was looking for a wife!"

Another rumor reached us when the tinker Aleko, on his way up the hill from the village, told us that the stranger was from Egypt and had come to marry Eva!

"What's that?" Mother exclaimed. "My sister never mentioned anything about someone wanting to marry Eva!" She turned and hurried out the gate toward our aunt's house. We were already dressed for church, so Ourania, Leonidas, and I ran after her, but we did not get far. Mother stopped when she was greeted by *Theia* Despina and *Theios* Yiannis—with their children Eva, Sophia, Nikos, and Stratis—coming down the lane toward us on their way to church.

"Despina, is it true that a stranger has come asking for Eva?" Mother asked abruptly, trying not to show her irritation at not being informed of such an important event in her niece's life. "Who is this man? How does he happen to be here for Eva?"

My aunt shrugged her shoulders. "We are truly as amazed as you are, Magdalene. *Kyria* Aliki just now came to tell me about it!"

"I do not know any Egyptians!" *Theios* Yiannis declared loudly. "Where did he come from, and how dare he talk about my daughter in public? You will see, my dears. At church we will learn that someone started the rumor by mistake, and it has nothing to do with Eva at all." He walked faster than usual and left us as he joined *Kyrios* Zacharias and hurried into church. When we arrived, we understood my uncle's impatience, since people were waiting outside, staring at Eva and at those of us who were with her. An Arabian horse was tethered at the coffee shop, and a young boy was standing beside it. When we took our places in the balcony, Ourania, Leonidas, and I could barely see the *xenos,* and we took turns pushing each other, devoutly of course, away from the front of the gallery. From what we could see of him, standing near the mayor at the altar, he did not appear foreign. He was dressed like an Athenian in a dark suit and white shirt. Throughout the service all eyes were on the visitor. Sophia said he had to be a Christian to come to church, but Ourania believed that he was a *Musulmanos*, a Muslim, who had left his turban at home. From early Christianity, as depicted in the mosaics of the great church of *Ayia Sophia* in Constantinople it was customary for women and children to occupy the *gynaikonitis,* the gallery, separate from the men, as in our village church. Thus, we were the last congregants to satisfy our curiosity after the liturgy. At dismissal, according to Greek Orthodox ritual, parishioners present themselves to the priest at the altar, where he dispenses the *antidoron,* a small piece of bread that he has blessed. By the time we had emerged from church, only a few people were standing around in the hope of seeing the mysterious stranger at close range, but we learned from *Theia* Aliki that the visitor had gone home with the mayor, *Demarchos* Alexandros, the leading citizen of our town.

When we reached our gate, we noticed neighbors standing in small groups up the road near *Theia* Despina's house. They waved to us although it was strange to see them outdoors at that hour instead of at home having their Sunday meal. My cousin Nikos was waiting at our door with a message. "Please, *Theia* Magdalene, mother wants you to come and help her." Ourania, Leonidas, and I did not wait for an invitation, and followed Nikos home.

As we passed them, the neighbors eagerly hailed my mother. "Anything new about the Egyptian? Is he coming to see Eva today? Are you going to help Despina entertain him?" Mother answered patiently, telling them that she knew as much as they did.

Theia Despina pulled mother into the kitchen saying, "The mayor tells my husband after church that he is bringing the stranger, *Kyrios* Diogenes Hatzis, today to see Eva! Did you ever hear of such a thing?" My aunt threw up her hands. "Even if he is an Egyptian, I have to serve them something. What else can I do? They can have *loukoumathes:* Sophia is making them right now, so they have something to eat when they arrive. Yiannis killed a chicken, and Eva is cooking it. With some macaroni, it will be plenty, don't you think? What else can I serve people when they come like this, at the last minute? *Onoma Theou!* In the Name of the Lord!"

Sophia was gently scraping portions of soft dough from a spoon into simmering oil and then lifting them out when they had cooked into golden puffs of pastry. Eva had sautéed onions and pieces of chicken in a large pan with thyme and bay leaf, and the appetizing aromas that greeted us were making me very hungry. With all the excitement, we had not had time to eat at home after church. Eva placed a lid on the pan, and turned to face us. Her plump hands on her cheeks, she raised her eyes to the ceiling. "What can it mean, Sophia? Ourania? A foreign country?"

"You will be fine wherever you go, Eva," my aunt said briskly. "It's this man I want to know about."

Sophia said doubtfully, "He seems a little old for Eva, Mama?"

"Is he from America?" I interrupted, enviously.

"No," my aunt replied. "I believe he is from Egypt."

"I do not think they are Christians there, Mama," Sophia observed. "What else do you and Papa know about him?" Sophia was not only pretty, but I thought she was very wise. Almost seventeen, she was taller than most girls her age, and slim with light brown hair and hazel eyes.

"Wife, I told you," *Theios* Yiannis looked into the kitchen for a moment. "This man is named *Kyrios* Diogenes Hatzis from Athens. *Demarchos* Alexandros told me that he is very polite, and he has apologized for not notifying us that he was coming. He asked permission to speak to Eva. He is the messenger of a friend of his who lives in Egypt. *Kyrios* Hatzis is not here for himself. He is a rug merchant in Athens, where he has a wife and a family, and he goes to church, according to *Kyrios* Alexandros. "*Katalavenis*? Do you understand? It is his friend in Egypt who has sent him here to see Eva; he is the one who wishes to marry Eva."

I looked at Eva, who was two years older than Sophia, but shorter. She had dark hair and brown eyes, and like my sister, she was clever with her hands. But unlike Ourania, who was a small bundle of energy, Eva was quiet and content to listen to the conversation around her, and rarely argued or gave her opinion. Where had anyone heard about my cousin that he would want to marry her, I wondered.

"But how does he know Eva? She has never gone to Egypt?" Sophia voiced my thoughts.

"We will have to wait and meet him when he comes with *Kyrios* Alexandros, and he will tell us everything we want to know," her father assured her.

The *loukoumathes* were tantalizing as Eva spooned honey and sprinkled cinnamon over them, but a look from mother suggested we would not be invited to have one, and that Ourania and I should go home. When mother returned later, after helping *Theia* Despina serve the visitors and clean up, she said that my uncle and aunt did not learn much more from the mysterious stranger during the short time he visited their house with the mayor that day. He had been pleasant. He spoke to Eva alone for a while. He told her that the suitor did not wish to have his name revealed or to give any more information about himself until he and Eva had met each other. *Kyrios* Hatzis ate a little chicken and some bread, but did not have any *loukoumathes,* saying that he did not eat sweet pastry. He said that his mission was accomplished. He had seen Eva, thought she was a lovely girl, and he would tell his friend his impression of her. More than that he could not say.

A month later, *Demarchos* Alexandros reported to *Theios* Yiannis that he had made inquiries about *Kyrios* Diogenes Hatzis. A friend of his in Athens assured him that he was a highly respected carpet merchant and a family man. Eva kept to her quiet ways, patiently sewing and embroidering everything her mother gave her to add to her trousseau, and not talking much about the strange visit. She was the center of attention in the weeks that followed. People would stop her for a casual chat as they had never done before, looking her over, as if trying to fathom what there was in her to attract a rich man from Egypt. Nor did speculation cease. What had brought this honor to our village? It was springtime, and love was in the air. Perhaps, along with the schools and everyone in the countryside, the unexpected visitor was another harbinger of the arrival of spring.

The first day of May, *Protimaiou*, brought the schoolroom out of doors, with a picnic to mark the day and to welcome spring. Joining hands, we sang "May is coming," *O Maios minas erhete*, and danced to usher in good weather. We had our lessons sitting wherever we could find a spot to spread our blankets; after recitations, as we were becoming restless, the teacher organized running and jumping competitions. The day before, Ourania and I, with our friends, had skipped about the fields and picked armfuls of yellow and white daisies, and all the other flowers—lavender, pink and red—that we could find. With lunch of bread and cheese and with cold spring water to drink, we sprawled on the rocks bounded by heather and wove the colorful flowers into wreaths. The smallest and prettiest wreaths we set aside to wear on our heads. Early on May Day, before school and the picnic, and wearing our flowery headgear, we ran through the village and placed the larger wreaths we had made at every door, as a sign of good luck for the coming season.

Elias Andamas, we were told, frowned at the wreath on his door. But he was known to be cranky, so we were not surprised. He continued to erroneously blame *Pater* Georgios for delaying his marriage to Eugenia, but finally a date compatible with the Easter Holy Days was agreed upon and the wedding took place. Only a few people in the village were invited to the wedding and to a small wedding feast that Eugenia and her mother had prepared. My parents did not attend, but *Theia* Despina and *Theios* Yiannis were there since my uncle was a relative of Elias.

"Why was Elias in such a hurry?" *Kyria* Stamata demanded of my aunt one day after the wedding, when they were drinking tea at our house. "He was so despondent when Roula abandoned him. Now, after his insulting manner when he proposed marriage to Eugenia, it is a wonder that she went through with it."

"He apologized to Eugenia, I am told. He said he wanted his life back to normal as soon as possible," *Theia* Despina replied. "With Eugenia as his wife, he knows he will have his meals ready and that she will be there to take care of his children."

"That poor girl!" Kyria Stamata observed. "I only hope she knew what she was doing, marrying someone as unstable as Elias! He does not know his own mind, if you ask me! At least he will have no problems with Eugenia. They say she is a virgin."

Pouring her a fresh cup of mountain tea, my mother frowned. "Stamata, you can tell me about that later. Her sister chuckled, as they glanced at me, standing by the kitchen sink. "Eleni is as curious as the rest of us to learn what the bride's sheet revealed on her wedding night."

I was grateful to mother for sending me out to the garden for the fresh mint she needed for *dolmathes*, grape leaves stuffed with meat and rice, that she was preparing. Stories about the groom's family being obligated to visit the bride in her home the morning after the wedding and making a judgment of her worthiness after viewing the nightgown became more offensive as I grew older. I had decided I would never marry, or if I fell madly in love, to make certain that the man I married did not observe such primitive customs. Droll tales were repeated from regions where the men sent ear-splitting pistol shots into the air to proclaim the bride's acceptance into their family. If the bride failed the test, she was sent home in disgrace. This was rare since most women were counseled by their sisters. Such customs lost favor as people moved away from an agricultural way of life. A few of my contemporaries were unable to escape this behavior, so they endured it.

Early one market day, Ourania was rounding up our goats to take them to pasture. Leonidas and I were helpfully patting their hindquarters to guide them out to the roadway, gleeful at trading household chores for a day with Ourania in the fields, when Sophia and Eva hailed us. Eva was pulling on the donkey's harness to make it go faster, while her brothers Nikos and Stratis were cheerfully prancing alongside, bawling at the animal to move ahead.

"On your way to market, cousin?" Ourania inquired, restraining one of her goats that was trying to stray.

Sophia shook her head in mock desperation. "Did you ever see it fail? All of us—Eva, Niko, Stratis, and I—have been trying to get this animal to hurry. It will take all day now to get our shopping done in Kastania and get back home! And this *yaithouraki,* donkey, chooses today to balk."

"What are you selling?" I asked wistfully, glancing at the full baskets suspended on each side of the feckless animal. I wished that I too had a reason to go to market and sell something.

The county seat of Kastania was a beehive of activity. Court convened there for the inhabitants of the surrounding villages to formalize contracts and settle grievances. Peddlers and farmers from afar—with items and produce to sell or trade—arrived before daybreak to set out their carts and blankets to display their wares in the town square. It was a privilege for my older siblings to accompany father when he went to the *pazari*, bazaar, and I yearned for the day when it would be my turn.

Sophia shrugged, "There isn't much, Eleni. I grew some winter spinach, and I hope there is someone who will want to trade for white flour and spices. Mother wants to do some baking."

Ourania, always quick, commented, "Mmm, sounds like you will be baking something good." White flour and spices for pastries were a rare commodity in our homes, used only for special occasions.

Taking the donkey's bridle from her sister, Sophia nodded with a smile on her lips. "It will be something good, and you will like it!" The donkey had finally yielded, and she waved to us and hurried after her brothers and Eva.

Ourania tittered. "Why do you think she was in such a hurry to get away, Eleni?"

I watched the receding figures and was puzzled, too. "I don't know. Sophia did not tell us much."

"White flour means an engagement party!" Ourania exclaimed. "And I'll bet it is for Sophia and Kostas Zaharias. He went to school in Sparta and will have all that property from his father. *Theia* Despina would not go to that much trouble and expense for just anybody."

I felt slighted that my cousin, who I considered my closest friend next to my sister, had not told me first about her engagement. "Now, don't you worry," Ourania consoled me. "Sophia cannot tell us anything. Can you imagine what would happen if the Zacharias family does not accept the dowry that *Theios* Yiannis proposes?"

"That would be very sad!"

"Not at all. Sophia would have to find another boyfriend!"

That summer I spent more time at the *Lefko.* With Eleni, my chicken, waddling beside me, I noticed that with little money to purchase feed for cattle, and with not much arable land, we kept a donkey to carry heavy loads. It subsisted on leaves that we collected from the nearby fields and sometimes seemed to live on nothing. We always kept at least one goat to supply milk. Goats, like the donkey, did not demand a delicate diet, although the goat browsed on everything and the donkey did not. When we had more goats, we sold their milk to the shepherd, who made cheese from it.

As for the pig, it was kept in a sty not too close to the house, because it was not considered a clean animal. Furthermore, it had the manners attributed to those people who are insultingly called *gourouni,* pig, and took anything that was thrown in the pen into its capacious stomach. Each year, our father purchased two pigs to fatten up in time for the important holidays of *Koimisis,* The Dormition (Assumption of the Virgin) on August 15th, and Saint Basil's Day on January 1, New Year's Day. Most families had at least one pig to supply winter provisions.

My father cleaned and smoked the pig in the smokehouse he had built at the *Lefko.* Each part was prepared and preserved for later consumption except for the internal organs that were not used for food. Herbs and spices made tasty pickled pigs feet. Pork sausages were fragrant with grated orange peel. Dried orange rind was used to flavor many foods, but was especially appetizing mingled with cloves and *thymari*, thyme, in pork dishes. The meaty pieces of smoked pork were cut into cubes and preserved in large earthen crocks in their own rich fat in a marinade of red wine, orange rind, and spices. This preserved ham was called *hirino*. After the lard was rendered, some of it was used to make soap and the remainder was saved. The crocks of hirino and other foods were stored in the cellar, away from the casks of wine and the area where the animals were kept. In winter, as a welcome change to our diet, mother would fry tasty morsels of hirino with eggs in a quantity of the lard, and spread a generous portion of the savory fat on slices of bread.

At the *Lefko* one day, Ourania and I were cleaning up after father and his helpers had finished eating. As the men stretched out wherever each could find some shade for his midday nap, Leonidas called out to Ourania and me, "I'll race you to our garden!"

Ourania, always faster than anyone else, sped out after him, and I hurried up the rocky slope with them. We tumbled together in a heap, laughing and breathless, when we reached the dusty patch of dirt the three of us had staked out as our own. Earlier in the spring, we had planted lentils, which push out of the ground within a few days, and some corn. After our seeds sprouted, though, our initial zeal waned, and since we returned to the village house and did not water them for days, one by one the little plants expired, and we came to use our abandoned garden as our personal play yard. Its situation between two boulders on a hill kept us out of sight of father, who might be looking for us to do chores, such as carrying water from the spring or looking for kindling.

The last time I was at the *Lefko,* I had concealed a stick doll that I had not finished. It was still in the crevice, where I had placed it, and I pulled it out to work on it. Sitting near my sister, I fished out a needle and thread I had attached to my underskirt and began to embroider a face on the cloth head. But soon I turned to Ourania. "I can't make faces," I complained.

She took the doll in her hands and with a few quick stitches sewed on a smile. We proceeded to discuss clothes, and when I wrapped some white fabric as a wedding dress around the doll, my brother protested. "Are we going to play with dolls? I might as well go down and help papa in the fields."

"I just want to finish this one to take home to show mama," I said, as I wound a kerchief and waistband around the doll.

"What is it supposed to be?" Leonidas asked without much interest.

"An American bride!" I answered.

"American! That's all you ever think of, Eleni." He shook his head in exasperation.

"I bet," said Ourania, "America really is different from Bordonia—like another world!" She stared at the distant horizon.

"Do you think one of our brothers will ever come back and take us there?" Ourania asked.

"Well, even if they don't," I declared with more bravado than I felt, "I am going to go there by myself some day." I pointed to the sky. "See that cloud over there—way past the mountain? That is where America is. I will live there one day and have lots of gold—and a beautiful house—and a handsome husband!"

"Not me," my brother broke in. "I don't want to leave Bordonia. I am going to be a soldier."

Ourania, who had been studying the doll, took it from my hands. "Let me fix her dress properly, Eleni. You will have to learn how to sew better wedding dresses than this, so that you don't disgrace the Louvis family when you go to America," she teased. When the corn was ripe and we had tired of dolls, we would braid the corn silk. My sister's fingers were so nimble that she braided the silk on twice as many ears as I did in the same amount of time.

Leonidas, however, was not much help. When my father asked us to dig a hole for a sapling he was transplanting, Leonidas would hand Ourania the shovel after he had dug for only a few minutes. It always pleased me when the hole was ready, and father had planted the tree, tamped the soil around it, and announced, "Watch this orange tree, children. It will grow taller than you and provide us with good fruit." Papa had a green thumb, and for many years our orange trees were the only ones in the village.

In front of our property at the *Lefko* ran the county road, *o demosios dromos.* Partially paved, it wound downhill to Sparta from the villages situated in the higher reaches of Mount Tai-getus. Treacherous and slippery as it was during the winter snows, it was the main route to the marketplaces in summer. With several groups of tired and thirsty travelers on foot or on mules passing our property each week, papa decided to set up a traveler's rest stop. He placed a wooden bench and a table under the shady branches of the large plane tree—the *Lefko.* When my sister, brother, and I were there, father let us serve water from the nearby spring to anyone who stopped to rest.

We now enjoyed not only the easygoing pace of life at the Lefko, which we loved so much, but also the excitement of see-ing new faces each day. From the free-flowing spring, we filled a pail with icy water and served the water to our customers in cups. Father had a bottle of homemade *mastiha* on hand, an anise-flavored liqueur preferred by men in the summer. The women who accompanied their husbands favored *visinatha,* a glass of cold water sweetened with wild cherry preserves.

Most who stopped were villagers and their wives on their way to the *pazari* in Kastania or to Sparta. Once there were some "real ladies." I thought they were beautiful, with their rouged cheeks, and wearing bright colors, and their hair cut short—unlike anyone I knew. In a society where even young girls wore ankle-length, long-sleeved dresses in summer, it was an event to see these women arrive with an older man from town. It made me uncomfortable, though, to hear them laugh aloud and twirl their parasols as they eyed my father, who looked silly as he grinned at them. I wondered uneasily if these women had been to America, and if this was how women behaved in the country of my dreams. If so, maybe, just maybe, I might stay in Bordo-nia after all.

Chapter 4

A False Start

Stolistike i nifi kai apomeine.
The bride, dressed in her finery,
was left at the altar.

— GREEK PROVERB

In summer, we were allowed to go barefoot most of the time, except for the long walk to the *Lefko*. The path to our farm was mostly unpaved and took more than thirty minutes from the house. "Put your shoes on!" mother called after us, as my brother, sister, and I would leave, carrying them in our hands. We did not like wearing our heavy leather shoes because they were hot, and as hand-me-downs, they did not fit well.

"I'll be all right, mama," Leonidas protested.

"You are the one who will suffer if you step on a scorpion— not I!" Mother retorted.

Although I did not step on any scorpions, I had my share of scrapes. One day, as I was on my way to the *Lefko*, I passed some mountain sheep, with their long, narrow tails and short legs. The last time I had walked this way, I spotted the newborn puppies of one of the sheep dogs, and I walked slowly, bent over, to find them. They were brown and cuddly, and I hoped to play with one of them, although I knew that these dogs were bred to be fierce protectors. Suddenly, my foot was clamped between the jaws of a ferocious dog. I fell to the ground and screamed. The animal, most likely the pups' mother, pinned me down forcefully whenever she felt me move. I was petrified. At last, the shepherd appeared, and shouted and tugged at his dog as she continued to grip me. Finally, the shepherd was able to move me to safety. He helped me up, and sent me home with a scolding for coming too close to his flock. I was shaken and cried all the way until I found my father at the farm. He examined my lower leg and foot, determined that the dog's teeth had not penetrated deeply nor broken any bones, and washed my wounds with our homemade soap and spring water. In his nosy way, Leonidas had pushed close to papa in order to watch the procedure, and he imitated mother's voice: "Good thing you were wearing your shoes, Eleni." I joined everyone else, laughing through my tears.

The faithful dogs that guard the sheep remain untamed since they protect against all threats to their owner's flock. It was fortunate that the shepherd had been near enough to hear my cries. Usually shepherds had several flocks at a distance from one another, and they roamed the foothills to observe each flock, leaving their dogs in charge until their return. I had trespassed too close to the sheep (or to the pups), and the dog had acted on instinct. That night, as I lay gazing at the sky, I imagined that America was more civilized, and that people did not have monstrous dogs that attacked without cause. But I did not remain angry with the shepherds. As night fell, the lonely ballads of the *floyera,* the flute, pierced the twilight from deepest ravines to highest hills and meadows. In the clear air, we could hear echoes of romantic and mournful ballads as the shepherds bedded down too.

The life of a shepherd was a lonely one in summer, since each man took his sheep and goats (as well as those of neighbors who had hired him) to the mountainside where he found, or rented, grazing land. Usually robust, he moved the flocks from pasture to pasture, but returned each night to his tent to milk the ewes and the goats. In the hot Mediterranean summer, he preserved the milk by methods that had been practiced for centuries before refrigeration. He made cheese and yogurt cultures, and from them, produced yogurt and several cheeses—from the semisoft, unfermented *mizithra* to barrels of pure white *feta* in brine and wheels of *kefalotiri,* a hard cheese. Most of the cheese he traded or sold was eaten along with bread and olives. The harder cheeses usually were grated and served over pasta and rice.

Sometimes, during the summer, the shepherd's family moved with him to the fields, or he came home for a festival. Most wives made at least one trip to their husbands' tents, otherwise remaining in the village home, tending the garden and the children, until their husbands brought the animals back at summer's end.

Another summer, I was again injured, and had no one to blame but myself. When Leonidas, Ourania, and I happened upon a mule loosely tied at the *Lefko,* I announced, "I think I'll ride it before we call papa to tether it." My sister and brother did not think I would dare to do this and teased me. "Not a little girl like you, Eleni! Only big men ride mules."

"It's very easy," I persisted, "Anyone can ride a dumb mule."

"Now she thinks she is an equestrienne," Ourania laughed.

Too late, I learned that I had chosen the wrong steed for my first experience on mule back. As I struggled to clamber onto its back, it galloped away as I held on to its mane. Then it reared and stopped short to shed me on a stony patch. The rocks tore the skin on my right arm, and my sister and brother, distressed at what had happened, helped me hobble painfully to find father. As soon as he saw me, he sat me down and sent my sister to the garden for an onion. He sliced it in half, then rubbed the cut side all over with salt, and placed it on the wound. The pain was intense, but my father's calmness reassured me, so that I did not scream as loudly as I wanted to. Although the scar remained to remind me of my folly, father's germ-fighting measures successfully fought off infection.

Despite my wound, father agreed that I could sleep at the *Lefko* that night instead of returning to the village. My wound won his sympathy, and he granted Ourania and me permission to sleep on the crown of one of the mulberry trees. Although we always slept on mats outdoors in the summer, when we stayed at the *Lefko*, we were rarely allowed to sleep on a tree-top. We laid branches of the feathery scrub pine, crisscrossed on top of the mulberry tree, which grew to the height of my father. Ourania, taking the entire burden upon herself, while I sat quietly nursing my injured arm, collected downy soft ferns from the stream, which she placed over the scrub pine branches, and on top of everything, a blanket. Ourania helped me scramble up beside her. We felt privileged indeed to be sleeping on top of the mulberry tree. The sky was clear and the constellations of *Pegasus*, *Perseus,* and *Alevotravos* (the Plow, also known as the Big Dipper) were old friends. We fell asleep while counting shooting stars. The only disadvantage to sleeping on a tree top was that the sun awakened us the moment it peeked over the horizon. It was bright and hot, and we quickly scurried down from our perch.

However, it was not enjoyable to spend the night at the *Lefko* in bad weather. The donkey, mule, sheep, and goats had their stalls under the same roof, separated from us by a wall. We could hear them stirring and munching hay all night long, with a steady crunching sound.

The morning after I had fallen from the mule, Leonidas asked father to let him climb up to the lookout post. The *berraka* or *beryetsoula* was a perch with a thatched canopy high up in a tree. Farmers sometimes shared an inspection post that overlooked several acres. As their crops ripened, and before they were ready to be harvested, the owner, or someone hired by several owners, climbed into the *berraka* and stayed there for hours, on the alert for poachers—animal and human. Father had had enough of injured children by then, so he refused Leonidas that day; but instead, he promised to take the three of us fishing.

The small stream that ran through our property was used for irrigation and as a source of fish and seafood. We loved to go fishing with my father. He harvested from local waters in a manner that was both unusual and illegal. First, he dammed a section of the shallow tributary of the Eurotas River that ran through our property; then, he fashioned a channel to trap the sea creatures in the pool he had made. Last, we joined him in poisoning the pool with a weed called *phlomos* that grew wild in the fields. *Phlomos*, related to mullein, exudes a milky toxin when the stalk is cut, similar to milkweed. Excitement mounted as father sent my brother, sister, and me to gather the pale green bundles of *phlomos*. We watched him drop the plants into the water, leaving them overnight. The next morning, we waded into the stream, and with our bare hands, gathered all of the minnows, crabs, and eels we could carry away in pails. The creatures were not dead, but rather confused and sluggish from the noxious *phlomos*. Father instructed us to be careful of the weed, and to take note that, while he used only enough for the desired result, he had ascertained that the stream was flowing freely before he dammed that one section. After we had harvested all of the sea life in the pool, father opened the dam, and the stream rushed away on its path, diluting and dissipating the weed's ill effects. Similar methods are used in other parts of the world. In ignorant hands, this strategy is unsafe, and rightfully banned because it sickens the cattle and other animals that drink from the tainted streams and contaminates their milk. Washing our catch with spring water and cooking it purified it, so that it did not adversely affect our own digestive tracts.

No stream is worth much if on a sweltering summer day, children cannot dive and splash in its refreshing waters. Boys romped in the waterways whenever they wished, improving their swimming skills, but the girls were rarely given permission to hike up their skirts—when no boys or men were around—to wade and splash too.

As much as I liked playing on the farm, I did not want to be away from the village whenever an itinerant peddler arrived. He came on foot in the morning, carrying a large woolen sack on his back, and set it down in front of the *caffenion*, where people congregated. The man who repaired copper kettles had a donkey, and he would call out, "*Chalcomata na yanoso! Chalco-*

mata na yanoso!" (Let me repair your copper and brass!) The boys ran after him, raucously chanting their own crude rhyme: "*Kai sto kolo sou na hoso*"—which rhymed ass with brass. Our large kettle, the *harani,* used to boil water for washing and for bathing, was copper-lined. It periodically needed a new coating of copper because it was set directly over an open fire, and the bottom frequently burned through.

My favorite peddler was the *pragmatefthees,* who sold a variety of household necessities that we could not make ourselves. He would ring a brass bell as he called out, "*Velones! Klosthes*! (Needles! Thread!) *Mantilia!* You will not find such fine kerchiefs at the *pazari* in Kastoria!" The neighborhood women clustered around him, examining his wares. He set down his bundle as each woman chose what she wanted and could afford.

If I had saved up a few pennies that one of my brothers had given me, there was nothing I enjoyed more than standing next to my mother and looking over the pretty handkerchiefs. In the days before paper tissues, people made do with cotton, silk, or linen handkerchiefs. I inspected all of them—some with a little embroidery or edged with colored thread—and then made my selection. My love of these linen squares even drove me to take one that did not belong to me. It happened a few days after the peddler's visit. Mother and I had just finished spreading clumps of dough for *trahanas* on two large, cotton sheets stretched out on a table on the balcony. *Trahanas* is a pasta-like staple—made of flour, yeast, and milk—in small kernels that brings sighs of contentment to those brought up on it. It was used as a macaroni product and eaten at any meal. On cold, wintery days, it made a comforting and filling breakfast. Mother would add about two cups of *trahanas* to two quarts of water and simmer the mixture for half an hour. It was served plain or with sugar as a cereal. Or it was dropped into boiling broth, as done with rice or noodles. For supper, mother sometimes browned the *trahanas* in olive oil or butter before cooking it with tomatoes and onions.

Trahanas dough was made only in summer, in large quantities to be dried and stored for the rest of the year. One day, mother had mixed all of the ingredients, had let the dough rise, and then had carried the bowl to the balcony. I was helping her, using both hands to crumble fists full of dough over the sheets. That was when Leonidas came running through the courtyard: "Mama! Papa is coming with three men!" In dismay, mother cried, "What? Now?"

"Yes. They are at the *caffenion*, and Papa said to tell you to be ready when he gets home."

"That man!" She exclaimed, more to herself than to Leonidas and me. "Why can't he come home by *himself* one time, instead of bringing home everyone he meets on the way?"

She turned to me. "Eleni, I will put the *trahana* back into the bowl. We will finish tomorrow. Go to *Theia* Despina to see if she has three or four eggs. *Grigora!* Hurry!" She called Leonidas. "Cut me some greens and bring any ripe tomatoes you can find. Then sweep the courtyard and the balcony after I have moved the sheets with the *trahanas.*"

We went into action. I ran to my aunt's house. But her door was locked and no one was at home, so I ran to another relative, my father's cousin, *Theia* Euterpe Louvis. Uncle Louvis owned the general store in the *plateia,* village square. Their house was adjacent to their store. All year his wife could be seen tending her pots of brilliant red geraniums, or green mounds of herbs on the twin balconies of her large house. In fact, most houses had pots of basil, mint, and flowers, but *Theia* Euterpe had more of everything.

Their gate was open, so I went upstairs to the porch and knocked on the door. It was ajar, and I entered. I could hear someone talking, and I followed the sounds, but found myself in the empty living room. It held more furniture than our house or Sophia's house. I had never been this far before, and cautiously proceeded toward the kitchen, peering into the bedrooms. Each had two beds and a tall dresser. I stepped into one of them, and saw a dresser with a beautiful yellow handkerchief lying on it. I crossed the room to get a better look and then picked it up, pressing it against my cheek as if it were my own. Just then, I heard voices that sounded as though they were coming closer, and I panicked. I was not supposed to be in this bedroom, and I rushed to the door, still holding the handkerchief. It was too late to return it to the dresser, so I stuffed it into my pocket and left the room. *Theia* Euterpe was in the kitchen, pouring cups of coffee for a man and woman sitting at the table. She was never cordial, but on this day, she was different. She placed an arm around my shoulders, and introduced me to her visitors from Sparta, adding, "Eleni's brother is prospering in America." To me she said, "What are you doing here?"

"I knocked, but there was no answer," I stammered. "Mama would like to borrow some eggs from you, please. Papa is bringing company home. Three, if you can spare them."

"My husband's cousin, Demetrios!" She exclaimed to her visitors. "He invites anyone he meets at the *caffenion* to his house for supper. I will get the eggs for you, Eleni."

I do not know how I stood there watching her reach into a cupboard and count out three eggs. I waited for her to go to that fateful bedroom and look for the hanky, but she merely placed the eggs in the bag I had brought with me. "*Entaxi*, all right, go on home." I thanked her and turned away, wanting to run as fast as I could from her house and all the way home, but instead I walked carefully with the bag of eggs in my hands, and the stolen hanky in my pocket.

I returned home still frightened at what I had done. I knew it was wrong to have taken the hanky, but I did not tell my mother. She was hurrying to fix supper for father and the unexpected guests, and I would have to keep my guilty secret to myself, always fearful that *Theia* Euterpe would expose me.

Leonidas had just finished sweeping the porch, and mother was shaking out a small rug when father arrived, as though this was a long-standing engagement. Mother greeted the guests graciously; by now she was used to her husband's habit of rarely giving her advance notice when bringing strangers to their home for supper. The men took seats in the courtyard.

Our main meal of the day was at noon, so in the evening we ate something as simple as bread and cheese. This would not do for visitors, however, for whom mother always cooked something more substantial.

Father was expansive: "Magdalene, I sent Leonidas home to let you know we were on our way this time." He brought out the wooden carafe, the *chotra*, filled with homemade red wine that he poured into his guests' cups. They drank slowly, and smoked, leisurely rolling their cigarettes, as they discussed politics.

In the kitchen, mother heated olive oil in a large frying pan, added sliced green onions and chopped tomatoes, then mixed in the three eggs. She grated a small mound of *mizithra* and mixed it with some oregano into the eggs. She had set the table and was preparing a salad of the greens Leonidas had brought in from the kitchen garden. To the greens she added fresh basil, salt and pepper, and dressed the salad with oil and vinegar. When she was ready, she placed everything on the kitchen table along with a large loaf of bread and glasses filled with cold water. She invited the men to the table . *"Peraste*! Come in!" Over the meal, they continued their discussion and, as was usual with father and his friends, the men talked into the night. My mother, sister, brother and I already had snacked on cheese, bread and olives, and we went outside to play with our friends.

The next day, mother and I went to work to finish the *trahana* while the weather was still hot and sunny. We stretched two cotton sheets on the balcony, and spilled the clumps of trahana dough onto them. They dried on one side, and then the other. After a few hours, we turned over the clumps, working them with our fingers into smaller pieces. At dusk, mother carefully shook the pieces into large bowls and took them inside. Every day, for the next two days, we repeated this process— dropping the pieces on the sheets to dry in the sun, crumbling them into smaller pieces, then bringing them inside at dusk. It was hard to resist snacking on these tough little bits of dough, but I occasionally popped a few into my mouth when mother wasn't looking. On the third day, we pressed the pieces through a coarse sieve, to their final shape as small kernels, and spread them once again under the hot sun. Finally, we stored the trahana in crocks for winter.

Only when peaches, apricots, figs, and oranges were ripe were they offered for sale at the open air markets in Sparta. Fruits did not come to us in any other way, and we enjoyed them sweet and in season so much that Ourania, Leonidas, and I sometimes helped ourselves to one or two from the bulging saddlebags of one of the farmers who stopped at the *Lefko.*

Our own back yard produced one of the sweetest fruits, easy to help ourselves to, but not always the wisest thing to do. Surrounding the lower garden of the house in Bordonia was a fence of cactus. In spring, when the olive trees were dotted with white buds, and the orange trees were fragrant with waxy, cream-colored blooms, the cactus plants would put on their show of yellow and pink flowers. The fruits they produced later in the summer were most refreshing. In order to savor them, however, we had to choose a day when there was no breeze because the slightest wind could direct one of the sharp cactus spikes into our eyes.

As soon as the aroma of the sweet *frangosika*, prickly pears, filled the air, I knew they were ripe, and informed my father. He attached a nail to the top of a long bamboo pole. Catching hold of the stems with the nail, I pulled down as many of the fruits as I wanted. I swept the skins with bunches of tough weeds to clear them of the tiny needles that covered them and then I tucked as many as I could out of sight in a hollowed-out niche along the bank of the shallow stream. They were concealed from others hungering for the sweet fruit, and they were kept fresh by the cold water running nearby. One sultry afternoon, I decided that nothing would taste better than a couple of sweet, cold *frangosika.* I downed one, but that wasn't enough, so I ate a second one. Soon, I had eaten more than I should have. The stomach ache I suffered that night was not as bad as the medicine my mother forced me to take: castor oil! Years later, I gave this medicine to my children only once because of my strong aversion to it.

At last the day arrived when mother sent me out with Ourania to take our goats to pasture. I waited impatiently for my
sister to fill a woolen bag with bread and cheese and olives
wrapped in oiled paper for our lunch. Then, we walked through
the village, keeping pace with the animals. We kept three or
four goats at a time, and because they were so voracious they
had to be taken to distant fields every day, so that they would
not defoliate the neighborhood trees and shrubs. Occasionally,
we raised sheep, but this depended on what my father wanted to
do each year. In general, we did not name the animals that were
raised to be sold for their meat, and the donkey for cash. However, we had a favorite milk goat, *Kopela*, Young Lady, for a
number of years. The bells worn around their necks announced
who they belonged to as we passed through town, then down a
hill, through a ravine, and into a field far from our village. My
sister found a place where she could safely tether the goats and
watch them from a shady spot; there we spread a blanket and
watched the clouds, took walks and returned with sticks for our
doll figures. We fashioned clothing for them out of scraps of
fabric that we had brought along; as we worked we told each
other the life histories of each of our creations. One story
described Marika, whose wicked stepmother made her work
like a slave and who dressed Marika in rags. We elaborated on
the girl's misfortunes and on her goodness and religious fervor,
which gave her the courage to endure. One day, a handsome
young man came to her village and carried her away to be his
wife and live with him and his kind-hearted mother. Marika had
an extravagant wedding, with an elaborate dress and a bridal
wreath decorated with field flowers. The kind-hearted mother
and the attendants were all dressed beautifully. Many guests
(made of more sticks) came. We were running out of sticks and
held the wedding feast early, as we ate our simple lunch. Then,
we put the newlyweds to bed for their wedding night, with
much giggling and naïve interpretations of what happened in
the nuptial chamber. After lunch, we stretched out to nap. The
goats, in the meantime, were under the watchful eye of my sis-

ter, who tethered them in various places, so that they did not strip bare the available foliage.

After our siesta, Tasia, a friend of Ourania called from a neighboring field, "*Ela*! Come over, Ourania! Bring Eleni and join me!" We moved the goats, so that we could visit her. Her friend Koula joined us, and they made dolls and added them to the play. That afternoon, all of the dolls married, had children, and led full lives. It was a wonderful day! Ourania and her friends knew all the popular songs, and when they were not singing them, they chatted about clothes, and boys, and the latest village gossip.

A few days later, I was weeding the garden when mother called me to tell me the mail had come, and I should come in. Leonidas was in the kitchen watching excitedly, as father held a letter in his hands, and Ourania hung on his arm to see if she could read it. It was from America! I could tell because it was written on thin paper and had many stamps.

"What does it say? Who is it from?" We all asked at the same time.

After we had stopped shouting, my father spoke quietly. "It is from your oldest brother, my son Andonis. He writes that he is going to marry the pretty lady Viola he had written to us about once before. He wants Mama and me to come to America for his wedding."

We were astounded. "What will we do without you and Mama?" Leonidas wailed. "Who will take care of us?"

My parents waited for our discomfort to subside. Then Papa spoke, "I cannot go, but Mama will go to our son's wedding. Andonis says that Eleni is too young to stay at home, so she must go with Mama, and since one of her sons should accompany her on the voyage, Leonidas will go as well."

Ourania stared at him hopefully, but it was mother who told her. "You will have to stay at home with Papa. He will need you to cook for him and for the men when he has helpers—and to take care of the house and the animals. I will come back, and then Andonis promises that he will send for you to come to America."

Father turned to me. "What do you say, Eleni? Do you want to go with your mother and Leonidas to America to visit your brothers and your sister?"

"Oh, Papa! Mama! When do we leave?" I choked—laughing and crying at the same time. "Why can't *Theia* Despina come and cook for Papa and the men? Eva and Sophia could help with the house and the animals. Ourania has to come with us!"

"Theirs is a large family, and we can not impose on your aunt or anyone else to take care of your father and our household in that way."

And so it was going to happen just as Andonis had written in his letter.

From that day until the day of our departure, two weeks later, I did my chores as if in a dream. Mother had often expressed the desire to see her children who had gone to America, and her eldest son Andonis had decided that this was the time. He was doing well in his candy business in Lancaster, Ohio, and would be my first brother to get married. He sent money to pay for mother's passage and for two of her younger children, since children under the age of twelve could travel free.

Ourania was very disappointed that she had to stay home, but she trusted that Andonis would keep his promise of inviting her one day soon. Given her cheerful nature, Ourania helped in any way she could with our preparations for the trip. Leonidas and I threw ourselves into preparing for our departure, which consisted mainly of getting in everyone's way. We were so happy to be leaving the village where we had spent all of our lives. "You are going to cross the ocean," father cautioned, "and go to a land where the people do not speak and understand the Greek language. Until you learn their language, you will have to get on as best you can, with the help of God, and with your brothers at your side."

The day for our departure arrived at last. My father would be shorthanded when it came time to harvest the wheat, corn, and olives, but he knew Ourania could prepare food for the workers and she seemed glad that mother had the opportunity to visit her children who lived in America. Mother had packed our few belongings in two woolen bags. She filled a third smaller one with dried, home-grown oregano, special tea leaves harvested from the mountain, and even some of the dried *trahana*. Leonidas and I could hardly contain ourselves. We were ready to go out the door barefoot and carrying our shoes, but father frowned at us. "You must wear shoes all the time, children." So, we dutifully pulled them on and tied the laces. As we were about to leave the house, Sophia came in and hugged us tearfully. I took out a folded handkerchief and handed it to her. "You can use it now, if you wish. It is for you." It was white, and I had embroidered her initial S on it. Everyone smiled, and Sophia cried, "I will think of you every time I look at it, Eleni. But I will not be able to use it because it is too pretty!" We hugged and wept some more. Then Sophia took my hand, and we hurried out to the courtyard, where the others were waiting. Everyone kissed and cried and hugged each other. Neighbors accompanied us for part of the way and wished us well. The women hugged me, and the men kissed me on my forehead.

"I'll miss you Mama! Eleni! Leonidas!" Ourania often cried. "Write to me every day. Send for me as soon as you can!" Father's gray eyes were solemn as he advised us once again: "Obey your mother always, Eleni." To his youngest son he added, "When you arrive in America, you must obey your older brothers."

My father had gone to the United States years earlier, but could not adjust to working in a factory, so he returned to Greece, to his beloved countryside, referring to his experience in the factory as "two years in a dungeon." *Theia* Despina and her family, as well as other friends, accompanied us to the village center, where we met the mule train that would take us to the market town of Kalamata. There we would get our passports and buy the tickets needed for passage to America.

A group of people had gathered outside of the *caffenion*. One of them, with a wide mouth and thick black mustache, strode toward father and clapped him on the shoulder. "Do not look so worried, my friend," he bellowed. "Are you going to insult me and declare to the good people of Bordonia that you do not trust Georgios to lead your family to safety?" Georgios and his mules served as the taxi service and guides for the surrounding area. Travelers taking the dangerous route over Mount Taigetus to Kalamata on the Gulf of Messinia planned their trips according to his availability, just as we had. "God be with you, you ruffian," father replied, introducing him to mother.

"*Kyria mou,* my good lady, you have nothing to worry about when you hire Georgios, the best mule driver in all of Greece!" He grinned.

"Enough of your bombast!" Father took him aside. "You are certain you know where to find Joanna, my niece in Kalamata, where you are taking my wife and children?"

"Of course! Everyone knows the house of Petros, who repairs the clocks."

The other travelers in the party included a man with his wife and their two young sons, also going to Kalamata. When Georgios motioned that he was ready to leave, father helped to seat mother on the saddle, so that both legs were on one side. Women did not ride astride. Then, Leonidas and I kissed father's hand and scrambled onto the mule provided for us. Ourania was small, so we helped her up and squeezed her in, so that we could be together a little while longer. Father stood near us as we started out. "Remember, Magdalene," he advised mother. "The papers are in order. Be sure you tell the man at the passport office in Kalamata that my son in America prepared them." He turned to Leonidas. "Remember. You are now the man, and you will have to watch over your mother and sister."

The procession of mules and well-wishers pressed on. I felt important as neighbors stood in their doorways calling out our names, waving to us, and wishing us well. "Send me a little piece of gold from the streets!" called *Kyria* Stamata.

"Ah, the wealthy men Eleni will meet." *Theia* Xenia bobbed her head, as she stood on her balcony above the road. "She will come back with her nose so high in the air that we won't be able to talk to her!"

We laughed to hold back the tears. *Theios* Yiannis cautioned my brother, "Don't forget us when you make your first million,

Leonidas! Just remember that we knew you when you stole old Tsomas's pig!"

This inspired the boys running alongside our mule to giggle as they recounted the details of their escapade with Leonidas. Tall, gaunt *Kyria* Aliki ran out of her gated courtyard, holding a package tied snugly with rope. "Magdalene," she spoke imperiously, as she pressed it into mother's lap. "This is my good coat and some dresses I am sending to my sister in Chicago. Just tuck it in your bag out of the way." Father's look of exasperation did not bother her, but he scolded her anyway. "*Sto Onoma Theou!* In God's name, Aliki! Your sister has a rich husband and does not need you to send her anything! Besides she lives in Chicago, and where Magdalene is going is not near Chicago!"

"It is all right, Demetrios," mother murmured. "I will find someone to take it to her sister."

Father was silent. He stopped the mule mother was riding and tucked the package under the ropes which held one of our own bags against the mule's flanks. "Thank you, Magdalene. May the Lord bless you and your children and speed you on your way." *Kyria* Aliki glanced at my father, and muttered, "Chicago is in America, Demetrios. Magdalene is strong enough to carry one more parcel." Then she moved closer to another neighbor and told her that she did not approve of "all this travel across the sea. If the Lord had meant for us to go so far, He would have made men us with fins and tails, as He did the fish."

"Ooooooooosht!" Georgios roared the start of the journey. Our descent out of the village was about to begin, and brought on more tears and final kisses from Ourania as she slipped off our mule and hugged mother's ankles. Then she and father stood by the path and waved us on. The squeaks and groans of the wooden saddles, and the steady clomp, clomp of the pack animals' hooves on the dirt and rock-strewn road accompanied our exodus from the village. It took half a day before we were beyond familiar fields and farms. The path grew steeper and more narrow. After we had breached the mountain pass we would be in the town of Kalamata. From the port of Kalamata we would board a small boat called a caique to carry us on the Ionian Sea to Patras, the port of embarkation on the west coast of Greece for steamships to America.

"Mama!" Leonidas called suddenly, "Way up there on the ledge! Do you see those people moving?" Georgios, the guide, laughed heartily. "Yes! Of course your mother sees the people up there. That's where you'll soon be. Maybe you will look into an eagle's nest. Who knows?"

I felt my brother shudder. One of the men on horseback was riding directly behind our mule. "Don't worry, my boy. You are better off on your mule on these mountain paths than I am with Blackie here." Whenever we came to a narrow ledge, I prayed that the mule was as good as the man had said, and would not accidentally rub against the sheer rock on one side and send us plummeting into the boulders below. But the animals plodded with measured steps up and around the winding goat paths. When the mule stumbled on a stone, as he sometimes did, I held my brother until we felt the steady pace resume. Stones plunged off the side of the path, ricocheting against the cliff on their way to the bottom. Both of us held our breath, fearing that the mule's next step would not be so sure, and we would take the same direction as the falling stones.

Kyrios Thivas, the father of the two young boys, closely followed the muleteer looking neither to the right nor to the left, and speaking to no one. His wife, on a mule of her own, held the reins tightly and spoke to my mother only when they were on a wide, level place on the path. "I would prefer to have stayed at home," *Kyria* Thivas confided. "I am so afraid of Taigetus. But we must go to my cousin's wedding in Kalamata. She is marrying a lawyer from Patras, and it will be a very big wedding."

Mother told her that she was going to America and spoke with pride of seeing her sons, and of the eldest, who was paying her way to come since he owned a confectionery store in Ohio, America. *Kyria* Thivas declared she did not approve of children moving away from home. "My sons would never leave their papa and me and go so far away. But when you have so many children, I am sure you do not miss them as much as I would since I have only two sons."

It had always seemed to me that my mother was very sad as each of her children departed, but she did not contradict the other woman. Just then, Omiros Thivas, the younger son, who had been listening said, "I am going to America some day, Mama. Maybe not right away, but probably when I am 15."

Kyria Thivas spent the next half hour in a long discourse to her sons about boys who leave home. Each was on a separate mule, so she had to raise her voice to be certain that she was heard. She stopped only when we reached a spring and Georgios dismounted for lunch. The mule driver strolled to the free-running water and filled his cupped hands with it, drinking noisily. Then he attended to the mules, while the rest of us dismounted and ate our meal. Georgios stretched out on a rock and sliced hunks of bread and cheese, offering them to anyone who might want some, lifting pieces to his mouth from time to time.

The two women spread out cloths on the ground. *Kyrios* Thivas cut slices from a large round of bread and handed them along with wedges of cheese to his family. Mother also had brought bread and cheese, and the families shared tomatoes, cucumbers, figs, and grapes. The men on horseback kept their distance from us, and walked around, pointing out the scenic vistas to each other. They accepted figs from my mother, commenting on the sweetness of the home-grown fruit.

After a nap, Georgios started us off again. The afternoon ride was a tedious continuation of the morning's trip, as we skirted more cliffs and ravines. My brother and I needed all the courage we could muster. All of our lives, we had been warned away from the steep tracks that led up to the mountain. Now, Taigetus proved to be a test of courage—one more step away from our village and toward the promise of America. Nor were any of us prepared to see such an immense body of water as the Gulf of Messinia, which we could see clearly from the foothills as we descended. "A boat can't stay afloat on so much water!" Leonidas exclaimed, without taking his eyes from it. An arc of mountains enclosed the long curve of beaches and the harbor.

"Ships have sailed there and beyond since before Odysseus," Georgios informed him.

"Wait until you sail past the Pillars of Hercules as you sail out of the *Mesogion*, the Mediterranean Sea, on your way to America," he added. "Then there is no turning back. You are on the ocean—bigger even than the Gulf of Messinia that you are looking at right now. The ocean circles the entire world."

Georgios led his caravan from the path into the busy road of the market town of Kalamata. It was the biggest city I had ever seen, since I had never been to Sparta, and I tried to look everywhere at once. Donkeys carried baskets of eggplant, squash, beans, melons. Fabric and clothing hung for sale on carts and from wooden beams. There were people everywhere.

"Here's your niece's house," Georgios said to mother at last, stopping in front of a modest gate. "Hey, in there!" he shouted, "Your aunt from Bordonia is here!" My brother and I slipped off the mule as best we could, while Georgios gave mother a hand and then our baggage from the animals. We exchanged a few words of farewell to the others on the mule train, and then, with a shout of "*Yiasas*!" Georgios waved to us and was gone, and we turned to greet our relatives. The street gate opened and a young woman came out with a little boy clinging to her skirts and another one holding her hand. "Aunt Magdalene! Eleni and Leonidas! *Yiasas!* Come in! Come in! We have been waiting for you!" She kissed mother, then each of us, and led us past the garden, which was fragrant with jasmine, and into the house.

"So you are going to America!" Ioanna Moras showed us to chairs in the large room that served not only as the kitchen, with a large hearth and sink at one end, but also as the living room, dining room, and from the mattresses on the storage bins against the far wall, even the children's beds and guest bedroom. She filled glasses with cold water from a pitcher near the sink and placed a sweet cake covered with powdered sugar on tiny dishes, one for each of us. The water was different from the clear mountain water we were accustomed to, and of a consistency that reminded me of castor oil. I was thirsty and drank it, but always remembered it to be a strange kind of water.

"My husband had to go to his mother's village to repair clocks early this morning, and he will not return until tomorrow night," Ioanna said. "I will take you myself, *Theia* Magdalene, to the Passport Office as soon as it opens in the morning. But come, you must be hungry. I have dinner ready."

We ate well—rabbit stew with potatoes—and slept soundly on mattresses Ioanna had placed on the floor by the hearth for Leonidas and me. Mother was taken to a bedroom.

The next morning, Ioanna tied a kerchief over her fair hair, and held one child by the hand; the other child took Leonidas's hand and mine. She led us to the government offices, stopping under the trees in the town square. "Eleni, here are some raisins to eat with the boys." She instructed me," You will wait here for your mother and me to return. Do not speak to anyone, and do not go any place else." My brother stood by stiffly, watching me. As soon as Ioanna left, the younger boy started to cry; then his brother joined in. I sat down on the ground, and told them stories and sang to them to quiet and amuse them. Leonidas paced nearby, but he too sat with us, and we passed the time quietly, telling stories and eating the raisins. I had followed Ioanna and Mama with my eyes as they walked up the steps of the building. My mother rarely left home to venture out on her own, even to carry on business in the village, as many women did, and I was afraid that once she entered the imposing building, she might not find her way out. With silent prayers that Ioanna would stay with her, I kept my eyes glued to the door.

In our class-conscious society, mother's black kerchief covering her hair and her dark, homespun skirt and jacket identified her as a villager. Her niece, on the other hand, with a light colored blouse and skirt, and shiny black leather shoes with a slight heel, was obviously from town and commanded somewhat more respect. Mother said that when they first entered the dark interior of the building, they were confused! Men and a few women pushed past them; all seemed intent on business, knowing where to go and what to do.

The first man they encountered was seated at a desk near the entrance. He wore a shirt with an open collar, and spoke to her brusquely. "Yes, what is it?" He held a cigarette in his hand and kept turning away to talk to others, who were stopping to ask him questions.

"When he turned again to me, and I told him we were looking for the passports for America, he directed us down a hallway, waved us away, and lit another cigarette from the lighted end of the first one."

A day later, Ioanna related the rest of the story to her husband while we listened. "We knocked on the door that he had pointed to, and a man's voice told us to enter. A young man wearing glasses was sitting at a desk; he did not look up at us, but kept on writing without saying anything. You know how it is? We did not want to interrupt him if he was writing something important, so we waited. Finally, he asked, 'What do you want?' *Theia* Magdalene gave him the papers and told him that she had come for her passport to America. 'My two children, Eleni and Leonidas, are going with me.' The man looked at the papers, then instructed, 'Wait here,' and went to an office at the back of the room. We waited a long time. I was afraid to say anything to *Theia* Magdalene in case our talking disturbed the important men in the other room.

When the man returned, he did not say anything, and sat down at his desk. I could tell *Theia* Magdalene was upset, but what could we do? After a while, the door to the office in back opened again, and a dark-haired man in a white shirt and tie, (unlike his helper who wore no tie) peered out. 'Why haven't you sent the woman in?' he barked.

'You only said, *Nai*! Yes. You did not say you wanted to see her right now.'

The man with the dark hair motioned us to follow him into his office. He was a nervous sort, the way he told us to sit down. He walked around to the front of his desk, and then sat in the chair behind it. 'Your passport is ready, *Kyria* Louvis.

You and your daughter may leave tomorrow for Patras.' 'Thank you, sir,' *Theia* Magdalene replied, and we stood up. 'And Leonidas, too?' *Theia* said as we started to leave. The man looked away, 'Of course, madam. I have said that you and the girl may leave. But not the boy, of course. He cannot leave Greece right now.' We were startled by this. 'But why not? His papers are in order. His brothers in America prepared them and are expecting him.' *Theia* was so upset when the man told her, 'It is not possible.'

Theia Magdalene told him that her sons in America did not want her and Eleni to go alone. She needed to have one of her sons with her, and Leonidas was the only one at home. She also told him that her sons had work for Leonidas in America, but the man shook his head. 'I am sorry, madam.' He smiled at us and said, 'It is not so bad, after all. The government prohibits all boys ages nine and older from leaving the country. It is the war at the Albanian border,' he shrugged. 'The Turks are helping Albania fight against Greece, and this may prove to be a long war. If all our young boys leave for America now, in five or six years, the nation will not have enough young men to fight for her.' *Theia* Magdalene appealed to him. 'But Leonidas is barely nine. We must go to America to see my sons. Tell him, Ioanna! You can say it better than I can.' I said, 'Can't you do something for my aunt? She and her children have traveled all the way over Taigetus from Bordonia . . . near Sparta. There must be some way that this one little boy can go to America with his mother.' But the man refused to help us. It was the law, he said. *Theia* Magdalene was so upset. But she knew that she could not oppose the law of the nation. We left that building with tears in our eyes."

Leonidas, Ioanna's children, and I had not moved from the tree where our mothers had left us. I could see that something was wrong the way mother held her head and the way Ioanna was holding her arm and patting it. They walked slowly toward us as we ran to meet them. Shaking her head sadly, mother placed her arms around us. "We are not leaving for America."

Leonidas cried out, "But when, tomorrow?"

"No, I am afraid that we must return to Bordonia and wait until your brothers can arrange another trip for us."

"But Papa said the papers were all right."

"They are, Eleni. The problem is the war with Albania. The nation is not allowing Leonidas to leave."

"But, mama, he is only nine years old! What does the nation want with a little boy?

"They told us that Greece cannot spare young boys," Ioanna said. "If it needs soldiers in a few years, there will be no one here to defend its people, so they are prohibiting the emigration of all boys."

"Mama," Leonidas blinked tears away. "You and Eleni go to America. I will return home with Georgios when he goes back to Bordonia."

But our mother shook her head. "No, your brothers wrote that you, Eleni, and I are to come to America— not just your sister and I. We shall return to the village together—the three of us. It is God's will that we do not leave Greece at this time."

We were an unhappy trio. Although Ioanna took us around the city to visit relatives and to see the beach at the Bay of Messinia, during the two days that we waited for Georgios and his mule train to escort us back to Bordonia we were depressed. As soon as the sun rose on the appointed morning, Georgios appeared at Ioanna's gate, and we climbed onto the two mules provided for us. The bitter disappointment of not completing our journey to America and the embarrassment of returning home so soon after our heartfelt farewells, made the mountain trek seem worse than it had been before. The ledges seemed narrower and the gorges deeper than they had appeared a few days earlier.

News of our return had already reached Bordonia, and we were greeted enthusiastically by those we met on the lanes through the village. "Welcome back from America! *Kalos Eilthate*!"

"How did you like the steamship? Not much, I guess, since you've returned so quickly."

"Back so soon? What marvelous American souvenirs did you bring us?"

Of course, *Kyria* Aliki stood waiting, demanding the return of the package intended for her sister in Chicago. For the first few days, my brother and I suffered continual teasing, but eventually our friends turned to other amusements.

CHAPTER 5

The Dowry

Alla logia na agapiomaste.
Say something else, so that
we can be friends.

— GREEK PROVERB

As melancholy as I felt after my dreams of becoming an American vanished, I had no time for tears or moping. The bounteous American tables filled to overflowing for my benefit had to be erased from memory, while my parents, my sister, my brother and I prepared for the wheat harvest that would now provide us with our next loaf of bread.

The foothills of Mount Taigetus had few open areas for cultivation. Planting wheat and corn in clearings between boulders, and later dividing these parcels among heirs or creditors, left a patchwork of arable land over the countryside. The *Lefko* was near one wheat field, but another plot belonging to father was a fifteen-minute walk in another direction in the middle of a relative's property. The dowry system was another reason for this confusing mosaic of small landowners, and land hunger caused many disputes over ownership. Brothers moved the boundary stones in the dead of night to assert a claim; cousins came to blows in the courthouse; and there were stories of more deadly confrontations. Such instances of belligerence were rare because, if they were to maintain their standard of living, people had to work together.

In these inhospitable mountain passes, where the sun dominated most of the year, a rain shower could ruin the farmer's
annual wheat crop if he delayed harvesting. Because everyone's
crop of wheat ripened at the same time, the men helped at one
farm, then hurried to the next one, working quickly against the
chance of a storm. Wheat becomes moldy and inedible if it is not
kept dry from the time it is cut, gathered, and the kernels separated and stored. Every able-bodied person assisted with the harvest, and if a dark rain cloud was sighted in the distant sky, panic
set in, and there was a mad rush to bring the wheat under cover.

When our wheat was ripe, Leonidas informed our relatives
and neighbors to come and help. Father moved out to the field
or to the *Lefko*, setting up a camping area, where he would stay
to manage the harvest. Mother spent the morning at our village
home, cooking and baking to supply food for the workers, while
I helped her cook and load the donkey. I recall seeing the wheat
field from afar as I arrived with the noonday meal. The sun was
shining directly on it, and I thought that I was looking at a sea of
bright yellow gold. Ourania had sent our goats out to forage
with another girl, and she met Leonidas and me and took us to
the field, where everyone was working so intently that they
hardly noticed our presence. The men would start at the head of
a row of wheat armed with a curved knife, grasp a sheaf of
wheat stalks in one hand, then rapidly slice it off at the bottom.
Without stopping, they let that bundle drop to the ground, and
immediately swooped down onto the next handful of stalks,
working with a rhythmic swish-swish, swish-swish, from one
row to the next.

As soon as a helper moved to a new row, the three of us
rushed in and gathered the fallen stalks, stacking them at both
ends of each row. There, some of the hands swept them into
sacks and secured the sacks on each side of the donkey's wooden
saddle to be hauled to the threshing floor.

There was a time when every plateau across the Grecian
countryside had an *aloni*, a threshing floor. These were made of
flat paving stones set in a perfect circle with a small hole in the

center. Many *alonia* dated back to the first inhabitants of the region. Worn down smooth from years of weathering and use, they served communities not only for processing grains, but also for village picnics and festivals. The machine age and emigration to the cities took their toll on small farmers and their outmoded methods. In Greece today, on a windy hilltop, a wanderer might stumble across one of these rare stone platforms, weed-covered, barely visible, and useless.

Father pounded a tall pole into the center hole of the threshing floor and tied the mule to it. The workers brought the bags from the wheat field and spilled out the stalks onto the stone floor while the mule trudged around in the circle, stomping on them. The location of the threshing floor was scientifically determined: Because the edible kernels of wheat are heavier than the superfluous chaff, the *alonia* were built on a hilltop with exposure to the gentle, steady breezes of *Zephyros*, the west wind.

Later, after the wheat was cut, some of the workers moved on to another farm. The ones who stayed joined father at the threshing floor with wide pitchforks. The mule was led away and the workers dug into the trampled piles of wheat on the threshing floor. Some pitched the hay to the side, leaving the husks of grain on the floor, while others gathered the hay into stacks.

Mother worked in the field only on the first day, after she had delivered the noonday meal. It was the busiest day of the harvest. That evening, she returned to our house in the village with Leonidas and me. Ourania, older and stronger—because every able hand was needed to bring in the harvest—stayed on to help.

The next day, my brother and I delivered food once again to the workers at the *aloni*. On some days, mother sent us with our donkey loaded with baskets of bread and a stew of green beans and onions with tomatoes and rice; at other times, she sent a casserole of okra or eggplant with basil, oregano, and grated cheese. Father kept her supplied with fresh produce from the small farm at the *Lefko*. When he sent word that it was time for winnowing—when wheat kernels were separated from the chaff—all hands were needed, and that included mother, Leonidas, and me.

The previous night, mother soaked a salted, dried cod, *bakaliaros,* in fresh water, changing the water a couple of times to remove most of the salt. The next morning, she cut the cod into pieces and sautéed it with onions, tomatoes, and beans to take to the workers. *Bakaliaros,* a staple of the Mediterranean, was purchased as a hard, dried fish and stored until the cook was ready to reconstitute it and cook it. It provided valuable proteins and minerals, yet it did not spoil in our hot climate if it was not used right away. Early that day, *Theios* Yiannis stopped at our house. "Demetrios sent me to tell you, Magdalene, there is no wind today, and to inform the other women. We've had the wind for three days. But today *Zephyros* quit on us. Demetrios says not to send lunch to the *aloni*. Instead, send it to him and the men at the *Lefko*. He's staying there to tend the vineyard near the ravine—until *Zephyros* returns."

Leonidas and I carried the baskets of food and bread to the *Lefko*, disappointed that we would not join the bustling harvesters. Like father, who scanned the skies while spreading out lunch for his fellow workers, my brother and I sat in our yard when we got home and tossed stray bits of hay into the air to test the velocity of the wind. It wasn't until two days later that father sent a messenger; then mother, Leonidas, and I set out, stopping briefly at her sister's house, where she called, "Let's go! *Lihnizoume!*"

On the hilltop, the *aloni* was filling with wheat from the sacks unloaded by the helpers. Ourania and I took our places next to mother, and my sister tied a white kerchief over my head, bringing the ends around, so that it covered all of my face except for my eyes. All the other women wore similar scarves to protect them from the hot sun as well as from the scratchy, fine dust of the chaff.

Mindful of the direction of the wind, the first woman bent over and took hold of a giant flat basket, the *koskino*, in her two hands. She scooped up a mass of grain into it, then lifted the basket with a quick upward movement, so that the wind carried away the chaff, but left the heavier kernels in the basket, which she emptied onto a blanket. The men continued to empty bags of wheat onto the *aloni*, while one of the women with a *koskino* scooped up the grain and repeated the action. Before long, all of us—men, women, and children—were covered from head to toe with golden dust. The rest of us sat by the *aloni* rubbing the kernels of wheat between our hands to remove their inedible husks, once more depending on *Zephyros* to carry away the residual chaff, and spreading the grains on blankets to dry in the sun.

At midday, everyone stopped for our meal, and we stretched out under a tree for an afternoon nap, *apoyeumatino,* then resumed our tasks. That night, after a light supper of bread, olives, and cheese, we sat, or stretched out, on blankets outdoors. As we relaxed, the men moved away so they could smoke their hand-rolled cigarettes, drink wine, and tell their stories.

Kyria Aliki stood up suddenly, commanding our attention. Everyone was quiet. She announced, "I have a story to tell. Who wants to hear it?" Her question was greeted with affirmative replies, and she settled back down on one of the blankets. She told a tale about a beautiful girl who lived in a village just like ours, and of her misadventures at the hands of evil pirates, and her rescue by a handsome prince, who married her. *Kyria* Aliki was a talented storyteller, who wove into her plots colorful descriptions, furnishing the castle's rooms with elaborate sandalwood chairs encrusted with diamonds and rubies, with silken tapestries of richest gold, and deepest red, and emerald green, and azure blue, and of treasure chests filled with pearls and other precious jewels. She could provoke tears and the next moment make our hair stand on end.

When she had finished, and no amount of coaxing could persuade *Kyria* Aliki to tell another story, *Kyria* Stamata started to sing a favorite folk song, and all of us joined in, including the men from where they sat. Later, as I made myself more comfortable on a blanket with Ourania, the shepherd Pantelis Kanaris, somewhere up in the hills, lulled me to sleep with the plaintive tunes of the *floyera*, a flute-like, reed instrument.

The next day, we repeated the dusty process of separating the kernels from the chaff, working quickly to finish, so that the men could move on to the next wheat field. If *Kyria* Aliki told her stories one night, *Kyrios* Alekos, the village tinker, waited for the next night to recount his tales of humans' scary encounters with the *kallikanzaros* at the stroke of midnight. The *kallikanzaros* was a scrawny, ugly, and unmannerly goblin who scrabbled down chimneys on New Year's Eve to spoil people's fun by frightening them, and peeing on their fires. On New Year's Day (Saint Basil's), children received gifts if they had gone to sleep the night before. But, if they did not sleep, they risked encountering the disgusting *kallikanzaros,* who might eat them. How we were supposed to sleep after hearing such tales, I do not know!

The grain was spread out on blankets to dry in the sun for two days, and when the kernels were ready, father filled woolen sacks and took them home on the donkey to be stored in bins in the winter room. He carted some of the wheat to the mill to be ground into flour. Because the flour was perishable, we did not mill more flour than we could use. I believe that the miller was paid one-sixth of the amount that he ground.

Soon after the wheat was stored safely, farmers looked to harvest their corn. The sun beat down on our village from the moment it rose one August morning when *Theia* Despina and *Theios* Yiannis with other neighbors and their families came to help with our cornfield. Ourania, Leonidas, and I happily trooped along with our cousins, but as before, mother stayed home, acting as coordinator; she took messages about weather predictions to relay to my father, and she baked bread, cooked, and washed.

Once we had gathered at the field, the men proceeded quickly down the rows of corn, detaching the ears of corn from the stalks. Kostas and Georgios Zacharias arrived soon after we did and asked father if he would like some more hands. They were made welcome and took their places in the cornfield. *Kyria* Stamata smiled knowingly at *Kyria* Aliki as they scooped up ears of corn into their large aprons. They were whispering when they emptied the aprons at the ends of the rows for my sister, my brother, our cousins, and me to toss the ears into large sacks. The men tied the heavy sacks and carried them to the threshing floor. Sophia and I had just finished filling one bag of corn when Kostas appeared and smiling at my cousin, said, "I will take this up to the *aloni,* Sophia." He lifted the bag to his shoulder, and we accompanied him to the threshing floor where he set the sack down beside the others. "It is kind of you to help my uncle today, Kostas," Sophia commented, looking only at the bag on the ground. She knew that all eyes were on Kostas and her.

"Your uncle and your father help with our harvest, Sophia." He smiled at her, ignoring the open stares of *Theia* Despina and the other women. "Besides," he added, "there are times when a man helps himself by helping others." *Kyria* Stamata passed by, heading directly for my aunt, no doubt repeating Kostas' words to her.

After that, my aunt remained at Sophia's side for the rest of the day. Even when we—Ourania , Eva, Sophia, and I—decided to walk to the mountain spring for water, my aunt accompanied us. She sat with us when we ate supper and later, as we worked at the threshing floor, she remained with us. With my aunt so watchful, Kostas did not attempt to speak to Sophia again. We spread our blankets in the field, but it was not time for sleep. As the sun set behind a distant hill, *Theia* Stamata stood up and held out her hand for my mother, who stood up and reached down and took her sister's hand, until all the women were standing in a half circle, singing as they danced the *syrtos*, a traditional dance. Not to be outdone by our mothers, Sophia jumped up and grasped her sister's hand, with the rest of us attaching ourselves to the line of dancers, until the mountains surrounding us echoed our voices.

Pantelis the shepherd brought out his *floyera,* and when we stopped to catch our breath, he did not lay his instrument aside, but continued with plaintive tunes of the mountain. Soon, *Theios* Yiannis could sit no more. My uncle was a stout man and not very graceful, but when he danced he became a different person.

He snapped his fingers and pivoted on his heels, then twirled from the hanky his partner held taut. Kostas and some of the other men joined the line, but not the women; in those days, we did not dance with the men. Instead, we clapped and accompanied Pantelis with our singing, until the evening's entertainment was over, and we had to return to work. The sacks of corn that had been left beside the *aloni* were now dumped onto the paved circle. We—the women and girls—took our places on blankets around it and began stripping the husks from the ears of corn. It was pleasant to spend a summer night on the hilltop working with our friends, except for one thing. I did not like to come across a fat white worm in an ear of corn. When I did find one, I would throw it into the husks that were fed to the horses and donkeys, although usually the chickens made it to the worm before the four-legged animals. As we finished for the night, Ourania and I passed *loukoumi*—squares of jellied fruit, also known as Turkish paste—and *mastiha,* the sweet, anise-flavored liqueur, to the women. Father poured small cups of *tsipouro*, the homemade liquor, for the men.

Everyone was awake before daybreak the next morning, spreading the corn on blankets to dry. We did not grow corn to eat fresh; rather, it was dried and ground into flour. For the next few days, throughout the countryside, cobs of corn lay under the hot summer sun. The kernels were then rubbed off and stored in wooden bins in the winter room, where they remained until they would be milled for flour.

Later that week, we were helping at *Kyria* Stamata's cornfield, when *Theia* Despina, *Theios* Yiannis, Eva, and the boys arrived without Sophia. Mother had just finished securing bags with our lunches of bread and cheese on a tree branch high enough, so that the goat foraging nearby could not reach them. *Kyria* Stamata never offered her workers any food, but she paid in coins—very little pay—yet everyone went to help her anyway. The men moved ahead to the cornfield, but Ourania and I stayed with Eva and our mothers.

"Eh!" *Theia* Despina said. "Do you see Yiannis?" She gestured with her head toward the retreating figure of her husband.

"I couldn't wake him this morning. He was out all night—at the *taverna*—drinking and talking. And who was he with, Magdalene? Just as I told you he would be—the matchmaker!"

My mouth opened in surprise, and Ourania jabbed me with her elbow to be quiet, so that we could hear the rest of the conversation. Eva merely smiled, and mother replied, "So, he has accepted Kostas as a son-in-law, and they have a tentative agreement on the dowry? Did they set the date for the engagement?" Mother then asked. "What pastries are we making?"

"It just happened yesterday, Magdalene, and I can hardly catch my breath!" Eva, Ourania, and I proceeded slowly ahead, listening attentively. "*Kyrios* Zacharias has a sister Dina, who was at his house last night, and she told Kostas to wait until next year!"

"You cannot listen to everybody, Despina. You and Yiannis should choose the date best for you, whether it is in the next few weeks, or after *Panayias,* the Assumption."

"I do not think Sophia and Kostas want to wait as long as next year, Magdalene. Yiannis will be lost, too, if we put it off too long; he likes Kostas, and looks forward to having another man around the house. When he came home last night, he said I was to keep Sophia home, so she would not harm her complexion in the sun. She is not to help me with the wash tomorrow because she might ruin her hands in the harsh soapy water! For a week now, I have had this trouble with my back, and still I came here to Stamata's, and this morning took care of the goat and the chickens by myself. What did he do yesterday? He said to me, 'I'll take the donkey to the mill and get some flour.' But instead of getting my flour, he met with the matchmaker, and after that he stayed at the *taverna* toasting everyone. So, early this morning, Eva had to go to the mill, and Sophia is home baking bread for me."

It was not long after that day that Sophia came to our house and announced her plans. "It is too soon to have the wedding before August 15th," she told mother over a cup of tea one afternoon. I had just arrived from school, and she had waited for my return. August 15th was a date next in importance to Easter, and weddings were held either fifteen days before or after that date. "We will have the *arrevones,* engagement, on papa's nameday celebration, on September 23rd, and the men can discuss the dowry at the same time."

"And the wedding date?" mother asked.

"It is the first Sunday in October."

With the crops in, farmers could pause in mid-August for the festivities in honor of *Panayias,* The Virgin Mary. Father came home from the *Lefko* and, early on the morning of the holiday, he and Leonidas, along with *Theios* Yiannis, would load the donkeys. One was packed with skins of wine, sacks of cheese, olives, bread, and blankets for us to sit on, for the feast after church services. The other carried the slaughtered pig that father had raised for this occasion. They made their way to the isolated country chapel dedicated to *Panayias*, where the liturgy would be held, and set up the spit in a clearing next to another group.

Everyone wore his Sunday best. That morning, I chose my favorite hanky, with a pink edging, and tucked it securely into my dress pocket. The men and boys wore their good pants (that is, not their work clothes), clean shirts, and some wore caps. My mother had donned her good blouse and skirt, and wore a dark silk mantili on her hair. Ourania and I were in our best dresses, made of homespun cotton, and wore our hair in braids. In the predawn darkness, we walked in family groups up the steep mountain path away from the village. The steady clip-clop of horses and donkeys accompanied our subdued chatter. "*Hronia Polla*!" We greeted one another as we met others on the track, "Many years, to you!"

"The *meltemi* (a north wind of summer) was fierce yesterday, wasn't it?" *Theia* Despina remarked to mother when she spotted us. "It is much quieter today. Maybe it will die down altogether by the time church is over. I can't stand it! Day after day it keeps blowing!" The hot etesian winds, annually sweeping over the Grecian hillsides, could be ruthless, pelting hot sand into nostrils and eyes.

"I'm so hungry, I could eat one of those birds without bothering to roast it!" Ourania pointed to a hawk flying overhead. A fifteen-day fast from meats and dairy products had preceded *Panayias.* Anyone who broke the fast could not receive Holy Communion.

"Mm," said Leonidas, who had left father with the roasting meat and had run back to walk the rest of the way with us. "I think I'll wait for the roast pig."

"Don't talk about food,"Ourania protested, "or I'll faint right here on the road, and you'll have to carry me the rest of the way." My brother and I choked back laughter at the sight of her rolling eyes and tongue hanging out of her mouth. Mother shushed us, so we behaved ourselves as we arrived at the small white chapel, silhouetted against tall pines and cypress trees. A tantalizing aroma from the clearing beyond the church announced that the roasting of the lambs and pigs was nearing completion. Father saw us and left his post to my uncle to come and light a candle with us in the windowless chapel. We waited our turn to take a tiny taper from a tray near the entrance, and lit it with the flame of another, pressing them close together in a sand-filled dish in front of the icon of the Virgin Mary. The room was small and without pews. We stood shoulder to shoulder, the women with the children on the left side of the aisle—since there was no balcony—and the men on the right side. At this point father left us to finish preparations for serving the pig; we stayed until the end of the liturgy.

We flew out of church after the dismissal and raced to the picnic area. Dripping and hissing on the coals, the juices from the roasting meat filled the air with their fragrance. Father motioned us to come closer; and from the tip of his knife, we took bits of the mouth-watering *kokoretsi*, grilled morsels of lamb kidney or liver basted with lemon juice and oregano. Most people cooked a pig at *Panayias,* but a few also had lamb. The women spread blankets under shade trees and placed wine, bread, cheese, and olives on them.

The cooks poked long testing forks into the roasting meats, sometimes slicing off a piece to hand to a taster. The carving began and our plates were filled after *Pater* Georgios delivered a prayer. We ate hungrily, either seated on blankets, rocks, or standing by the spits. The cooks carved lamb and pork until nothing was left and the bones were picked clean. Without refrigeration, food was never left over.

Magic, superstition, and fortune-telling intrigued us. *Theios* Yiannis had been served the translucent, flat shoulder bone from the lamb that Pantelis Kanaris had roasted; after my uncle had eaten all the meat, he rinsed the bone, and handed it to *Kyria* Aliki. This was the fortune-telling bone, and she was the village psychic. Like the priestess at the Delphic Oracle, she held one end of the shoulder bone carefully in the tips of her fingers, and bent over, thoughtfully gazing at it from all sides; then she held it up to the light. She slowly turned it around and examined the back and again the front. Finally, she pointed to a spot on the bone. "Hmm, see this? It is a bag. Heavy. It could mean some money. But maybe not for you, Yiannis. Here! These lines. See the waves? It is the sea—a journey."

"There you are, Yiannis!" *Kyrios* Alexandros, the mayor, declared jovially. "A sea journey and a bag of money! What more can a man ask for?"

Kyria Aliki shook her head mysteriously. "Again, the trip is not for you. It is for someone close to you."

"The Egyptian for Eva!" *Kyria* Stamata declared loudly.

"Oh! Oh!" The fortune teller frowned. She had not finished studying the bone, and she held up a finger of caution. "There is sickness—sadness. A mother, a father—crying. But it is not a death." She looked puzzled. "It is very strange. Something magical is attempting to interrupt the reading. I do not like it."

I shivered and moved closer to Ourania. My uncle stood up abruptly. "Enough of that, Aliki. Come, Pantelis! Cheer us up with your music, so that *Kyrios* Alexandros can start the dance."

"I cannot play." Pantelis shied away from him. "It is a bad omen to have the reading of the bone tell of sickness." He motioned to his wife to prepare their son Themistocles to leave, and he started to pack up their utensils and other articles to return home.

"It is not a death, Pantelis!" But the shepherd and his wife helped their son onto the donkey and headed home.

"See what you have done, *Kyria* Aliki. You have made us all so glum with your predictions! Tell Yiannis some good news, so he can go home as happy as when he came here today."

The fortune teller squinted at him. "I do not make this up. You know that, *Kyrios* Alexandros. I read only what I see in the bone." Nodding solemnly, she stared at the bone once more. "See this curve here? It shows happiness—a large portion of it. But after that comes the sickness." She shrugged and handed the bone back to *Theios* Yiannis. "That is what I read," she proclaimed. Unsure of what to do with the offending bone, he handed it to his wife.

The following month, on September 23rd, my uncle and aunt invited everyone they knew in the village to the engagement party for Sophia and Kostas. *Theios* Yiannis had been named after Saint John the Evangelist, so he did not celebrate the more popular feast day for Saint John the Baptist, whose feast day is January 7th.

A week before the party, held on Saint John's Day, mother helped my aunt bake sweet breads and pastries: *kourambiethes,* crescent-shaped cookies, dusted with sugar; *mellomakarona,* honey-soaked oval cookies flavored with orange and cinnamon; and *koulourakia,* butter cookie twists. They were placed at one end of a long table that was set up in the winter room. On the day of the party, the table also held platters of roasted lamb, *hirino* marinated ham cubes, pickled pigs feet, and macaroni covered with grated *kefalotiri.*

A *bouzouki* player and a clarinetist had been hired; as soon as they had tuned their instruments, they saluted my uncle, who then began to dance the *tsamiko,* a dance with both fast and slow dragging steps. Georgios Zacharias, who considered himself a good dancer, took his place next to my uncle, offering him the end of a handkerchief. The one who dances next to the leader is usually a strong dancer. By holding the handkerchief tightly with his right hand, he supports the leader in his athletic movements. With a nod to Georgios, *Theios* Yiannis took the handkerchief with his left hand while Georgios clasped Kostas's right hand, forming a chain with three other men who joined them. Georgios held the taut handkerchief aloft as my uncle clung to it and performed a series of deep knee bends alternating with jumps and slow kicks.

Ourania and I attached ourselves to a line of women dancers, and we danced nearly every dance until we were ready to drop. Exhausted, we looked for a place to sit before it was time for the priest to announce the formal betrothal of Sophia and Kostas. Instead of a rest, we found Eva, who was washing and refilling platters in the kitchen. She offered each of us a sugar cookie if we helped her, so Ourania and I cheerfully joined her at the sink. When Eva's father appeared at the door, we fell silent. *Theios* Yiannis wiped his face and neck with a handkerchief. Hands on hips, he looked out at his family and friends, who had come to celebrate his name day. Sophia, bringing dishes into the kitchen, stopped on her way. Her father patted her arm awkwardly, and when Kostas came in, *Theios* Yiannis said, "Tell your father that I want to talk before we start the betrothal formalities."

My uncle sank down heavily on a chair at the table. This sent Ourania and me scurrying to remove plates and cups. My uncle indicated that the chair next to him was for Thanasis Paladinos. The man most often called upon to negotiate business arrangements for the villagers, *Kyrios* Paladinos was tall and lean—bald except for a fringe of dark hair circling his crown. Now, he stroked his thin mustache and waited respectfully for Kostas's father to be seated. Ourania, Eva, and I kept wiping the same dishes, not talking, our eyes cast down at the plates and cups.

As host, my uncle opened the discussion, nodding expansively toward his two visitors. "Then is it as we agreed, yesterday, eh?" he asked hopefully.

Kyrios Zacharias, Kostas's father, shook his head. "*Ohi!* Tell him, Paladinos! He has to do better than the wheat fields, a few olive trees, one goat, and five sheep." Andonis Zacharias was well-built, with a full mustache that bristled as he stared at

Theios Yiannis. "A couple more of those wheat fields of yours are all that is needed to add to Sophia's dowry."

"You're a bandit, Andonis." My uncle protested, "I cannot spare even one field. In the name of God, how would I feed my family? What do you think I am?"

"Come, Yiannis. Your girl deserves better than that" *Kyrios* Zacharias appealed to the matchmaker. "Am I not right, Paladinos?"

"They are a harmonious couple," the matchmaker murmured.

With a grunt, *Kyrios* Zacharias pressed on. "All right, then. What about that vineyard of yours—off by itself—at the *mikrogkremos,* the Little Cliffs. You've got some olive trees there. Maybe Kostas will find it in his heart to accept these and a few more goats."

"Not one penny more! Look at all the beautiful rugs and blankets Sophia brings with her! Her home will be the showplace of your family, Andonis. Let me tell you! Sophia is better than any other woman with a needle. She has more clothes and linens packed in her trunk, made by her talented hands, than any other girl in Bordonia . . . and Sparta, too!"

Kyrios Zacharias shook his head. "That is all very good, Yiannis, but remember this: Kostas is very handsome and strong. He attended the *gymnasion* to learn the latest developments in farming. He is the most eligible bachelor in Bordonia!"

My uncle held up his hand and bent each one of his fingers down against his palm as he slowly counted off, one by one, the extent of Sophia's dowry. "Besides the properties we already agreed upon, you and the matchmaker have taken from me: five olive trees more than the original five that I had planned to give Sophia, as well as the gold sovereigns, and two mattresses. I do not have any more to give. I have two sons and one more daughter. After my property is divided between Nikos and Stratis, I will barely have anything left for me and my wife! And then there is the possibility—I know it is not likely—that we may hear from the Egyptian. So, it is my habit always to plan ahead.

Eva will need her share. What will happen to Eva if Sophia takes it all, and there is no dowry for her?"

"No one wants you to give up everything, my friend." *Kyrios* Zacharias was becoming impatient. "S*to diavolo!* The devil take it! Sophia cannot disgrace Kostas with such a paltry dowry. Paladinos agrees, don't you? Forget about your wheat fields. I'll settle for a few more olive trees. You can throw in the vineyard at the Little Cliffs, if you wish. That's all. The boy is a hard worker."

"I cannot do that! You can have a few more olive trees, but not The Little Cliffs. It was my wife's dowry and belonged to her grandmother before her."

"I tell you what. Keep your olive trees. If the Little Cliffs has passed down on the mother's side, then it should go to your wife's daughter. We can shake hands on this right now and be done with it." He studied my uncle's expression.

"Out of the question! That vineyard remains in my family!"

"Of course," *Kyrios* Zacharias continued, lowering his voice, so that we could barely hear him. "I love that girl of yours as though she were my own, The Little Cliffs are so close to my *karidies*, my walnut grove, that I am wondering something: If you add it to Sophia's portion, I will turn ownership of the *karidies* over to Kostas. The Cliffs are far from your other *horafia,* properties, and you have to go out of your way to attend to that vineyard. And look! You will make your daughter an important woman by doing this if Kostas becomes the owner of my walnut trees. They are the biggest producers of fine walnuts in all of Lacedaemon! Come, man. She is marrying the Prince of Bordonia! In a few years, that boy will be taking care of you and me—both of us!" Noting my uncle's coolness as he listened to these remarks, he ended thus: "When Kostas first looked upon Sophia, Eros struck, and that was the end of it right there. She was the only girl for him."

The matchmaker again murmured, "A very excellent young man has chosen the finest of young women."

My uncle nodded impatiently. "*Nai, nai*, yes. We know all about Eros. Not the Little Cliffs!"

Each man had spoken. Now it was up to the matchmaker to bring the two together. He had listened politely and had responded genially. "An excellent choice for both children, indeed. *Kyrios* Yiannis has proposed a very fine dowry for his daughter Sophia. Do you not agree, *Kyrios* Zacharias?" Thanasis Paladinos had finished high school in Sparta, but before he could finish his law studies in Athens, he was diagnosed with tuberculosis. An elderly doctor had told him his only chance of survival was to return to his parents in the mountains and eat wholesome foods. In time, his health improved, and he turned to farming. The dual roles of legal adviser and of matchmaker, however, soon took precedence. His stately, pedantic manner had served to moderate many a hot-tempered negotiation. He prided himself on his skill, discretion, and tact in handling even the most difficult situations, and he was usually able to predict the outcomes. Today's challenge he considered an easy assignment. Both families stood to gain by this union, so he felt certain that neither party would let property negotiations stand in the way of what fate had ordained when this couple fell in love.

Kyrios Zacharias brushed aside the matchmaker's comments and continued energetically, "I said to my son, 'Kostas, if she is the girl you want, then she is the girl I want for you also.' Those were my exact words. And I meant what I said then—just as I am telling you now. I will not stand in the way of my son's happiness for a few sheep and goats."

"Then it is agreed: Andonis, you accept the offer of *Kyrios* Yiannis?" The matchmaker knew that it could not be this easy, but he had to say something at this juncture. We held our breath as we waited to hear the answer.

Andonis Zacharias hesitated a moment. Then he stiffened. "We are close, but." He pressed his lips together and his face turned red as he remonstrated. "It is a disgrace, Louvis! Such a meager dowry does not respect the true worth of my son, Kostas!" He slapped both hands on the table—his eyes bulging slightly, his moustache bristling. He eyed my uncle. "Your daughter will not be happy in my house!" *Kyrios* Zacharias shoved his face close to my uncle's face.

It was *Theios* Yianni's turn to glare. "What are you saying, Zacharias? Do you plan to mistreat my daughter if she does not take all of my property with her when she marries your son?"

Kostas's father ignored the matchmaker's warning glances, then realizing his mistake, tried to control himself. "Of course not, my friend, but we are realists, are we not?"

"Go to the devil, Zacharias!" My uncle alarmed all of us as he stood up. "And while you're at it, you can forget about my daughter! She does not have to marry your son and take all my vineyards and fields with her in order to be a part of your clan. I do not intend to give my daughter and my entire fortune to the Zacharias family!" He strode around us to the sink where he poured himself a glass of water from a pitcher and drank it down. Belatedly, he realized he had broken a cardinal rule of hospitality, and hastily filled two more glasses and set them in front of his guests, standing over them.

Eva, Ourania, and I had been arranging and rearranging the pastries on a platter. A change in our position would have called attention to us, and we did not want to lose our listening post. I stopped breathing when *Kyrios* Zacharias and *Kyrios* Paladinos stood up. The two fathers would never reach an agreement, and the wedding was off! I knew nothing of such deliberations, and I was greatly relieved when *Kyrios* Paladinos intervened: "Your daughter is a prize for the Zacharias family, Yiannis. We all know that Andonis already loves Sophia. He will be like a second father to her. It only remains for you both to look into your hearts and bring this union to fruition. *Na kathisoume.* Let us sit down," he pleaded. "*Oli mazi,* all together, one more time."

Kyrios Zacharias wiped his wet brow with one hand and nodded to Kostas, who had just then stood in the doorway. My uncle sat down. The three men sat silent—deep in thought. Sounds of music came from the other room. *Theia* Despina looked in to tell her husband that the priest was asking whether it was time to begin the *arrevones,* the betrothal ceremony. "Not yet!" She withdrew with a nod.

"Eva!" My uncle caught sight of his older daughter. His call made the three of us jump, but his tone was pleasant. "Bring us wine." Eva filled three glasses with wine from a carafe and carefully placed a glass in front of each man. She retreated into the shadows with Ourania and me. Although my uncle did not seem to object to our presence, Ourania sent me out of the kitchen with a plate of pastries. On my return she motioned with her head, and raised her eyebrows at us, as she signaled Eva and me to act busy.

The men drank the wine and turned their attention once again to the negotiations. My uncle nodded and shrugged. "Maybe it is best. The Little Cliffs should go to Sophia."

Kyrios Zaharias set down his glass. "Kostas is a worthy young man, Yiannis. As you already know, he is better even than Paladinos in figuring out accounts. He has a nice house in mind for the wife he takes. Remember this. In a few years, you and I will need that boy more than he needs us."

Theios Yiannis smiled. "Zacharias, I think that you have always wanted that vineyard at the Little Cliffs. But there is one more thing you must agree to before we shake hands." He demanded the full attention of the matchmaker. "The deed for that vineyard will be in Sophia's name. It will state that—should she die without children—the Little Cliffs will revert to my family."

Kyrios Zaharias frowned. He stared at the table, working his mouth. After a long pause, he turned to face *Theios* Yiannis and *Kyrios* Paladinos. "*Entaxi!* All right! What am I worried about? Sophia and Kostas will have many children. It will be Zacharias property despite having a woman's name on the deed."

My uncle stood up. "So, it is settled. It is time these two children of ours were engaged! Eva! Ourania ! Eleni! Tell *Pater* Georgios that we are ready."

CHAPTER 6

The Wedding

*Kaliteri katohi tou anthropou
einai mia sympathitiki gyneka.*
Man's best possession is a
sympathetic wife.
— *ANTIGONE,* EURIPIDES 450 BC

With the negotiations for the dowry settled, Kostas was free to visit Sophia, but they were not allowed to be alone. Sophia's mother always managed to be in the room whenever he came to see Sophia. Eva usually was with her when Sophia walked to the spring for water; if Kostas happened to meet them, Eva moved discreetly out of hearing, but she did not leave. Despite this lack of privacy, they came to an understanding of what each expected of the other as they made plans for their wedding and their future together. The women of the family helped Sophia and her mother with sewing the finishing touches on a dress for my aunt, or buttons on new shirts for the two boys, Nikos and Stratis, or even helping to sort and fold blankets and linens. Everything had to be ready by her wedding date. Kostas, too, was occupied with preparations for his new role as manager of his father's vineyards and soon as full owner of more proper-ties. He turned to harvesting the grapes—as did everyone else—and stocking the wine cellars.

Theios Yiannis and a neighbor came to help father gather the dense clusters from the low-growing vines and stack them into large baskets. The donkey then carried the grapes to the cement cisterns for the first steps in wine-making. We did not have a large vineyard, barely three or four acres, but no matter how small the property, the production of a good barrel of wine depended on the vintner to supply good rootstock in the right soil with the proper amount of rainfall and sunshine. A constant vigil required spraying or picking off the various pests and fungi that attacked the roots, stems, buds, and fruit of the grape; in addition, the barrels that held the juice to ferment into the final product had to be sufficiently aged oak and the contents oxygenated at proper intervals. Even with such close attention to these details, the outcome—a potable wine—was uncertain.

Our participation was required at this stage of the wine-making process. Leonidas, Ourania, and I, after washing our feet in a nearby trough, took over the first pressing. We stepped on the purple grapes and squished away with peals of laughter, the juice splattering us, and our parents not scolding us for the mess. The lightness of children's steps squeezed the grapes without mixing inedible crushed seeds and skins into the juice. After we were lifted off the fruit, the clear juice was run off into casks as the first pressing; the remainder went to the wine press. As with everything that we grew, nothing was wasted. The skins and pits from the last pressing were returned to the concrete basin; these dregs were left to ferment with a certain amount of sugar, then distilled into pure alcohol spirits, such as *tsipouro* (also called *raki)*, or with the addition of aniseed as *ouzo,* or with sweetened mastic resin as *mastiha.*

From the wine press, the juice was emptied into large goat-skin bags and poured into seasoned barrels stored in our *katoyi,* cellar. In due course, with father's judicious addition of sugar, the juice was fermented at the correct temperature and became table wine. *Retsina* was the native wine of Greece. It was up to the winemaker to add as much resin to the fermenting grapes as his taste dictated. Legend has it that resin was first used because of its antibacterial properties; others dispute this, asserting that the addition of resin was merely a tradition and of no benefit.

Nevertheless, resinated wine had its supporters. At times when the wine did not ferment successfully, the barrels were labeled "wine vinegar" and used for salad dressings and for pickling meats and vegetables.

In autumn, our house became a miniature warehouse of supplies for winter. The rafters were strung with ropes of onions, garlic, green peppers, oregano, thyme, basil, mint, and mountain tea. Beans, figs, and almonds were spread out, each in its season, on the large, heavy cement lids of the cisterns. They dried in the hot sunlight and then were stored in wooden bins in the winter room. Green quince and bright red pomegranates were harvested as well. The quince is a hard, virtually inedible fruit when fresh, but when it was chopped up and cooked with sugar, it made a flavorful preserve. Pomegranates were eaten fresh, since the fruit lasted within its skin for a long time after it was picked. The dried pasta *trahanas* was stored in its bin in the kitchen.

Every day, we brought vegetables from the garden into the kitchen for mother to cut up for dinner, or to process for later use, or for father to sell. On market day, father would go to Sparta to trade baskets of tomatoes and beans for salt and kerosene: the former to preserve foods for the winter and the latter as auxiliary fuel to augment the brushwood that had been gathered throughout summer.

"Come, Magdalene!" Mother's sister arrived one morning. "The currants are ready!" We did not grow these bushes with their small, sour, purple berries, but my uncle's were top quality, and he sold them to commercial winemakers in the area. *Theios* Yiannis and his helpers had already brought the currants into their house. All of the furniture—tables, dressers, chairs—had been removed from the kitchen and the winter room, and set outside in the courtyard. Inside the house, blankets were spread on the floors; these overflowed with freshly-picked currants. We picked over them, separating stems and leaves from the fruit, and then spread the berries to dry. The entire process took place indoors because the weather was unpredictable in autumn; often we returned for another day, sometimes two days, to finish picking over the currants until all had been spread out to dry.

The mornings became cooler and a sudden rain shower forecasted cold mountain winds. Mother and the other women did not wash clothing in the cold water of the river any more, and it fell to me to help at home one sunny day the end of September. As we carried the clothes out to the garden, mother announced that she thought her son Stavros soon would be coming from Sparta to visit. It was time for him to leave for America. She always seemed to have a sixth sense when it came to her family, and often would predict what would happen without benefit of any external forms of communication. I watched as she set up the iron *tripodo,* tripod, in a clearing, and lifted a *kazani,* a copper-lined tub, onto it. As she started a fire under the *kazani*, I asked her how she could know these things. "Eleni, mothers just know," she replied. She smiled and added, "Stavros said that he was coming back this month, and the month is almost over." I toted buckets of water from a barrel that caught rain water and watched her drop the clothes, one by one, into the *kazani,* and add chips of yellow, homemade soap. When the water was boiling, she damped the fire and let the clothes soak. We walked around the garden, where we picked green beans, some late tomatoes, and a handful of mint to add to the meal she had planned for the day, and we went inside to cook dinner. When we returned to the wash, mother scattered the fire wood to put out the fire, and together we removed the wet sheets, skirts, shirts, and pants—one by one—with a long, sturdy pole and carried them to a boulder at the side of the garden. Mother slapped the garments with a bamboo cane to remove the excess water, and we stretched the clothing on rocks and shrubs to dry.

Despite my mother's sensible explanation, I was surprised when Leonidas ran home that afternoon and announced that Stavros had arrived in Bordonia and was right behind him. At the age of sixteen, Stavros was not as tall as Soterios, but slender, like all of my brothers. He was the nervous type, his dark eyes darting from one person to the other as he described working on the busy streets of Sparta—earning money by sweeping stores and restaurants and carrying packages—any work he could find. He finally had earned enough for his passage in steerage class on a ship leaving for America the following week. It was hard for my mother to see each of her young sons leave home, but she knew that their future in Greece was either as farmers in an impoverished land where one failed crop could lead to starvation, or as lowly workers in a city, where their inexperience and lack of family capital and connections made them vulnerable to exploitation. Certainly, Stavros would have more opportunities with his brothers in America than he would have in his own country. I was very excited for him. Ourania and I wasted no time in brushing his clothes and doing whatever he or my parents asked of us to help him prepare for the journey. He was the last of my brothers to leave Bordonia. Leonidas, the youngest, was destined to take a different path.

Before I was born, two of my brothers—Spiros and Anthony—had left Bordonia for Sparta. Each of my brothers followed: Yiannis (who joined the Greek army to seek his fortune), George, Theophanis, Stavros, Peter, and Soterios. One by one, with the exception of Yiannis, they worked at anything a young boy could do in Sparta to earn enough for a ticket to America. Mother had given birth to fourteen children; twelve had survived. Based on our best calculations, my sister Arista was five years older than I; Ourania was two years my senior; Leonidas was born two years after I was.

When the day of Stavros's departure arrived, we tearfully said our goodbyes. He kissed each of us, but we could tell he was eager to be on his way. He had been ready before dawn, dressed in the simple woolen shirt and pants of a worker; his bag was packed with clean clothing to change into once the ship landed in America. He lingered long enough over his farewell to mother, and with a final hug—long before it was time to go—he took father's arm and they hurried off to the village square. There, father rented Stavros a mule that would take him to the train station in Sparta; from there, he would take the train to the ship in Piraeus.

Our sadness soon was replaced with the excitement of preparing for Sophia's wedding. From the day that she could hold a needle, Sophia, like all girls in the village, worked to fill her hope chest. By the age of eighteen, she had sewn hems on enough sheets, pillowcases, and towels for her future home, and she had decorated many linens with examples of her fine embroidery. By contrast, my own efforts were much slower, and I doubted that I would ever finish sewing a pillow I had started. I was happy to set aside my project and attend to Sophia.

Each day during the two weeks before the wedding, I stopped at Sophia's house after school to learn who had visited her and what household goods or foodstuffs she had prepared, or had received, for her new home. We talked about the seamstress who was sewing her wedding dress and her second new dress. She did not have these yet; they would be delivered to her before the wedding. They would be of a finer fabric than what the village looms could produce. *Theia* Dina, Kostas's aunt from Sparta had proclaimed—as she exited church on one of her visits to Bordonia—that she "loved Sophia very much, but hoped that she would not disgrace the Zacharias family with her countrified wardrobe." It was *Theia* Dina Arnopoulos who insisted that Sophia have a second new dress to wear on important occasions.

My mother took a dim view of my absenting myself from home and neglecting my chores, so there were days that I could not visit my cousin. The eggs had to be gathered daily; water had to be fetched from the spring at Ayiannis three or four times a day, and there were lessons to be completed before dark. (Lamps were not lit for studying; they were lit only when we expected company.)

A week before the wedding, Sophia and Eva set out all of Sophia's finery in the winter room for well-wishers to admire. Ourania and I ran over as soon as we heard that her trousseau was on exhibit. A cabinet and a dresser had been cleared of the pictures and trinkets that usually were there, and the new apparel was arranged on them. A large trunk stood open on the floor. It held linens and clothing. Pans and pots lay beside it, along with an oil lamp and a lantern. Two small gold coins lay conspicuously on Sophia's new clothing.

I thought that the new petticoats—of fine cotton and trimmed with lace—were the prettiest of all, and I examined each one with a loving eye. Ourania had our wedding gift to Sophia in her pocket. Mother had given my sister a small gold piece. When Ourania handed it to Sophia, she hugged us both and said, "I will carry it on my wedding day and think of you." She placed it on the dresser next to her new dress. She hugged us again. "You are so dear to Kostas and me. You must come and visit me every day after I am married. We will have tea together on the balcony and gossip like ladies." Then she left us to greet *Kyria* Stamata and *Theia* Xenia.

"Ah, here's the tablecloth you started three years ago, Eva!" Stamata exclaimed. "It looks good now that it's finally done." Eva blushed, aware of her reputation of being "sweet but slow." Ourania made a face—crossing her eyes at Eva and me—and made us giggle.

"So beautiful!" *Theia* Xenia was holding up a hearth rug in both hands." I remember when Sophia wove this on my small loom. To think! I am still alive to see this happy day when my dear neighbor takes it to her new home as a bride!"

Sophia invited them to sit down and have *tsai tou vouniou,* tea gathered from the mountain plant similar to chamomile, so that they would have time to comment on each new gift, as they had done every day of the prior week. They admired the gift from Ourania and me and complimented my mother. Our ears perked up when Stamata lowered her voice and, pressing a gold coin firmly into my cousin's hand, advised, "Now, just tuck this away. Kostas does not need to know about it. Between you and me, Sophia, the day may come when you may need it. Men do not always turn out to be all that we think they are when we marry them, child."

Had she known that Kostas's *Theia* Dina was standing at the door, I don't think *Kyria* Stamata would have given Sophia her gift just then. "Bah! What are you saying, Stamata?" The large woman pushed her way into the room. "You brought your tongue with you—here on the eve of my nephew Kostas's wedding—

making trouble, as usual!" Her shiny black hair was swept up into a bun and covered with a black silk scarf. Her dress was dark gray wool, cut in the latest mode. She wore leather pumps with a slight heel, and she carried herself like the wife of a well-to-do merchant, which indeed she was.

Kyria Stamata cast her eyes downward only momentarily; then, she drew herself up to her full height—equal to that of *Theia* Dina—and pressed her lips together. "If it isn't Madame Moderne, herself! Please come in, so that you may insult your old peasant school mates."

Ignoring the scornful exchange and smiling sweetly, Sophia stepped between the two women and took the new arrival by the hand, as she kissed her cheek. "How nice of you to come and visit, *Theia* Dina. Look at all of the beautiful things our friends have given Kostas and me for our home." Sophia secured *Kyria* Stamata's gold piece deep inside her pocket, and nothing more was said about it that day.

With a glance and sniff, *Theia* Dina assessed the gifts. "I see that some of the people around here have parted with a few of their possessions. No one will be able to give as many gold pieces as *Kyrios* Arnopoulos and I have set aside to give Kostas." She looked up when *Kyria* Stamata called out, "Ahh, *Kyria* Dina, please! It would be inappropriate for me to leave before I can see how many gold pieces you and *Kyrios* Arnopoulos are giving the couple. Are they real gold or fake? What should I tell the populace when they ask me?"

These two formidable women had been sparring with each other since their early school years. The fact that Dina had married a wealthy businessman from Sparta and Stamata, a farmer, had not changed their mutual antipathy. Dina derived pleasure in coming to the village and confronting Stamata. Yet their attacks on each other lacked true hostility, and they often ended their confrontations with a cup of *tsai* and a *koulouraki* at Stamata's house.

Dina extracted from her bag a large tortoiseshell comb, which she held up for everyone to see. "Not that nasty thing for

Sophia!" *Kyria* Stamata exclaimed. "I doubt if you have washed it since your grandmother last used it seventy years ago!"

Ignoring the taunts, *Theia* Dina announced, "I shall be here first thing Sunday morning to properly comb your hair, Sophia. Is it not beautiful? It was my grandmother's. Your hair will look so much better after I arrange it on your wedding day." She waved the comb in the air and turned back to *Kyria* Stamata. "This comb is valuable, and Kostas will frame it, and one day the museum in Athens will offer him thousands of drachmas to purchase it for their walls."

Someone choked back a snicker and another whispered, "The museum, indeed!" She carefully put the comb in her bag and nodded to Stamata, who shook her head and left. Sophia and Eva brought out the tea in cups, along with a plate of *koulourakia,* and served each of us. This would be the only time my sister and I would be permitted to accept a sweet since it was the first day Sophia had her trousseau on display. Cookies were made of sugar and other costly ingredients, and therefore were reserved for special occasions and special visitors, which we understood but regretted. Children were not in this category. Mother had instructed Ourania and me to refuse tea and cakes, or to go home before they were served. But this one day we were allowed this indulgence. Today, we also drank our tea slowly and listened politely to *Theia* Dina's conversation with my mother and my aunt.

"I return to Sparta early because I have a fitting with my seamstress, *Kyria* Basilena. I wanted my dress to be in the finest silk for the christening of Dr. BIakadermos' son. Do you know of the famous doctor, Despina? Magdalene? He is a very important friend of *Kyrios* Arnopoulos. Kostas will be coming with me to the christening though I do not think you will care to, Sophia. You will not feel comfortable among important people like the doctor and his wife." She said this without a smile, staring at my cousin as she sipped her tea.

"I will go wherever Kostas wishes, *Theia* Dina," Sophia replied innocently.

Her mother made a dismissive motion with her hand. "Isn't it a bit strange, *Kyria* Dina, to think of Kostas attending the christening of a stranger with you but without his bride?"

"It is done in Sparta when the bride does not fit in!" Kyria Dina swallowed the last of her tea, brushed cookie crumbs from her skirt, then stood up to go. "I will return to this house to comb your hair on Sunday." She fixed Sophia with another long look and walked to the door with *Theia* Despina.

I felt bad for my cousin, but she did not seem to mind the aunt's mean remarks. On our way home, Ourania imitated *Theia* Dina's affected, mincing walk and asked, "Don't you think there is something strange about that lady?"

"I think she is old and jealous that Kostas will have a pretty wife."

My sister shook here head. "Mama is fifty, so she is old, but *Theia* Dina is younger than that. Maybe it is true what people say—that she wanted Kostas to marry a rich girl who lives in Athens. The shepherdesses were talking about that the other day. They think that she wants to stop Kostas's wedding, so that he can go and meet that other girl."

"How can she stop the wedding now?"

"There are ways. What about M*ati,* the Evil Eye? She looks like that gypsy witch we once saw in the village square. She could put a spell on Sophia to harm her, and then the wedding would be off!" We were impressed by witches, the occult, and their invincible powers, but we also did not hesitate to question their powers.

"If *Theia* Dina is a witch, then why didn't she get the girl she wanted for Kostas in the first place?" We argued about this the rest of the way home.

Three days before the wedding, Kostas, his father, the match-maker, and the mayor arrived at *Theio* Yianni's house with Xenophon and Stelios, two cousins of *Kyrios* Zacharias. The *koumbaros*, best man, served as sponsor of the nuptials, and *Kyrios* Alexandros had accepted this honor in the absence of

Kostas's godfather. In his capacity as *koumbaros,* he not only exchanged the wedding crowns, but also served as the couple's advocate for their guidance toward a Christian life. The *koumbaros* was considered as close as a brother, and he and his family always were treated with deference by the newlyweds and their families. Depending on the circumstances, a *koumbaros* generally presented the couple with a substantial gift.

That morning, my parents had been invited to the house of my uncle and aunt, and my sister, brother, and I went with them. This was the day on which the items in Sophia's dowry would be tallied and delivered to her new home. Ourania and I did not miss a thing as people milled about. My aunt and her daughters served cold water and *gluko tou koutaliou*—a spoonful of home-made fruit preserves served on a small dish—to each of the participants seated at the table. The rest of us stood and watched without speaking. Thanasis Paladinos held up the dowry papers and started to read aloud as he walked around the room: "Two mattresses, four sheets, four blankets, two pillowcases, two pillows, five towels, rugs, mats according to size and use." The matchmaker continued: "One large, copper kettle, three iron pans, two large wooden spoons, two wooden bowls . . ."

Sophia—along with Kostas's mother, *Theia* Dina, *Theia* Despina, and my mother—counted the items for her *kasela,* hope chest. As the inventory continued, Kostas accompanied *Theios* Yiannis and my father to round up the animals that comprised the remainder of Sophia's dowry. After the large chest had been packed, Kostas's brothers placed it on a sturdy cart they had brought along for this purpose. My sister and I lost interest when it came time to count the number of olive trees, fields, and vineyards, so we turned our attention to the final preparations for relocating Sophia's dowry.

Friends and neighbors brought gifts for the couple and left them in the courtyard: Crocks of preserved fruits; a jar of *ortikia*—a delicacy of tiny quails preserved in olive oil and herbs; baskets of chestnuts; wooden bowls filled with raisins;

strings of dried figs; and earthenware jugs of wine—all for the new household. Finally, after all of the terms had been reviewed, and the papers had been signed by *Kyrios* Zacharias, *Theios* Yiannis, the matchmaker, and *Kyrios* Alexandros—according to the agreement that had been reached between the two fathers—Kyrios Zacharias stood up and the parade began. With the pots, pans, and baskets tied to the saddles of the mules and donkeys, *Zanis,* the fiddler, led the way. Everyone in the procession carried something as we chatted and strolled through the streets, transporting Sophia's belongings from her father's house to the home in which she and Kostas would live as man and wife.

On the day of the wedding, my mother would not let Ourania, Leonidas, and me leave until she had looked us over. We had had our baths the night before, our hair had been brushed and combed, and we wore our best outfits. As soon as we were ready, we hurried to Sophia's house. Kostas and his family would come to escort her to church; her parents and the rest of us would follow. Even in their Sunday best, the younger boys chased each other around the courtyard, as usual.

As we entered the house, we sensed that something was wrong. Sophia was not at the door to greet us, smiling and showing off her wedding finery. Ourania pushed ahead of mother and me into the bedroom, where we stopped and stared. Sophia stood in front of the mirror, with tears streaming down her cheeks, while *Theia* Dina, standing behind her was grimly pulling at her hair with the tortoiseshell comb. Ourania and I mumbled *hronia polla*, and shared a low stool near Eva, who had a sad face as she watched Sophia. Their mother looked pretty in a new gray silk blouse and skirt, but at the moment she was frowning at *Theia* Dina. We sat silently, not knowing what to do, as we observed the scene. Despite her discomfort, Sophia looked beautiful. Her new white dress was made of fine cotton that was gathered at the waist, and fell as smoothly as if it were silk. The high neckline and long sleeves were trimmed with a small border of delicate white lace, and on her feet she wore black leather slippers whose thin soles would feel every pebble on the path to the church. All she needed now was to have her hair combed, and to wipe away her tears.

In stark contrast to Sophia's white radiance, *Theia* Dina loomed large and dark. Wearing a black satin dress and head kerchief she looked as though she were on her way to a funeral rather than to the wedding of her nephew. (Mother explained later that *Theia* Dina was wearing black in mourning for the death of a distant cousin.) She clucked and fussed as she roughly pulled the comb one more time. "Your hair is the color of chestnuts, Sophia, but it needs more care. It will now be prettier than ever." She stood back and observed my cousin.

Theia Despina finally lost her patience. "My dear Dina, please stop this. It is time for me to braid Sophia's hair or we won't be ready when Kostas comes to take her to church!"

The other woman nodded, and moved aside next to my mother. "Go ahead, Despina. Braid her hair. I am surprised that you still find braids stylish." She thrust her old tortoiseshell comb into my mother's hand, and folded her arms across her chest. Before mother could put it down, we heard a cry from *Theios* Yiannis at the outer gate.

"*Ela lipon!* Come! Despina! Sophia! *Sto Onoma Theou!* In the name of the Lord! *Erhonteh!* They're coming! The Zacharias family is on the way. Let's not keep them waiting!" Kostas's aunt uttered a little cry and hurried out, stumbling over my brother and cousins, who were in her way.

Theia Despina took over and arranged Sophia's hair, while my mother placed the offensive comb on the dresser, where it slid out of sight. We all turned to Sophia. My aunt gently wove Sophia's long hair into a glossy plait, arranging it on top of her head to resemble a diadem. Mother sent Ourania and me to the kitchen to bring cool water for Sophia to drink; and also a moistened cloth with which she patted Sophia's eyes and face. Eva fluffed out her sister's skirt, and soon the bride was herself once again, happy and smiling, when Kostas arrived. We were unaware of the superstition that it was bad luck for the groom to see the bride before the wedding, so we were happy to see Kostas. He said *yiasas* to everyone as a group with a polite nod of the head but only had eyes for Sophia and went to her; they spoke to each other quietly. We were left at leisure to admire the handsome groom, his dark brown hair combed back, and his manly, robust frame splendid in a new black suit. Without a word, he took Sophia's hand in his and ceremoniously led her out of the house. Kostas nodded to Zanis, the fiddler, who walked ahead of them, playing a song for the bride and leading the way to the church. Kostas's father, mother, brothers, and aunt gathered around the couple and walked with them. Then came *Theios* Yiannis, *Theia* Despina and their children, and after them, our family. The neighbors stood along the road or on their balconies; the older women wiped their eyes, and everyone called out their good wishes, while some pursed lips to create the sound Ptoo! Ptoo!—a simulation of spitting—which was done to ward off the Evil Eye. In Europe and elsewhere, there were those who believed that any person could possess the Evil Eye, and could curse a bride, a child, or anyone else, without the accursed party's awareness. Therefore, unless the curse could be prevented, it could bring doom on the person who had been cursed. Ptoo! Ptoo! was considered a defense against such a curse. There also were small blue stones with a black center, like an eye, that reputedly had the same effect.

Our church had few windows, but its shadowy light was comforting. Flickering candles revealed baskets of fresh flowers placed by Sophia and Eva the night before in front of each of the icons on the *iconostasion,* the altar screen. Lighting a candle as we entered, we took our places beside our parents as women and children stood with the men for the ceremony. At the altar, Kostas and Sophia approached a small table that held the two *stefana*, wedding crowns, on a silver tray; a book containing The Gospels; a cup of wine; and two large candles. *Pater* Georgios and *Kyrios* Alexandros—who was the *psaltis,* the chanter who assisted the priest, as well as the mayor, and for today, the *koumbaros*—began with hymns and prayers extolling marriage and the love, peace, and harmony that would reign in the couple's home. *Pater* Geor-gios handed one large candle to Kostas and the other to Sophia, lighting each with a candle from the inner sanctum.

The two wedding crowns were wreaths of delicate, white orange blossoms and other flowers and buds made of wax, which were connected by a white satin ribbon. *Kyria* Stamata, standing behind us remarked to her husband that *Kyrios* Alexan-dros had not bought the most expensive crowns, but that they were very nice ones, and that Sophia would not be ashamed to display them in a frame after the wedding. As the priest intoned, "Oh, Lord, our God, crown them with honor and glory," the *koumbaros* stood behind the couple and switched the *stefana* three times from the bride's head to the groom's—and back again. The couple was crowned king and queen of their house-hold; the ribbon that joined their crowns signified that they would reign jointly. The Dance of Isaiah followed as *Pater* Georgios placed Sophia's right hand in Kostas's left hand and led them slowly around the altar, each holding a lighted candle. *Kyrios* Alexandros followed closely behind, holding the white satin ribbon that joined the wreaths, and doing his best with his free hand to steady Sophia's crown, so that it did not slip from her braided headdress.

Prayers and readings from The Gospels, commending the axioms of love and respect from Saint Paul's Letter to the Ephe-sians, and Saint John's counsel that a wife must respect and sub-mit to her husband. Finally, the couple drank from one goblet to signify that they would share their lives in love and joy, in pain and sorrow.

Kostas's parents were invited to congratulate the newlyweds at the altar, after *Pater* Georgios's blessing, and to escort the couple outside. We tossed flower petals at them as they passed us. *Theia* Despina and *Theios* Yiannis hugged their daughter and new son-in-law, and the rest of us followed. From the church, the newlyweds, accompanied by the Zacharias family, left for dinner at their house. Only Kostas's family attended; everyone else returned home, as was the custom. The next day, with the blessing of the groom's family, after they had been assured of the bride's chastity, the couple came to visit us and to thank us and everyone who had attended their wedding and to invite us to the celebratory wedding feast at the home of the groom's parents .

Most of the residents of Bordonia were there, as were relatives of both families from other villages, and a few from Sparta, like *Theia* Dina and her husband *Kyrios* Arnopoulos. Since morning mother had been helping *Kyria* Zacharias and *Theia* Despina cook and prepare for the feast. By late afternoon, platters of food had been set out: lambs roasted on the spit, *pastitsio* (ground lamb layered with macaroni), roasted chickens, vegetables in savory tomato and mint sauce, and fresh-baked loaves of *psomi*. Ourania, Leonidas, and I, along with the other young children ate whatever morsels our parents placed in our dishes always with a hopeful eye on the pastries: *mellomakarona*, honey cookies or sugar-covered *kourambiethes,* and *diples,* folded strips of crisp pastry, coated with honey and cinnamon. *Diples* were made especially for weddings; *diplo* meant a doubling of the years allotted to the young couple. Rarely were any of these confections left for us. A violinist arrived with two other musicians who played the *bouzouki* and the *floyera.* We listened to the music, danced, and watched the dancing. By the time the youngest children had fallen asleep on the laps of their parents, I too was ready to go home and to bed.

The week after the wedding, I was in the kitchen shelling peas while mother fixed dinner. *Theia* Despina stopped in with some pastries for us. "Isn't this silly of me?" She wiped tears from her eyes. "I am so happy for Sophia, but today I cannot stop crying. Kostas is a fine boy, and they will make a nice home and raise many children."

"Yes," mother agreed, "so why are you crying, Despina? Has something happened?"

"I don't know what to tell you. It is such a small thing. You remember Dina, the sister of *Kyrios* Zacharias, who was at my house with that ugly comb? But you probably don't remember her from school. She was a few years after you, Magdalene. She always talked about her rich cousins in America, and how they were sending a wealthy American to marry her."

Mother nodded. "I had forgotten all about the sisters of Andonis Zacharias until I saw Dina that day at your house. I don't know if it was Dina, but I recall that one of them asked me to go with her to have our fortunes read by the gypsy. But I was afraid, and I did not know her very well."

"Dina is the one who likes to go to the gypsy. Her sister married the man in America. Dina is determined to interfere in Kostas's life. She comes from Sparta every day to give Sophia instructions on how to clean and how to sew! She is worse than a mother-in-law. *Kyria* Zacharias never tells Sophia what to do."

"You must help Sophia find a way to stop this," mother replied. "She will have to leave the house when she knows the aunt is coming."

"But you know the village. It would not be long before someone could say exactly where Sophia is and what she is wearing! And she cannot come to my house or yours because we could not lock the doors on the woman. Would you tell the aunt she cannot come in?"

"Kostas's parents must talk to her. What does Dina do when she goes every day?"

"I do not think Dina is well. Do you remember how she shoved that ugly comb through Sophia's hair on her wedding day? She insists on combing Sophia's hair as soon as she enters her house. Is that normal? And then the day this past week that she dragged Sophia to my house to find that tortoiseshell comb. She was muttering and crying out until we found it under the dresser. And when she leaves Sophia's, she goes directly to see the gypsy woman who lives down by the creek."

"That must be costing her money!"

"Her husband has forbidden her to go, but she persists."

"Yes, I have heard that he is a devout churchgoer, and believes that the gypsies and their Black Magic are wicked and unchristian."

"*Kyria* Zacharias told me that Dina's husband has told her seamstress that he will not pay for any more dresses if she does not stop visiting the gypsy."

"So, why does Dina go against him like this?"

"That is why I believe that she is not right."

Mother glanced at me, noticing that I had filled a bowl with shelled peas, and sent me to the garden to bring in some greens.

I did not see Sophia very much in the days after her wedding. Her new house was on the other side of the village, and I was kept busy with school work and helping mother string onions and herbs, and fill the storage bins for winter. Only crocks of olives and olive oil had not yet been replenished, so as the cold blasts of air swept down through the mountain passes, and the wind whistled at the cracks in doors and windows, we bundled up and set out to gather olives.

As much as I liked to eat olives, I did not like gathering them. They only ripened in the autumn and winter, and they were not harvested until cold weather had set in. Because it took twelve years for an olive tree to develop and bear fruit, a mature tree was a valuable commodity, no matter whether it had been planted in a grove or had sprouted along a byway near a stream. When my father was ready to harvest our olives, he and a helper carried ladders and six-foot wooden poles to the grove. Mother, Ourania, Leonidas, and I came after, with the donkey and the mule carrying sturdy burlap sacks. As the men set up the ladders, mother tied cotton aprons around our waists; they had large pockets in front, which we filled with olives.

Father and his helper climbed up their ladders and struck the tree limbs with the heavy poles. Olives rained down on the blankets that we had spread out under the trees. The process continued until each tree was empty of its fruits. After the men moved to the next trees, mother, Ourania, Leonidas, and I collected the olives into the aprons tied around our waists. As our apron pockets filled, we emptied them into the heavy burlap bags tied to the donkey and the mule. When my father dragged the blankets to another tree, we scooped up the stray olives that had escaped the blankets. Rain was always a calamity at harvest time. If it rained, the olives would be hidden in mud, and we would have to search with our fingers to retrieve them. The wind whipped at our skirts and tore at our jackets, and we shivered, as we searched in the mud to find all of the fugitive olives. Because the oil is just below the skin of the olive, crushed and muddied olives were not desirable, so we had to be careful not to step on any, even as we scrambled about to find them. It was chaotic, wet, and cold, and I did not like it at all. By the end of the day, my fingers were scraped and bruised, and I could not get the chill out of my bones until later that night, after I had snuggled under piles of woolen blankets.

On the last day of the olive harvest, father already had climbed the ladder when *Theia* Despina and *Theios* Yiannis, accompanied by Sophia, Eva, Nikos, and Stratis, came by on their way to their olive grove, which lay beyond ours. We stopped work and gathered around them. I had not seen Sophia for two weeks. I was surprised at her appearance. She looked haggard, and when she smiled, it was not in her old, cheerful way. Even her hair, which she always had worn in a thick, glossy braid, hung loose beneath a dark *mantili*. The men and boys walked away. My aunt wiped her eyes as she spoke to my mother. "Sophia's hair is falling out by the handful! What are we to do, Magdalene? She is wasting away! She eats nothing!"

"Is she pregnant? Could that be it?"

"The midwife says no." She lowered her voice and added, "I think it is Kostas's aunt. Remember how she has been using that old comb? And she keeps visiting the gypsy. It is the Evil Eye! She has placed some kind of curse on Sophia!" She wiped her eyes as she spoke.

Such an accusation was not made lightly. But mother was not prepared to encourage her sister to believe in witchcraft. "You cannot know that, Despina!" Ourania raised her eyebrows in a question to Eva, who responded with a nod of agreement. Sophia joined in weakly, "Kostas thinks so too. He asked *Pater*

Georgios to meet me here today. We did not want any of his family to know anything—just yet."

"Yes," *Theia* Despina agreed. "Especially Dina!"

A few minutes later, the priest arrived, and we stood by expectantly. He waved cordially to the men who were talking together by the ladders; then he approached Sophia and looked at her with alarm. "You do not look well, my child. Your mother tells me you cannot eat and that you are feeling weak and sick. And the midwife does not believe there is any reason for you to feel this way—is that not right?"

Sophia nodded. *Pater* Georgios studied her for a moment. Then he asked, "When did your sickness begin?"

Sophia thought for a moment. "It was a few days after the wedding. I thought I was just tired with all of the people coming to visit. Kostas's aunt has been coming every day to comb my hair with an antique comb. Now I do not have the strength to lift my arms, and I cannot tell her to leave me alone, since she is performing a service by helping to comb me."

Long, knowing looks passed between my mother and my aunt. *Theia* Despina spoke up. "I do not like to say this, but I believe something evil has possessed Kostas's aunt."

"But," the priest was doubtful, "how could such a thing happen to a church woman such as Dina? She would not wish to harm Sophia, my dear Despina?"

"I think someone needs to look into this, *Pater*. Here is what has happened. Dina brought along an ugly, old comb, and she combed my daughter's hair with it just before the wedding. Three days later, Dina marched Sophia to my house and demanded that I find that comb right away. She was mumbling and shouting like a crazy woman—forgive me for saying this about a church woman, *Pater*."

The priest looked at her sternly as she continued. "We searched all over and finally Stratis, my youngest, bent down and looked under the chest of drawers where the comb had fallen. She did not even thank Stratis, but rather seized it from his hand and left. When Sophia fell ill soon after the wedding, I thought right away about that comb. Sophia keeps getting worse, and Dina continues to go to her house and comb Sophia's hair every day!"

"Have you washed the comb thoroughly so there is no unusual substance on it?"

"Yes, *Pater.* Kostas scrubs it with soap every day," Sophia answered weakly.

"Are there no prayers you can say, *Pater*, that will protect Sophia from any . . . evil?"

He looked at Sophia gravely. "The midwife says you are in good health otherwise." He mused, "We cannot let this continue. I will have to try it."

"What is it, *Pater*?" *Theia* Despina was apprehensive.

He answered solemnly, "No one can be certain. But I believe I must recite some prayers with you to guard against *Mati*, the Evil Eye."

CHAPTER 7

Parting

Ola ta daktyla then einai ithia.
All fingers are not the same.

— GREEK PROVERB

"The Evil Eye!" My aunt gasped. "I knew it! All along I've been thinking that was what was ailing my daughter, but I did not dare believe it! Why would anyone want to place a curse on Sophia?"

Pater Georgios held up one hand, expressing caution. "No, Despina. Do not repeat what you already have said about Dina. As irritating as she is, she may not be the person who possesses the power of the Evil Eye. Many people profess knowledge about curses, but nobody in this world truly knows how to be free of them. We can only try." He turned to Sophia. "Is there anyone who affects you when you are near them—perhaps someone you pass on the road—and after they have gone by, you are left with a feeling of weakness?"

My cousin shook her head and replied feebly, "No."

The priest continued, "*Ela!* We must go to the church. I cannot promise that I can be of any help. It is an awesome thing to attempt to expel the Evil Eye. Despina, you, Magdalene, and Eva—all of you will come with Sophia. Ourania, you and Eleni go home to your mother's garden. Collect some onions and all the beans that you can find, a little mint, and prepare a *fasolada,* bean stew. I will come home with your mother and take some to

125

Despina's family. Sophia must stay at her mother's house for two weeks. She will remain inside the house—never outside except for the balcony—where she will receive no callers. Only her parents, brothers, and sister may approach her. No one may visit Sophia—not even Kostas! I will explain everything to Kostas and his parents. If you are no better by that time, my child," he directed his gaze to Sophia, "then you must go to the hospital in Sparta."

The hospital in Sparta! I did not know which I dreaded most—the exorcism of the Evil Eye, Sophia's going to the hospital, or Ourania showing me how to prepare *fasolada.* Mother reviewed the instructions with Ourania for lighting the *tzaki*, the stove, and cooking the meal; then she accompanied *Theia* Despina, who put her arm around Sophia's waist, and Eva, as they followed *Pater* Georgios to the church.

Ourania and I walked home slowly. "Have you ever made *fasolada?*" I asked my sister. "It's easy," she shrugged. "I've helped mother a hundred times. I'll do the onions. I have to chop them up and cook them in the pot with a little olive oil. You go out and gather all the green beans you can find in the garden and wash them. Pinch off the tips of a handful of mint, too. Then snip off the tough ends of the beans and add them to the onions; with the chopped mint and a little water, we will leave them to cook." We prepared the stew as my sister had instructed. She chopped the onions, and then waited for me to harvest the beans and mint, pull the strings from the beans and wash them, while she sat on the balcony, crocheting a sweater that she had started the day before. We stirred our stew often, perhaps too often, mother chided us later. The beans had broken up into smaller pieces, but they were tender and tasted good, and there was enough sauce for all to dip their bread into any left on their plates.

Word of the exorcism spread; it became the main topic in our village and the surrounding communities for many days. Although most people knew what an exorcism meant, the practice was so rarely invoked that no one could say precisely what was supposed to happen. Exorcism was shrouded in superstition and fear since it involved the sinister ways of the Devil. How were we to deal with it, when merely mentioning the Evil One was presumed dangerous? Falling into a well could be an accident, or it could be attributed to an ill-advised conversation. *Pater* Georgios was not forthcoming about his methods, nor did my mother say much about it. *Pater* had said prayers over Sophia and had read aloud passages from the Bible that she had never heard before. That was all she would say. We did not see Sophia for two weeks and missed her during the last phase of the olive harvest, when the olives were brought indoors for sorting.

Because of Sophia's seclusion in her parents' home, her father's olive harvest was delivered to our house. For the next week, it was difficult to walk around because every evening the men dumped sacks of olives onto blankets that were spread out over every inch of floor space. We all worked at picking over the olives, separating them and removing the leaves and stems. The ripest would be pressed into olive oil first. The biggest and best olives were set aside to be sold to a dealer who would add olive oil, vinegar and herbs to them and sell them from crocks in his store. Other olives we preserved in crocks with olive oil and tangy vinegar for home use; the remaining olives we sent to the olive oil press.

Every day we hoped for news about Sophia's improvement, but we heard nothing. Meanwhile, Father loaded heavy burlap bags filled with olives on the mule and donkey and transported them to the factory, the *elaiotrivio*, where they would be pressed into olive oil. Because it was located at a distance from our village, my father and the other men whose olives also were being processed camped out at the mill for the two or three days it would take to finish their lot. It was a long walk for Ourania and me to bring father his midday meal, but we did not mind it too much. We usually met other neighborhood children on the way to the old stone building, and our fathers always were happy to see us. We brought them loaves of bread and pails of stewed vegetables and pasta, and all of us contributed to the commotion. Our shrill voices had to be raised over the sound of gallons of water splashing along the mill race, turning the old, creaking waterwheel, and washing the olives. Then there was the huge screw press with its screeches and groans, vying with the shouts of the men and the mill owner. They approached all issues loudly, from discussions of weight at the clanging scales to the direction of the mules. Two mules in harness trudged around the press in slow motion, causing the giant pad to descend and flatten the olives on mats that served as strainers. These thick pads, made of compressed goat hair, mashed the olives into a pulp, but did not exert enough pressure to crush the seeds. The pads oozed with glistening oil that dripped into a large container positioned beneath the press. This first pressing produced the purest, heaviest oil, which was called virgin. The virgin olive oil and the seeds and skins were channeled into separate containers; then, heavier pressure was applied to the remainder of the olive pulp. It took twenty-four hours after the first pressing for the oil to filter through a sieve made of coarser padding.

My father remained at the site until all of the olives had been processed, and he had received the correct allotment of oil, which depended on the weight of the bags he had brought to the mill. I was told that the mill owner kept ten percent of the count, storing whatever he kept for himself and selling the excess. The seeds and pulp were pulverized and compressed into slabs, which were fed to the pigs.

One day, as we arrived with father's meal, we found him lined up with the other men in front of the huge scale, where the growers confirmed the weight of each bag of olives. Ourania and I were startled when one of the men shouted angrily. "That's not right, Vasilaki! You have changed my allotment in your book!"

It was *Theia* Xenia's oldest son, Heracles, a man whose demeanor was usually quiet. He was hunched over the mill owner's book of figures. Vasilaki, the miller, stood stiffly beside him and declared, "Everyone knows, Heracles, that my figures are correct!"

I was afraid that Heracles would hit Vasilaki; he looked so angry. He shouted again. "How could you do this to me? I brought in seventeen sacks of olives, and you have me down for only fourteen. Your figures are not correct this time!"

"You are mistaken, Heracles. It was fourteen bags that you brought, and fourteen bags that I wrote down in my book! See there! You were with me. We counted them together. Now step aside, please, and let me get back to work."

"What! And let a Messenian like you cheat me? Not on your life! I brought seventeen sacks, and I expect full measure when I leave. Ask Elias Andamas. He was standing next to me as you were weighing the bags and counting."

Elias stepped forward, but the miller held up both hands to stop him. "This has gone far enough! *Se Parakalo!* Please, Heracles. You are holding up the line. I did not make a mistake!"

"Look, you!" Heracles cried, "Don't try to make me go away. I am not leaving until you give me my correct measure. You came here from Messenia, married my wife's cousin, set yourself up in this factory, using her dowry, and now you cheat real Spartans! I will kill you before I let you cheat me!" Heracles fell upon Vasilakis, grabbing his shirt.

Just then, *Kyrios* Alexandros, the mayor, advanced upon the combatants. Pompous and indolent as he appeared, nevertheless, he stood for the voice of reason. Quietly and firmly he spoke: "Stop, Heracles! Let go of your cousin!" Since his words had no effect, two other men separated them, and held them apart. The mayor continued, "Now then," he beckoned to Elias Andamas. "Tell us whether you witnessed the number of sacks that Heracles brought to the press."

Elias came forward again and faced the truculent son of *Theia* Xenia. "Heracles," he spoke apologetically. "I am your friend, and I fear you will be angry with me, but the truth must be told. You know I would never do anything to harm you. But this time you are wrong. I must remind you that I have seen this happen before, my friend. You have sometimes mistaken the number four for the number seven. It is true that, when hastily written, these figures can look alike. Vasilakis is right this time."

Retaining the anger in his eyes, rigid lips, and tight fists for a moment longer, Heracles then relaxed visibly. His jaw slackened, the anger left his eyes, and tears welled up. He stepped forward and clasped the miller. "How could I have accused you of wrong doing, Vasilaki? Forgive me for what I said—for what I was thinking—my friend, my cousin. Elias is right," he hung his head. "This has happened before. God help me, I do not know what it is with that four and that seven! I can only place the blame on Mayor Alexandros's *retsina*. I had an aperitif of two glasses of wine before lunch, an hour ago."

The men who had been standing with my father shook their heads and chuckled as they made their way outside to eat lunch. It was a mild day, and they settled on the ground or on one of the boulders that were everywhere. "That was clever, Heracles— trying to claim three more bags from Vasilakis," someone teased as the men around him laughed. The mill owner brought out a gallon jug of wine and passed it around. "If the mayor's wine made Heracles belligerent, my wine will make all of you as tame as *kounellakia*, bunnies." He raised his glass and toasted the success of the olive harvest and of their meal with a hearty, "*Kalophageto!* Enjoy your meal!"

My sister and I stayed with father while he cut two wedges of bread from the loaf we had brought. We followed him like slavering guard dogs trotting behind their keeper at feeding time. Succulent *boukouvala* would reward us back at the press near the open fire that was kept going to heat the water in which the olives were washed—and that kept the patrons warm, as well. Ourania and I watched quietly as father speared the bread on the ends of two sticks, then toasted the bread over the fire. He then dipped the toast into the thick, freshly-pressed oil and handed one wedge to each of us. Ourania and I walked home, happily munching on the warm, rich toast.

With the last of the olives picked and processed, father stowed enough olive oil and crocks of olives in our basement storeroom to last the year. Sophia went back to her new home with Kostas. The townspeople attributed her cure to the exorcism, but our priest denied this, insisting that it was the many prayers for her recovery that had turned the tide. My cousin soon was looking like her old self—happy and cheerful as before. *Pater* Georgios spoke to Kostas. Sophia was permitted to attend church on Sundays, but visitors to their home should be limited for another month.

In the privacy of our family, Ourania could not help observing "If *Theia* Dina did not have the Evil Eye, then she was a very mean person, who had coated the comb with poison." Mother scolded her for talking like this. Whatever it was, we did not see *Theia* Dina in Bordonia again for a long time, and Sophia's health was restored.

"That is how the Evil Eye works," *Kyria* Aliki intoned at the general store inside the *caffenion*, where mother sent me to buy coffee one day. "Nobody knows."

Kostas's mother told my aunt that *Theia* Dina had become very religious along with her husband, and that *Kyrios* Arnapoulos—driven by a need for contemplation and prayer—took up residence for a month in one of the thirty-three monasteries (where women were not allowed) on Mount Athos, the Holy Mountain in northern Greece, while his wife lived with the nuns in the cliffside monastery of *Elona*, the Healing Mother, in Kynouria.

It did not snow often in our village. So, whenever it did, unexpected changes occurred. The ridges of the mountains were more pronounced, the gullies were deeply etched, and the familiar outlines of houses, trees, bushes, and rocks were transformed into mounds of white cotton. Ourania, Leonidas, and I could not resist running out in bare feet to savor the unspoiled expanse of the courtyard. We packed the snow into large balls and rolled them down the hill behind the house, watching them break against the dark green leaves of the orange tree or crush the *tri-fylli*, the three-leafed clover that was favored by the goats. This winter pasture of theirs was none the worse for the rough treatment of our snowballs.

Fodder for the donkey and the goats was stored where they could not reach it, and small portions were doled out to them each day when they could not go out. Father had filled all of the storage space under the balcony and against the house with bundles of brushwood that our donkey had carried back from the fields throughout the summer months. This wood was an important source of fuel and was covered with odd pieces of sturdy cloth, or whatever we could find to keep it dry, and it was closely guarded. We seldom made a fire in the daytime, so when mother worked at the loom in the winter room, she wore several sweaters. On very cold days, she would make a fire and cook, and at night she would sit close to the embers and spin thread from a basket of fluffy wool on the floor beside her.

One dark afternoon, it was snowing hard as I returned from school. Mother had washed a few things, and was hanging them to dry over the backs of chairs near the fire. She wiped tears from her eyes as she told me. "It is *Theia* Xenia. She died this morning."

My heart grew heavy as I thought of the old friend who no longer would be in my life. Although not a relative, she had been like a grandmother to me. Whenever I passed her house in the summer, she invited me to come up to the porch to admire the basil and the *katifes,* marigolds, that she grew in pots. Then she would cut a bouquet of the bright orange and yellow marigolds mixed with fragrant herbs for me to take home to my mother.

That afternoon, as our family approached *Theia* Xenia's house in the deepening snow, we could hear the funereal chants even before we reached the door. It was customary that the funeral and burial be held within twenty-four hours of a person's death, and all day her friends made their way to the home in which the deceased had spent the last years of her life. *Theia*

Xenia lay in repose in a wooden coffin that was fresh with the fragrance of newly-planed pine. She was dressed in her black dress, her arms crossed over her chest, an icon of the saint she considered her patron, *Ayia* Sophia, in her hands. She seemed very small and as though she were asleep. A brass incense burner topped with a crucifix stood on a small table beside the casket, and an icon of the Blessed Virgin had been placed next to it. Huddled on stools near the coffin were five women, dressed in black robes with cowls pulled over their heads, concealing their faces. They slowly rocked back and forth, chanting the dirges we had heard as we approached the house: "*Kai yiati na fiyis simera? Afises ta paidia sou, oooh!*" ("And why did you have to leave today? You left your children, Ooh!")

These women were not relatives of the deceased. They were *miroloyes,* professional mourners, who appeared without invitation, according to ancient custom. Some families paid them, while others asked them to leave. Many of these women were accomplished performers capable of delivering a large repertoire of emotional chants that had them wailing and moaning well into the night. It was comforting to some to hear their doleful chanting, but to others it was depressing. *Theia* Xenia's sons and their families did not seem to object, as they stood near their mother's casket, but perhaps they were too sad to notice anything. Mother addressed each of the family—adults and children—in turn. Ourania, Leonidas, and I followed suit, murmuring appropriate words of condolence that mother had told us to say before we left the house. Father had come with us, but as soon as he could, he stepped outside with the other men. They preferred braving the cold to being cloistered in the small house; they stayed to accept a glass of brandy from one of Xenia's sons, and drank to her memory; then they left. As I made the sign of the cross near the coffin, the mourning women who had been humming, resumed their eerie lamentations, weeping and pulling at the hoods covering their heads to dramatize deep grief. Then, the bony hand of one of these women in black reached out and pushed me closer to the casket. *Kyria* Aliki, who was standing near me, grasped my arm firmly and whispered, "You must kiss her, Eleni. Kiss your old friend goodbye." Death was always present in agricultural communities. Pets, work animals, and wild life died before our eyes and we were familiar with the duties necessary to attend to them. Nevertheless, I was unwilling to approach *Theia* Xenia in her coffin, and hoped that she would forgive me.

"The child does not have to kiss her, Aliki," *Theia* Despina declared. How I loved my aunt at that moment. As I turned to leave, however, she stopped me, and I withdrew the generous feelings I had felt for her a few moments earlier, when she said, "It is enough if Eleni kisses the icon of *Ayia* Sophia that *Theia* Xenia is holding in her hands." Fortunately, Sophia came to my rescue. Ignoring her mother, she shooed me toward the kitchen; Ourania and Leonidas quickly came after me. One of Leonidas's friends teased us: "If you don't go back and kiss her hands, Eleni, her ghost will haunt you whenever you are outdoors at night."

I replied bravely, "I have never seen a ghost, Menis. Maybe *Theia* Xenia would be a nice ghost to have around."

"You shouldn't make fun of ghosts," he declared solemnly with a smirk.

"I'm not!" I retorted.

"Well, then," he responded, "what about *Mati*, the Evil Eye? It could rise up out of a well and draw you in so fast that no one would ever know what had happened to you—not your mother or your father or even Ourania!" I must admit that I was afraid of the Evil Eye, but before I could respond, we heard angry voices in the front room. We pressed around the door as *Theia* Xenia's sons began to shout at each other. "*Vreh!* Heracles, this house is mine!" the younger brother exclaimed. "Mama had said so to me—right here in front of Anna—last week."

"*Ohi!* No! You are wrong!" cried Heracles. "She bequeathed you the *ambelia*, the vineyards! I remember very well. How could you have forgotten, Agamemnon?"

Heracles seemed to thrive on disagreements, quite unlike his peaceful and gentle mother. Agamemnon spoke bitterly. "The house is mine—the *ambelia* are yours! It was Easter, Heracles. *Sto Onoma Theou!* In the name of God!" The younger brother continued. "You were roasting the lamb outside on the spit, with your sons, when she called us to her side, right on her terrace. She told us that she did not want us to ever argue once she was gone, and that the house would be mine because my house is not so fine as yours, and besides I have three daughters to marry off, and therefore would need a better house. You must remember our mother saying that, don't you? Or is your memory failing you?"

"Yes! I remember. But when I explained to her that it would not look right for the younger son to be given her house, she backed down, and told both of us that the vineyard would stand you in good stead, and that it should be yours. Then, she brought out the *mavrodaphne,* her favorite wine because it was so sweet, and we toasted our mother and were happy. We all agreed that day."

"*Paidia!* Boys! What is this?" Mayor Alexandros stepped forward. "Your revered mother is not yet in her grave, and you are disgracing all that she held dear by shouting about houses and vineyards. Shame! How do you think your mother's soul— *o Theos na tin synhoresi,* May God forgive her sins—feels at this moment? Here she lies in dignity, waiting for everyone to pay their respects, yet her sons cry out in anger and revile one another." He shook his head. "This is a sad moment for *Theia* Xenia. Everyone loved this gentle lady. Now she lies dead. And her sons cast shame on her. Enough of this! Heracles, what is happening to you? You are the elder. You must show the way to your younger brother and calm yourself. Tomorrow, after the funeral, after your mother has been laid to rest, then both of you will come to me, and we will speak—like men—not like petty children." He patted each man on the shoulder as he pushed them out of the room.

Kyria Aliki started to sniffle. She was seated in the winter room with some of the women. "I was with her near the end. Her daughter-in-law, Maria, was holding her hand, and I told her,

'Let her go, Maria. She cannot die when you are holding her. Charon will refuse to cross the River Lethe until you let go of her. And truly, as soon as Maria took her hand away, Xenia breathed her last."

"It was so peaceful. Like a little bird flying away." Maria wiped her eyes.

The loud voice of *Kyria* Stamata interrupted. "Ehh! Do you remember the time we had with old Chumbalas? Fighting and kicking, he was."

"Oooh, what a death that was!" *Kyria* Aliki rocked back and forth, and closed her eyes as though trying to fix the memory behind her eyelids.

"Ahah, hah, hah!" Stamata laughed, then remembered where she was, and moved away from the *miroloyes*. Other women pressed around her, recounting old memories. "Ah," continued *Kyria* Stamata, "I was thinking of Chumbalas and how he loved those goats of his. Remember when we found him asleep out on the *cambo*, the field, and Xenia took a little white *katsikaki,* kid? We were all laughing so much we thought he would wake up and catch Xenia sneaking away with that little goat, but he slept on."

My aunt chuckled. "Yes, yes—that was Xenia. She hid it right here in her kitchen."

"What a sight. Chumbalas was searching all over the hills for it!" Aliki sighed.

"Xenia almost convinced him that maybe he had counted wrong and never had two baby goats in the first place!"

There were smiles among the old neighbors until *Theia* Despina reminded everyone, "Better one of his goats missing than his own daughter."

The women murmured in agreement. Stamata added, "You know that daughter of his, Xanthippe, is living in Tasopolis—just as brazen as you please. She has a nice house, has children, works in the fields, just like everyone else—can you believe it?"

"Old Chumbalas never got over Xanthippe marrying the Turk."

"What is this world coming to?" *Kyria* Aliki shivered. "If my father had been alive when this happened, he would have led the entire village down to Tasopolis, and they would have thrown that Turk into the river. That's how much my father stood up for his principles. Now, it seems as though nobody cares. Girls marry anyone they please—even our arch enemy whom their grandfathers fought against in the war."

"Shh! The priest is here!" *Kyria* Stamata stood up. The *miroloyes* had stopped their chanting and listened while everyone stood near the coffin and participated in the *Trisagion*, the Requiem Service, which began with a three-part invocation: *Ayios o Theos. Ayios Ishiros. Ayios Athanatos. Eleison Imas.*" God is Holy. God is Mighty. God is Immortal. Bless us." Afterwards, *Pater* Georgios announced that there would be no funeral service tomorrow at the church; rather, the service would take place here in *Theia* Xenia's home, with only brief prayers at the cemetery. He knew that *Theia* Xenia would have been the first to agree with his decision. The snow was deeper and the paths were slippery with ice. Indoors was not much warmer unless we huddled near the fireplace.

Maria and Anna, the wives of *Theia* Xenia's two sons, passed trays holding small glasses of *tsipouro,* and the visitors started to leave. The immediate family, and those who wished to, remained for the overnight vigil, along with the five *miroloyes,* until the funeral the next day.

During the night, the snow continued to fall, and by morning it was so deep that walking was difficult. In the worst snowstorm that any of our elders could remember, only a few of the older men—along with *Theia* Xenia's sons, their wives, and children—ventured out to carry the coffin from her house directly to the cemetery. Most of the men had been out all night in the bitter cold digging emergency paths and caring for their livestock. Mother wrapped us up in woolen scarves from head to toe, and with our mother, Ourania, Leonidas, and I shoveled snow on the path to aid the funeral procession. The cemetery was located on the outskirts—as it was in most villages—away from habitation, so we had a long, uphill walk. The cemetery was easily identifiable from a distance by the row of dark green cypress trees that stood as sentinels around the small chapel and the graves. It was the custom, in the dry, rocky terrain of the Peloponnesus, to remove the bones from the coffin after three years, wash them, and reverently label, wrap, and store them in the funerary chapel. Since it had been impossible to dig a grave in the frozen earth for *Theia* Xenia, another grave from which the bones had been disinterred a month earlier was cleared of snow and *Theia* Xenia's coffin lowered into it.

"*Aionia,i mnimi,* May her memory be eternal." *Pater* Georgios chanted the ageless words that acknowledged the sadness of death, while consoling the living with the promise of life everlasting. Because of the intense cold, everyone wanted to go home as quickly as possible, but mother stopped us momentarily, indicating *Kyria* Aliki and her three sisters stumbling through the deep snow. Their sobs had been curiously audible during the ceremony. Now, they began to wail as they struggled to reach the chapel. Having arrived, they fell upon the snow-covered ground, sobbing, their arms stretched out. I looked at mother for guidance. The rest of the mourners had followed these sisters, and mother responded by lowering her eyes, so I followed suit. *Theia* Aliki and her sisters, in unison, cried out, "Oh, little brother, here you are! All alone without us, your dear sisters, to tend your needs, wash your clothes, and prepare your supper."

I thought this outpouring of grief was for a person recently deceased, but Ourania whispered to me that these laments were for their brother, who had died more than twenty years ago. He was only nineteen, the only son among four girls. He had been working in Tripolis, and had died of food poisoning. Every holiday, the sisters—bearing oil lamps and incense—visited the chapel. On the anniversary of his birth each year, they removed the bones from the shelf on which they were stored in the ossuary, reverently washed them, and returned them to their wrappings. They continued to express their loss in front of us as we stood and shivered in sympathy.

I was glad when mother told us to follow her back to *Theia* Xenia's house for the memorial lunch. *Theia* Xenia's neighbors had prepared *bacaliaro yahni*—dried codfish that had been soaked overnight then cooked in a savory sauce, and others had brought *makaronada* and *fasolada*. After the meal, there was brandy and coffee, and unsweetened toast called *paximathia.*

Weeks passed, the days grew shorter and the sun rose from behind a different hill in the east. School was out for the Twelve Days of Christmas, the *dodekameron*, when the birth and baptism of the Christ Child were celebrated. First, however, came Saint Nicholas Day, on December 7. We attended vesper services the night before, and in some areas, children awakened the next morning to find a coin from kindly Saint Nicholas. I do not remember this custom in my village, but we received treats on another holiday, a few days later.

Although Christmas, on December 25, celebrating the Birth of Christ, was an important Holy Day, we did not celebrate it with gift-giving and Christmas trees. Instead, we observed a fast from meat and dairy for two weeks before the holiday and attended church for most of Christmas Day. The traditional celebratory meal began with Christmas bread, c*hristopsomo* and *avyolemono soupa*, egg-lemon soup. The bread, made with white flour, was topped with a sprinkling of sugar or icing or other additions the baker might wish to add, such as chopped dates or raisins.

The first day of *Ianouarios,* January, was also New Year's Day and Saint Basil's Day, *Ayios* Basilios. In his youth Saint Basil gave away most of his considerable fortune to help orphaned children. Later he became Bishop of Caesarea, an important metropolis in the 4th century. Children loved Saint Basil because we believed that if we had been good all year, and placed a shoe outside the door before going to bed on New Year's Eve, he would leave us a gift. The next morning, we woke up fearful that our shoe would be empty. Yet, there always was a gift—an orange or a tangerine or a cube of sugar—to bring joy to our hearts. Once the excitement of finding this precious gift had worn off, Ourania, Leonidas, and I, wrapped in warm scarves and jackets, hurried out to join our friends and others who were promenading through the village streets, singing New Year's carols: "*O Ayios Basilios erhete, apo, apo tin Kaisaria . . .* Saint Basil is coming from, from Caesarea . . ." This carol predicted the appearance of the kindly, white-bearded Saint, who was coming to bring "sweets wrapped in paper."

Later, at supper, mother placed a large loaf of New Year's bread in front of father. *Vasilopeta*, Basil's Bread, had a coin concealed inside. The sweetened loaf was ceremoniously sliced, and my father handed out slices in order: the first slice was for the house; the second slice was for Papa; the third slice was for Mama—and so on, in order of the ages of the children. This year, Ourania found the coin in her slice, and she glowed in the knowledge that this brought her good fortune all year long.

On Saint Andonis's Day, January 17, *Kyrios* Andonis Zacharias was at home receiving friends because it was his name day. Sophia told us later that she had been offering the tray with *loukoumi* and glasses of cold water to *Pater* Georgios and his wife, when Phillipas *Kyria* Aliki's grandson pushed the door open and ran to the priest: "Your guests are on the way, *Pater.*"

"I do not expect any guests today," the priest replied, puzzled.

"But *Pater*. They are coming. They are on horseback, all three of them. One man is so beautiful! He is wearing red and green and yellow! The *geros* is the one that came last time. You know who they are—the people for Eva,"

"But, my parents did not know they were coming!" Sophia looked with alarm at Kostas.

"And I had no notice of such a visit!" *Pater* Georgios stood up. "Send for Mayor Alexandros and Thanasis Paladinos, the matchmaker. They will know what to do. Go, Phillipas, and tell them. But first! Where are the guests going? What did they say? Are they coming here to *Kyrios* Andonis's house, or to my house?"

"I told them that you were here—when the old man asked me."

"*Entaxi.* Go then, to the Mayor. I will stay here to greet them."

Sophia ran to her parents' home and sent her brother Nikos to tell my parents that *Theia* Despina needed them to be at the Zacharias house when they met the visitors.

"What else did Sophia say?" Ourania asked Nikos, while mother wiped our hands and faces with a wet cloth, so we could go visiting. "Is it really the same *geros* who was here last time?"

"One is the old man," Nikos replied. "The others are not. Phillipas said that one of them is dark like a *peiratis,* pirate, and he wears a *tourbani,* a turban, wrapped around his head. His shirt has big shiny sleeves, and his pantaloons are puffed out and of many colors! He is the rich one. He has gold chains around his neck and wrists and golden rings hanging from his ears! The third man is the one in charge, Phillipas says. He is wearing a suit and a necktie like the milords wear."

"An English?" Ourania asked. Milord was another term for Englishman.

Mother stopped our questions. "That is enough, Nikos. Go on home, so you don't keep your mother waiting. Tell her we will be at *Kyrios* Andonis as soon as we are ready. We will see these visitors for ourselves soon enough."

When we arrived at the Zacharias house, mother politely nodded to the exotically dressed man standing by the horses, and she proceeded inside, leaving my sister, brother, and me to gape. We could not take our eyes off the man in his turban of twisted red and yellow scarves and his vivid shirt and pantaloons. Aware of our fascination, he sought to impress us further by sweeping his arm, in a billowing sleeve of deep blue silk, as he gestured toward the stairs of the house.

When we entered, Eva was standing next to a short, dark-haired man wearing a well-cut suit, similar to what the King of England wore in pictures we saw in newspapers. She introduced him to us as "*Kyrios* Dinos Rolas." He shook hands with each of us in a friendly manner. Ourania and I took our seats on stools near mother while Leonidas ran outside to join Nikos and the other boys. We sat and stared at *Kyrios* Rolas. His cheeks were pockmarked, but he had kind eyes. I thought that, even though he was not much taller than Eva, he looked nice enough. *Kyrios* Diogenes Hatzis, the older man, the carpet merchant from Athens who had visited Eva months before, stood on the other side of *Kyrios* Rolas, until Sophia invited them to be seated. They settled down to business after *Pater* Georgios, Mayor Alexandros, and *Kyrios* Paladinos arrived, and we were free to whisper among ourselves what we thought of the pirate outside.

An exclamation from *Pater* Georgios drew our attention to *Kyrios* Zacharias who objected to something *Kyrios* Rolas had said. Then my uncle cried, "In two days! Six months! You do not take Eva anywhere, sir! How dare you come to me and ask for such a thing? I do not know your father. I do not know you or who your grandparents were! Do you think that Eva is a kitten or a puppy that we hand over just because you say that you like her?"

Kyrios Rolas looked stunned. His lips parted, and we waited for his response. After a moment, he said, turning from my uncle to face the priest. "*Kyrie* Louvis! I do not understand. I wrote to *Pater* Georgios three weeks ago telling him that I was on my way to Athens, that I planned to stop in Lenithi, and that I would come to meet your daughter, Eva. In the letter, I wrote in detail about my family. My father was Greek and the owner of a small fleet of ships when he met my mother in France. I was ten when she died. My father raised me in Alexandria, where he had a brother. I also enclosed a letter of recommendation from the Mayor of Alexandria, and a copy of my birth certificate. *Pater* Georgios was to give my letter to you if you approved of my proposal. I had planned to spend some days with your daughter, so that we could become acquainted before I returned to Alexandria. If she wished, we would marry before I left. If not, I would return in three months. If you disapproved of this plan, *Pater* Georgios was to write me back. And so, I am here. I never would have come had I known I was not welcome!" He stood up to leave. "I am embarrassed to have presumed that you were expecting me." He held his chin up, and his back was very straight. I held my breath. I was so afraid that he would leave, and Eva would never have a husband who had a servant who wore a turban.

Kostas rose, trying to calm *Kyrios* Rolas. "Please sit down, and let us finish our discussion. You and your friends are welcome in my father's house and in the Louvis home as well. *Kyrios* Louvis has no objection to your asking for Eva's hand. But we need to know more. We cannot go on with this misunderstanding. What could have happened to your letter?"

Pater Georgios nodded. "The world cannot be left with the impression that you and *Kyrios* Hatzis have disrespected our small community. It would appear dishonorable for you or your representative to arrive in this village twice without prior notice to press your suit for the daughter of one of our leading families."

"*Despinis* Eva, Miss Eva! *Kyria* Louvis! You must not think such a thing!" *Kyrios* Rolas turned to Eva and her mother, stumbling over his words as he looked with apprehension at Eva. .

Kyrios Hatzis jumped to his feet. "Believe me, Madame, when I say that neither *Kyrios* Rolas nor I could be a party to such an arrangement! Let him tell you. We have nothing but respect for you and for your family!"

The priest nodded. "Please. Be seated. I must be clear about this letter that you say you sent me. I do not want to bear the stigma of one who cannot relay a message. Tell me, *Kyrios* Rolas, where did you mail this letter?" The visitor frowned. "I gave the letter to Telis, my bookkeeper in Alexandria. He said he was going directly to the *tahidromeio,* the postal office."

"Is Telis a trusted employee? Does he carry out his duties as he is directed?

"He has been with me for one year, and is a good man. He came to me when Socrates, who had been with me for twenty years, moved to Athens to live with his son. It was he who recommended Telis, his neighbor."

Kyrios Paladinos, the matchmaker spoke. "*Kyrie* Rolas. Did Telis know the contents of the letter?"

"I keep no secrets from him. He knew I was traveling to Bordonia to propose marriage to a beautiful girl." He glanced at Eva.

"Might he be angry with you, sir, for any reason?" Mayor Alexandros inquired.

"*Nai!*" The matchmaker looked up with a sudden thought. "By any chance, has your bookkeeper recently introduced you to a young woman?"

Kyrios Rolas was quiet. He stared at *Kyrios* Paladinos for a long time, then pursed his lips and nodded. "He has a daughter. He talked about her often." He sighed. "I trusted him. How could I know that his fatherly hopes would lead him to such dishonesty—that he never mailed my letter to *Pater* Georgios?" He turned to my uncle. "May we speak together, sir? I will take care of Telis when I return home. For now, please accept my humble apologies?"

They settled down around the table again, while Ourania and I followed Eva into the kitchen. Sophia was handing Kostas glasses of wine to take to the men in the other room, and counseling her sister. "You will wait six months, Eva. You cannot marry someone you have known for only a few hours."

"But I believe he is a good man, Sophia. Don't you agree with me, Kostas? Mayor Alexandros, and the man from Athens both speak well of him, and I like what I have seen so far. He is respectful, and father and *Kyrios* Paladinos are looking at his papers. Mayor Alexandros can authenticate them by sending a messenger to Athens."

Kostas cleared his throat. "It is not a proper subject in front of young women, but you must know the truth, Eva, men in Egypt can have more than one wife at a time."

My quiet cousin shook her head, and replied. "He spoke to me about that at once. He reminded me that he is a Christian."

"Christos Hatzakos has met him and has seen his friends. We can write to him and ask him," Sophia commented.

Theia Despina burst into the kitchen with my mother. Ignoring us, my aunt said in a strained voice, "Whoever heard of such a thing, Magdalene? He wants no dowry, no trunk—just my daughter Eva, as she is! He said he will buy her whatever she needs on the way to Alexandria. Is this not an insult to her mother and father?" *Theios* Yiannis appeared in the doorway and frowned at his wife.

"*Ela, gyneka!*" Come, wife! Don't walk out on me!"

"Yiannis!" His wife chided him. "*Ta ehases?* Have you lost your mind! What proof can there possibly be that could convince us to allow Eva to go with this stranger to a foreign country—tomorrow?"

My uncle spoke calmly. "*Akou!* Listen! He brought along copies of his papers, the ones he put in the letter that we never received. *Kyrios* Hatzis, the carpet merchant, and Mayor Alexandros, and the matchmaker—they all agree that the papers are genuine and that they verify that he is Dinos Rolas, a Greek who owns a small merchant fleet based in Alexandria. He offered—I did not ask for this—to sign papers as soon as the priest has married them that ensure that Eva will own one-half of his possessions."

My aunt shook her head defiantly. "I need to know more!"

All of us returned to the winter room, and *Theia* Despina turned to Dinos Rolas. "I am not convinced. You cannot marry Eva tomorrow. I do not know the kind of person you are. For instance, why did you find it necessary to travel so far to find a wife, when you could have one from your bookkeeper? And, how could you possibly have heard about Eva from so far away as Egypt?"

He nodded courteously. "I do not know how it really came to pass, *Kyria* Louvis. I truly believe that it was written in the stars for me to meet Eva as I did. You see, I was to be married ten years ago to a young woman I met at a friend's house. One week before the wedding, she told me that she had no feelings for me. My face had been marked with the smallpox from childhood, so, as a youth, I always worried that no girl would ever like me. When first she loved me and then rejected me, I lost all perspective, and decided to lose myself in hard work. I took a job for a year as an ordinary seaman on one of my ships. I learned that love is fickle for many reasons—and not just disfigurement or what we think may be the correct reason. I came home to Alexandria, where, whether I was with my cousins or my friends, the conversation seemed to turn to my finding a wife. One night at dinner with my friends, someone mentioned that his wife's sister was perfect for me. I had heard this too often. I would have to invite the sister out or hurt my friend's feelings, so to change the subject, I announced that I had made a decision: I would marry only a girl who had six fingers on one hand."

"Whatever in the world made you think of such a thing?" Mayor Alexandros inquired.

"I do not know! The words came out of my mouth without my realizing it. My only reference to multiple fingers and toes occurred many years ago, and I had not thought of it since. As a child, I had a nurse who told me wonderful stories, and I loved her dearly. One day, we were at the beach, and she was wearing sandals. I pointed out to her that she had an extra toe on one foot. She was from an island, she said, where only the kindest and the smartest people were permitted to have either an extra toe or an extra finger. To me she was very kind and very smart. She could tell when I was hungry and gave me only food that I liked best. Why I thought of her at such a moment in the restaurant is beyond me."

"But how did you learn about Eva?" Sophia asked.

Kyrios Rolas smiled. "You will find my answer to your question just as strange." His eyes met Eva's, and they smiled at each other as people do when they share many memories. "At the restaurant the same night, our waiter overheard our conversation. He was Christos Hatzakos, the son of *Kyria* Olga Hatzakos of your village, who knew about Eva and her six fingers. As I stood up to leave, he apologized for eavesdropping, but admitted that he could not help it when he heard me talking about a girl with six fingers. He told me about Eva."

The room was hushed as we waited for more. *Kyrios* Rolas rubbed his cheek and went on. "I was doubtful. What kind of girl did this young waiter know? My impression of Christos, however, was of a young man with the intelligence and ambition that would take him beyond his present position. Occasionally, I thought of his description of the girl in Bordonia, and I would chuckle at my old nurse's encomium for those who possessed an extra finger."

He shrugged. "The sea has a mysticism of its own. I was on my yacht *Annoula* one evening at sunset. The breeze was cool and the stars filled the skies. A beautiful girl beside me would make it perfect. One by one, I rejected the women I knew—my bookkeeper's daughter, the relatives of my friends—and then I remembered Christos. He even had the audacity to suggest that Eva would be an ideal match for me!" *Kyrios* Rolas smiled again at my cousin, who lowered her eyes when she realized that everyone was staring at her.

"Before I could change my mind," *Kyrios* Rolas continued. "I wrote to Diogenes Hatzis, my father's boyhood friend in Athens, who has often visited my family in Egypt. I asked him to learn what he could about Christos and about Eva. I asked if he would visit Bordonia. As soon as he received my letter, Diogenes sought friends of his from Sparta and confirmed what Christos Hatzakos had told me about himself, and then he hired a genealogist to inform him about Eva's family."

Kyrios Hatzis explained. "When Dinos makes a request, I take it seriously. After I ascertained that the young waiter had spoken the truth, and that there was indeed a family with your name in Bordonia, I made it my business to come to your village and to meet the young lady as soon as I could. That is why I arrived so unexpectedly on that Sunday."

Theia Despina stared at him. "And who is that man who waits outside with the horses?"

Kyrios Rolas smiled. "I must apologize for Ibrahim. He is an Egyptian and a friend who has worked on my yacht for many years. He did not believe I would make an impression on you without an exotic servant to indicate my importance.

My uncle poured wine for those who wanted it. Ourania and I were fascinated by *Kyrios* Rolas and his story. It was all so romantic. He loved our quiet cousin, and we hoped that she loved him too. He approached Eva, and took her hand. "I won't insist that you come with me when I leave tomorrow. I will return in three months. If, during that time, your decision is not to become my wife, then you must write and tell me this. I would prefer it if you could come with me now, but I know this will not be possible."

Kostas was not prepared for *Kyrios* Rolas to stop there. He had become better acquainted with Eva during the time that Sophia was ill and thought he could now speak on her behalf. "There is one thing I believe that our family would like to know. If your letter had reached *Pater* Georgios, were you prepared to marry and leave with Eva at once? How do you feel about that now?"

Kyrios Rolas face flushed, and he reached for Eva's hand. "I would marry her this minute if she would have me."

Eva held his hand in hers while the rest of us stared. "Shall we take a walk?" she asked. My aunt remained speechless while her older daughter left the house to decide her future. My mother took us home. Later that same day, Eva's brothers—Nikos and Stratis—came to tell us that the wedding would take place tomorrow in the morning, and that mother, Ourania, and I were expected to be there early to help the bride dress and prepare for her trip.

As soon as she greeted us the next morning, my aunt lamented. "Why, Magdalene, does it have to be so sudden? *Kyrios* Rolas does not want to wait for us to prepare a proper wedding for Eva, as we did for Sophia." I noticed that Sophia was crying. Her sister would be leaving today, maybe forever, and I wanted to cry with her.

We were wearing our best clothes and had arranged each other's hair in well-brushed braids with ribbons in them. Ourania whispered in my ear that indeed it was not a proper wedding. "We have not had time to sew new dresses. And, what kind of a wedding will it be without music, dancing, and sweet pastries?"

Theia Despina collected a mound of linens and clothing from a bedroom and spread it out on the kitchen table: "Embroidered sheets and pillow cases, and a stack of linen towels," she chanted. She folded a blanket and petticoats for Eva.

"Mama, they will not fit in her valise." Sophia stopped her. "*Kyrios* Rolas said Eva is to bring only one small bag. He said he wants to buy his new wife gifts of clothing and when they arrive in Alexandria Eva is to go shopping for everything that she will need in their new house."

"I have to take something from home, don't I?" Eva said softly. "If he is as good and as generous as he seems, he will understand." She smiled as she filled a *kasela,* a small chest, with favorite embroidered pieces, trinkets, and clothing. Sophia left the house abruptly, telling us that she would return soon. When she came back, she was carrying her wedding dress and insisted that Eva wear it.

It was an exciting day: Eva was marrying a stranger, departing with him across the Mediterranean where we would not be able to see her for a long time. Best of all, she was sailing to a foreign land and shopping for beautiful new things with her husband and his servant.

Sophia helped her sister into the lovely white dress, pinned up the skirt where it was too long, and adjusted the shoulders and waistline to fit Eva. The bride looked beautiful as we followed her and her family to church. Ibrahim, the turbaned servant, bowed low as she approached, and held the church door open for her. *Kyrios* Rolas came forward. "Are you still firm in your desire to marry me, and to come away with me, Eva?" He asked her solemnly.

"Yes, I am," she said demurely. They approached the altar where *Pater* Georgios was waiting. *Kyrios* Diogenes Hatzis stood to the right of the groom, as his *koumbaros,* best man. My aunt and uncle took their places to the left of the bride, with Sophia, Kostas, the younger brothers, and the rest of us behind them. Ibrahim stood in the rear of the church. The Sacrament of Marriage was as beautiful as the ceremony that had united

Sophia and Kostas. After the wedding, we crossed the pavement to the *caffenion,* and remained there long enough for a simple wedding repast that *Theios* Yiannis had ordered ahead of time. The proprietor was from the island of Andros, so he had prepared one of his island's specialties, *fourtalia,* a savory omelet cooked with homemade sausage and browned potatoes. The owner had also baked sugar-covered *kourambiethes* as a wedding treat.

After we had finished eating and toasting the couple, Sophia, Eva, and their mother went home, where Eva changed into a traveling dress and a bonnet. *Kyrios* Rolas was pacing in the street, impatient to be on his way. They would ride on horseback with *Kyrios* Hatzis and Ibrahim to Sparta, where they would rest for several days. From there they would travel to the eastern port of Lenithi, where the Rolas yacht was docked. As everyone gathered around her, Eva's brothers arrived with her *kasela,* which they had carried from the house. They set it down next to the horses.

"What is that?" *Kyrios* Rolas asked brusquely.

"My trunk," Eva replied.

"My dear, Eva," he frowned. "I told *Mitera*, your mother, that you need take only one small bag."

"My dear *Kyrios* Rolas," she smiled at him. "Don't you agree that a girl who is going to live so far from her family is entitled to have a few mementos of home?"

His frown disappeared as he smiled slowly. "My new wife has taken over already!" He ordered a mule to carry the trunk to the port. Then, after tears and hugs and kisses, the newly married couple departed.

Magdalene Louvis, Eleni's mother, 1880.

Demetrios Louvis, Eleni's father, 1880.

Six of Eleni's brothers: (front) Spiros and A. D.; (back) Theophanis, George, Peter, and Soterios, 1919.

Eleni age 15, with her sister Arista and fiancé James Poulos, Lancaster, Ohio, 1916.

Eleni's brother Leonidas, in Greek Army, 1920.

Eleni's sister Ourania with goat.

Viola and Eleni, Ohio.

A friend with Eleni and mandolin.

Eleni (second from left) with friends, Ohio.

A. D. at soda fountain with crystal bowls of flavored syrups.

Newlyweds: Eleni's brother A. D. dressed as a Greek evzone, with his bride Viola, Lancaster, Ohio, 1914.

Display window of A. D. Louvis Confectionery, Lancaster, Ohio, 1915.

CHAPTER 8

The New World

Ela, file. Fage. Fige.
Welcome, friend. Eat. Then, go.
— GREEK PROVERB

Sophia's illness had not prevented her from giving birth to a little boy, Andonis, that summer. At first, I rushed over to see the baby every day, but I soon lost interest because *Theia* Despina or *Theios* Yiannis were always there. Now that she was *yiayia,* grandmother, and he was *papou,* grandfather, they would not trust anyone but themselves to hold the precious newborn and entertain him. Patting a piece of soft white cotton on his head and pressing a few kernels of rice into each of his tiny palms, my aunt would sing a favorite lullaby that began, "Little stranger from another land . . ." The lyrics went on to wish that Andonis would live long enough to have a head of white hair (signified by the cotton) and to have many sons (signified by the kernels of rice.)

In February, my brother Soterios arrived from America. It was his first trip home in three years, and we were very excited to see him. He was not as "American" as I would have liked him to be; he was tall and handsome, but he was wearing a Greek Army uniform.

"Well, how do I look?" He asked us as we stood around and admired him. Mother was tearful and hovered close to him. Yiannis, her second oldest child, had died while fighting at the

155

Albanian border a year earlier, so another son wearing an army uniform did not give her comfort. Not moving from Soterios's side, mother saw to his needs.

"Bring *hirino*, Eleni, and some eggs!" I hurried down to the *katoyi,* the cellar, where I filled a bowl with the mouth-watering morsels of ham, then found some eggs in the straw near the hens, and rushed back, so that I would not miss any of my brother's visit. Father was asking, "So, you have decided to come back and fight for Greece?"

Soterios nodded. "Yes, papa. Some of my friends from America are here too. We are prepared to fight Albania and Turkey to preserve Greece's northern borders."

"Isn't he the handsomest man you've ever seen?" Ourania nudged me.

Before I could agree with her, Soterios turned to us and handed each of us, including Leonidas, a small gold coin. No matter how small, a piece of gold was precious, and we were more impressed than ever by our tall, imposing brother. "Do not spend it foolishly," he warned. "Save it for something important." He then placed a pouch in mother's hand. My sister and I pressed against her, trying to see how many gold pieces it contained, but froze in place when my brother said, "Mama, your sons and your daughter Arista in America miss you very much. They cannot all afford to come to Greece, so they want you to come to America, and this is for your journey. This time, you will bring Ourania and Eleni." Ourania let out a whoop of joy. Before any sound could escape me, Soterios frowned at her. Not wanting to incur his disapproval, I did not utter a sound, and he went on. "The nation needs Leonidas here at present. Because that is so, my brothers and I will help him live in comfort, so that papa and you will always have one son at home with you."

Leonidas did not know whether to laugh or cry; later he proclaimed that he would be proud to stay in Sparta to fight for our nation, if called on. He knew his brothers would send for him to come to America when he was older. My sister and I were transfixed as Soterios continued.

"In six months, I will be back on leave; at that time, I will take the three of you as far as Sparta for your papers and passage to America. You will live with Andonis in Ohio."

Once more my hopes were raised, but since I already had experienced one disappointment, I determined not to make plans for my departure. One purchase, however, would not hurt. Easter was coming, and father always went to Sparta to the *pazari,* the bazaar, to shop for new clothes and treats for the holiday. For the first time in my life, I had money to spend for something special, and the most special thing I could think of was a new pair of shoes. We wore our shoes until they fell apart, and even then our "new" shoes were usually hand-me-downs. So, I asked father to buy me a pair of red shoes with the coin that my brother had given me.

At the *pazari,* farmers and other tradesmen gathered to buy and sell their wares. This colorful bazaar stretched along the main square of Sparta and other towns and displayed the fresh crops of the season grown on local farms. In summer, colorful mounds of red tomatoes, green peppers, and cucumbers were for sale, as were leafy greens, beans, and squash, and melons in season. One section sold shoes, pots, pans, and farm implements; another area off to the side had donkeys, pigs, and goats for sale.

Father always brought a treat; my favorite "candy" was cubes of sugar. Once, when Soterios was nine and still at home, he accompanied father to the *pazari* in Sparta, so that he could become acquainted with the city. He returned home, quite excited about a pair of sandals he had bought. He said that father had given him a choice between two delicacies: *stragalia*, chickpeas, or *loukoumi, Turkish paste*. His enthusiastic descriptions of the *pazari* made our hearts ache to go and see for ourselves some day.

When father returned home from the bazaar with my new shoes, I was thrilled. This was the first pair of shoes I had ever had that was a simple slipper without shoe laces. I loved those red shoes from the minute I saw them. I put them on and walked around in them for only a few minutes. I wore them to church at Easter; after that, I wrapped them in a soft cloth and did not wear them. But I unwrapped them often to polish and admire them. If I really did go to America when Soterios returned, I would have a pair of beautiful red shoes to wear.

It was early August when Soterios returned on leave, as he had promised, and announced to my parents that we should be ready to travel in three days. My sister and I could hardly contain ourselves. Once again, we said our tearful farewells, but this time they were more subdued. *Kyria* Aliki made a sarcastic remark about people who refused to carry parcels to America as a favor for their friends, but I was so happy to be leaving that I hugged her goodbye anyway. Soterios rented three mules for our ride to Sparta, and father and Leonidas helped us mount—my sister and I on one mule, and mother and Soterios on the other two. Father made a final check of everything we needed to have with us and led the animals out of the town square and toward the county road.

"Oh, wait, Eleni, Ourania!" Leonidas shouted. He reached into his shirt. "I almost forgot to give you the ribbons I got for you." We were touched. Hiding her tears, Ourania responded, "That would have been bad, wouldn't it? Since, if you had not given them to us, you would have had to wear them yourself. And how silly you would look wearing ribbons, Leonidas!" This set us all laughing as we made our way out of the village.

At the intersection of the village lane and the county road to Sparta, we once again shed tears as we said goodbye to father and Leonidas. Although I would miss my father, brother, and our home, my tears were not laden with sadness. All I could think of was that I was on my way to the land of my dreams.

My sister and I had never been to Sparta, but mother had been with father two times before this. We asked Soterios many questions on the way to Sparta. What was it like? What was America like? Where would we sleep at night? And we recited our itinerary to each other: Soterios would take us as far as Sparta, the county seat of Lacedemonia (or Laconia, its popular name), then leave us. We would then take the bus to Tripolis, the capital of Arcadia. At Tripolis, a bustling metropolis in the heart of the Peloponnesus, we would board the train for Athens and its port, Piraeus. We did not know what it was like to ride on a bus, and we had never seen a train. The words "bus" and "train" were exciting in their unfamiliarity, and my heart leapt at imagining these vehicles and the exotic places to which they would take us. Finally, we would board a ship that would take us to America in two weeks.

We could not picture a ship that was large enough to hold the three of us and many other people as well. Nor did we understand why it took two weeks to cross the ocean on such a vessel. We had grown up near a tributary of the Eurotas River, which ran in torrents for a few weeks during the rainy season, but much of the year was a dry river bed. For now, it was enough for me to know that we were approaching Sparta, the fabled capital of our state. I sat behind my sister and clasped her waist as the mule made its way down a steep hill into a tree-lined, paved street. Ourania and I stared with amazement at the houses and the people. Modern Sparta in 1915 was a large town—balconies overflowed with flowers, and trees grew on each side of the wide streets, which were lined with shops, one after the other! Even the hotel where my brother took us to stay that night was like something from a storybook. We ran our fingers over the soft bed linens, marveled at the toilet with a chain that, when pulled, caused water to flush out of sight and come back clean, and we were appalled at the amount of money it had cost Soterios to house us there.

Before we set out for a walk around Sparta, I reached for my new shoes, which I had clutched in their cloth cover for the entire trip. Very carefully I unwrapped them, removed the old, worn pair from my feet, and proudly put on my new red shoes. How pretty they were! I could not take my eyes off them, and I kept looking down to admire them. When it was time to go out, Soterios came to our room. Noticing my inattention, brother commented, "Very nice shoes, Eleni. Where did you get them?"

"Father bought them for me at the *pazari* at Easter—with the coin that you had given me," I answered, flattered that Soterios had noticed.

There was an edge to his voice as he inquired, "How does it happen that you have new shoes, but Ourania does not?" I looked down at my hands and did not answer. "It's all right," Ourania murmured, "I didn't want to spend my coin on shoes."

"No," he said sternly. "This is not right. Each of you should have new shoes, or neither of you should! Eleni, take those shoes off and put them away." I was overcome with shame at incurring his displeasure. I quickly exchanged shoes, tucking the new ones back into their wrappings and out of his sight. If this had happened today, I believe that my modern-day daughters would have challenged their brother... that my granddaughters would have defied him... and that my great-granddaughters would have disregarded his orders altogether. But I felt that Soterios was doing so much for me, and that the least I could do was obey his wishes. We went out to explore the city, and both of us put the incident behind us.

On our stroll that afternoon, we came upon a handsome building, *the gymnasion*, the public high school. Although publicly funded, its student population consisted mainly of boys from wealthy families. Students who attended the *gymnasion* had to live in Sparta, and with room and board so costly in Sparta, children from our village rarely could afford to attend this high school. After graduation from the *gymnasion*, a boy was set for life, as long as he achieved the required grades. Universities and graduate schools always favored the graduates of this elite group. Girls also attended the high school, but again only the daughters of affluent families. I rarely saw any of these young women, because they were "a breed apart" from poor village girls. Although some women did enter professions, most married professionals or successful businessmen and remained in the background, without publicly revealing their academic accomplishments. Successful men had their pick of marriageable girls with large dowries and usually remained single for a

few decades after graduation. These were the gray-haired, digni-
fied gentlemen seen beaming at their first baby's baptism, standing beside a young, wealthy wife.

Soterios pointed out the *kreatopoulion,* the central meat
market. The building was painted white and looked very clean;
guards were stationed around it. My brother told us that sanitary
conditions were strictly maintained, daily, and that the guards
were there to prevent anyone from entering the building until the
state examiners had inspected the meat. Only after the meat was
certified to be fresh and free of contamination could it be
released to the town butchers to sell to the public. He told us that
purveyors of diseased or unclean meat were prosecuted.

Later, Soterios took mother into an office building near the
hotel, instructing Ourania and me to wait. When they returned,
they told us that our papers were ready for the trip to America.
Next, Soterios bought bus tickets to Tripolis, where we would
transfer for the train to Athens. One adult ticket included accompanying children. The next morning—because he had to return
to his military unit in the North—Soterios escorted us to the bus
station. He told us what to do when we arrived in Tripolis,
described the place where we should wait for the train and—
after we arrived at Piraeus (the port city of Athens)—how to find
the hotel. As usual, we all cried as we said our goodbyes to Soterios, while he helped mother, and then Ourania, and then me,
and our bundles onto the bus.

I looked out of the window as the bus left Sparta and crossed
the narrow bridge over the Eurotas River. Behind us, Mount
Taigetus glared from his icy, snow-capped peaks. The excitement of traveling so far from our village was heightened by our
arrival in Tripolis, the hub of the Peloponnesus. This is the
southern, mountainous peninsula of Greece, shaped like a hand
with three fingers and a thumb and linked to northern Greece
and Athens by the Isthmus of Corinth. Buses and trains from
North and South crossed here; some were headed for Patras and
the western Peloponnesos; others announced their destinations
for Athens and Piraeus at the other end of the line. We even

heard the announcements for the bus returning to Sparta. After leaving the bus, the three of us moved to the platform where Soterios had instructed us to wait for the train to Piraeus, the seaport of Athens. We stood for quite a long time until mother began to worry and turned to a woman with her family and asked if this was the right place to wait. The woman deferred to a young man beside her, who assured us that our train would soon arrive.

Sure enough, a black locomotive chugged its way into the station, erupting so much smoke and noise that all of us were terrified and questioned the wisdom of boarding the fearsome machine. It was not our train, however; it was full of soldiers headed for the front in Albania. We stood by silently, sharing in the sad drama that we had often experienced: sons and brothers bidding farewell to their loved ones, and going off to fight. At last, the train to Athens and Piraeus chugged into view and stopped. There were five passenger cars behind the awesome, grunting engine, and each car was full. The train stopped momentarily but then began to pull away. My sister and I cried out, fearful that we would be left stranded on the platform.

"Look!" The son of the woman beside us pointed. "It is stopping again. See! They are hooking more cars onto the back. It will not leave Tripolis without us after all." We had to push our way onto one of the added cars and managed to locate a compartment that was not yet overcrowded. We passed the remainder of the trip in reasonable comfort, although we had to squeeze together, along with our new friends, who had remained with us in the surge to enter the same compartment. They introduced themselves to us as *Kyria* Pantas, her son Lukas, and her daughter Elle. Elle was a plump, shy teenager, and Lukas was tall and thin and in his twenties. They were going to visit *Kyria* Pantas's mother in Piraeus, who lived near the grocery store where Lukas worked. It was after sunset when the train pulled into a station in the middle of fertile, verdant meadows. Someone announced that this was Corinth. It was already dark when we crossed the Isthmus of Corinth, the narrow waterway that separates Attica and northern Greece from southern Greece and that connects the Aegean Sea and the Ionian Sea. The train sped across the bridge over the Isthmus, but it was too dark to see the shorn cliffs that Lukas Pantas told us about. Later, we stopped in a place where there were lights along the streets, and many houses, also brightly lit. Lukas said we had arrived in Athens. We could not see much of the city, but were amazed by the brilliance of the electric lights, which shone in the windows of every building. It was unbelievable to us that they stayed on so late at night. And the people! There were so many walking on the streets—even at night! It was actually early evening when we arrived in Athens, but in our village after sunset our light came from a fireplace, a candle, or a lantern, and most people stayed home and went to bed.

"Do not get out at this first stop," Lukas cautioned mother. "The train first stops in Athens. Then it goes on to Piraeus, the seaport. You will get off there." Mother told him where we planned to stay for the night, and when we reached Piraeus, Lukas pointed to an inn across from the train station, where our brother had reserved a room. We spent three days in Piraeus, by the harbor, while we waited for our ship to sail. That first night, Ourania and I waited in the lobby for mother to register. Ourania pointed out a canary in a cage. We agreed that it was strange to keep a beautiful yellow bird confined like that, and we observed it for a while. It began to sing, and we were entranced by its music. I thought it must be tame and wanted to bring it out so we could pet it. I spotted the latch on the side of the cage, and—country bumpkin that I was—I lifted it, and opened the door. The little bird hopped over and stood at the opening poised to fly out. Just in time, the manager dashed toward the cage to prevent the bird from escaping. He was very angry at me. We never learned whether he had retrieved his little bird because mother hustled us away to our room. In the morning, we did not see the bird cage.

As we prepared for bed, we were again faced with unfamiliar modernity—the electric light. "How does the light go out?" I asked. Mother offered no suggestions and fell asleep while Ourania and I continued to ponder. "Blow it out as you do a candle," my sister advised. We blew and blew until both of us were red in the face, but it would not extinguish. We did not dare call the manager, since he was so angry at us. That first night we fell asleep with the light on; it wasn't until the next day that we learned the secret of the electric light switch.

On the appointed day, we took our bags and proceeded to the docks to find the great steamship that would carry us across the ocean to America. The date was August 15, 1915. I shall never forget it. Nor will I ever forget the name of our ship, the *Constantinos*. It lay at anchor in the calm blue waters of the Saronic Bay, some distance from the dock. I was amazed at the enormous body of water that lay between us and the *Constantinos*. As for the *Constantinos* (huge as it was), it did not appear large enough to stay afloat for two days, let alone two weeks, carrying all the people now clamoring to board it, and the immense cargo being hoisted into its hold. How would my mother, sister, and I survive on this vessel which seemed to us no sturdier than a twig in a raging storm? Our next trial was the small boats bobbing up and down in front of us, which I realized, in panic, were the vehicles for reaching the *Constantinos*, and which were rapidly filling with passengers. Men from the rowboats shouted, "Save drachmas! Ride with Manolis!" "*Grigora!* Hurry! The *Constantinos* leaves with the tide! Takis will get you there first." "That's the way, Mama! Your daughters won't get a drop of water on them in Panos's boat." In spite of these many assurances, mother could not persuade Ourania and me to board. The swaying movements of the vessels frightened us, and we did not move from the spot. Then Panos, noticing Mama's dilemma, swept me up and handed me to a man in his rowboat, who set me down on one of the wooden seats. Panos did the same with Ourania, and then he helped Mama board. We were the last ones to be seated in the rowboat, and just as I had feared, the small craft pitched and rolled all the way to the *Constantinos*, drenching us with spray. Trembling with fear, I prayed that destiny would not send me to the bottom of the Aegean before I reached America. In the confusion, it was difficult for an innocent from a mountain village to understand that we were not sailing to America in this vessel. By the time the rowboat bumped against the hull of the mammoth ship, I had become a lemming, blindly following everyone ahead of me up the rope ladder. Fortunately, Ourania was ahead of me, and mother was behind me, holding me tight and pushing me up and forward. The rope ladder was not stationary and swayed with all the people climbing it at the same time, so that when a sailor helped me on deck, I was thankful to be on a solid surface.

There were flowers in vases on this level. Mother held our hands as we followed the directions of the sailors to our place on one of the lower decks, where there were no flowers. We saw women in fashionable dresses and shoes, and men in neckties and Sunday suits, dressed as though they were attending a party, strolling along the quay. These were the first-class passengers, in their elegant attire. It was a rare glimpse of these affluent people, because second-class passengers and immigrant (third-class) passengers were required to remain below on their lower decks and to eat in their designated dining areas. Our small room had two bunks, one for the three of us, and the other for another woman and her daughter. It was extremely hot in the stuffy enclosure. As we were accustomed to open air; we looked for a window, but all we could find was a small, round porthole. We opened it as far as it would go, which was not much at all, but it did not give us relief. So, we bore the stifling August heat of Athens at night, while the ship took on its cargo. Finally, on the third day, the *Constantinos* put out to sea, and our small room became more bearable.

Twelve days later, we landed in New York City. Many of the people quartered in our level of the ship were—as we were—seasick throughout most of the voyage. Regular meal times were announced by the ringing of a bell. Those who were well enough to eat would form a line in an austerely furnished area called the third-class dining room. It was cafeteria-style, where we proceeded in a line, and picked up a tray with a plate, knife, fork, spoon, and napkin. A man wearing white stood behind the steam tables and served a portion of stew or casserole; the next server placed a slice of bread on the plate; the last man provided a cup of tea. I was not very hungry for most of the voyage, but I drank more tea with lemon than I have ever since.

Mother struck up an acquaintance with two women, and Ourania and I made friends with their daughters, each of us describing her expectations for our lives in America. We avoided our cramped quarters and walked or sat in the few public areas near open air as much as we could. Halfway through the trip, Ourania confided to me that the voyage was taking such a long time that she had come to the conclusion that the ship had made a wrong turn, and that we would never reach our brothers and the vast, fabled land we had dreamt about for so long.

Then, we heard rumors that we were nearing our destination, and Ourania and I strained our eyes, looking out at the horizon for hours in order to sight land before anyone else did. Finally, someone shouted, "There it is! The Statue of Liberty!" The ship listed to one side, because everyone ran to the deck that was closer to the bronze lady standing on the pedestal with her torch raised to greet us.

"This is New York harbor!" Ourania pinched me. "Eleni, you are looking at the biggest city in the whole world!" Mother stood beside us—the three of us overcome by emotion as we stared at the Manhattan skyline.

Once again, we watched as the elegant people from the first-class deck disembarked soon after the gangplank was lowered. After them, followed the tourist class. We were disappointed to learn that none of the immigrants could go next. I started to fear that, after our long journey I might not be permitted to get off the ship, never to set foot in America. I recalled how I had felt the day mother, Leonidas, and I had been turned back in Kalamata. We watched unhappily as those who were disembarking laughed and made their way to their destinations. Dock workers shouted in several different languages and lowered crates tied with thick ropes from the ship down to the pier.

"They will be taking us to *Caselgarri* on those small boats over there," one of our new friends told us. Sure enough, a motorboat came into sight, and we were herded down the ladders and into the boats, and taken to Ellis Island. It was called "*Caselgarri*" by Greek immigrants because early émigrés had been processed at the Fort at Castle Garden. Long after Castle Garden was vacated, the term *Caselgarri* stuck as the point of entry no matter what the actual name was

Caselgarri, actually Ellis Island, seemed to us beautiful and modern in 1915. It was a large building, bright and clean. First we passed through a fumigation area to rid us of the lice and fleas that were common in cramped quarters on shipboard. I do not clearly remember how this was done, but I don't remember that it was objectionable. Next, we were shown into a large, white-tiled room with toilets in cubicles, each with its own door, and with many sinks lined up against one wall. The attendant gave each of us a towel and a small square that was hard and white. We looked at one another wondering what the squares were. "Maybe it's cheese," Ourania said, and she put a corner of the smooth substance to her tongue. "Ugh, no!" She spat it out. An attendant smiled and came over to us. She rubbed her hands together as though washing them. "*Sapouni*!" We exclaimed. It was the first soap cut into neat white bars that we had ever seen—quite different from the crude yellow bricks that we produced in our galvanized tub in the back yard at home. After we had washed ourselves, we were shown a room where we would sleep. It was a dormitory with bunk beds covered in white sheets. An attendant motioned to my sister that she was to take the upper bunk, and I the lower bunk. When we were settled in for the night, Ourania began giggling and whispered down, "Remember how we always wanted to sleep on the highest branches of the mulberry trees at the *Lefko* in summer? I got the best place again!"

The next morning, after we had washed ourselves with the white soap, and had something to eat, we were taken to sit on benches in a waiting room. To our surprise, mother's name was called. A woman led her into a room not far from our bench. As time passed, Ourania and I became alarmed at being separated from our mother in this strange place. We kept asking each other what could have happened to her. Would we ever see her again? What would our brothers say if we lost mother here in *Caselgarri*? The people seated next to us could not answer our questions, so we waited anxiously.

At last, I could sit still no longer, and I walked to the door through which mother had disappeared. I pushed it open a crack and peeked in. To my surprise, mother lay on a table. She was covered with a sheet, but her arms, unfamiliarly bare, were resting on top of the sheet. A woman in a white coat stood beside her. Mother saw me, and through clenched teeth told me that she would be out soon. She explained that the woman was a doctor, who was checking to make sure that mother was healthy enough to stay in America. I reported to Ourania what I had seen. We had never heard of physical examinations, and waited even more anxiously for mother to return.

Our gentle mother did not seem happy when she exited the examining room, once again fully clothed. Shaken by the experience, she explained to us that the doctor had motioned to her to take her clothes off. "But I absolutely refused to disrobe in front of those strangers. They finally brought a woman who could talk properly. She explained in Greek that in America they had to make sure that I was in good health, and to do that they had to examine me with my dress off. I do not know why they needed to do that! The lady said that they would send me back to Greece if I did not submit to the examination by the doctor." The fear of not being able to see her sons in America overcame her modesty, so with great reluctance, mother allowed herself to be undressed and examined.

Fortunately, she was pronounced healthy enough to enter the country. Now we had to wait for one of my brothers to come and find us, although I wondered how he could in this huge place. We had not sat long before someone showed us the way to another reception room. After a short time, a man walked up to us and read our names out loud from a paper: "Magdalene,

Eleni, and Ourania Louvis." We stood up. My legs trembled as we waited for something to happen. We were escorted to an office where mother was questioned briefly by yet another man. Then, the door opened, and a young man who looked like one of my brothers walked directly toward mother.

"He is one of my sons!" Mother exclaimed. "He is either Peter, or George, or Theophanes, or Spiros, or Stavros." When he came closer, she recognized her son George—one of six sons she had not seen in many years. By the age of twelve, each boy had left home for America. Some were now in their twenties. Ourania and I greeted our new brother shyly and then hung back for mother to be welcomed tearfully by her son. George lived in Jamaica, Long Island, in the state of New York, and that is why he met our boat. My other brothers—Anthony, Spiros, Theo, Stavros, and Peter—were in the state of Ohio, many miles away. We were aware that Ohio was the place where our brothers lived, but we had not learned much New World geography in our village school. New York City, *Brookli*, and Chicago were in America, and we assumed that Ohio was far away since we would have to travel in a train to reach it.

George held mother by the arm and carried the heaviest bags, leading us to a motorboat that crossed the bay from Ellis Island to a pier in Manhattan. Then, he took us in a cab to a hotel room in Jamaica, near his own room, where we would stay overnight. After supper, he brought beer for mother, and a few bananas, two items that were unfamiliar to us and seemed quite exotic. Mother tasted the beer but did not drink much, declaring that it was bitter. Ourania and I ate a banana, and decided it had the texture of a fruit grown in Sparta called *skourouhia*.

The next day, George took us to visit a woman on Long Island who had been born in Bordonia. Mother called her Eugenia, the little Delouris girl. Her home was now in Jamaica, in a building with many balconies. I believe it was six stories high, but to us it appeared immense. Eugenia was tall and thin, with black hair worn in a tight bun. She greeted us wearing a sundress with red flowers all over it, covered by a blue apron. She was thrilled to see mother, who had been her mother's friend and confidante. Eugenia had married and had left home a year before, and she wanted to hear all the news of the village. As soon as we sat down in her living room, she served each of us a small dish of sweet, preserved grapefruit peel and a glass of cold water. Later we had dinner in her dining room. We ate roast chicken and potatoes that were savory with oregano and lemon— also *dolmathes,* ground lamb and rice wrapped in grape leaves in an egg-lemon sauce. I could not eat much. After that, she handed us glasses filled with chocolate ice cream and soda with a straw in each glass. I said I thought it was a peculiar American custom to have uncooked macaroni in a drink. She laughed and showed us how to drink with a straw. The soda portion was all right— seltzer water mixed with chocolate syrup—but the chocolate ice cream was too cold for my taste, and neither Ourania nor I could finish it.

While mother and George talked to Eugenia, I stood on her balcony. On the street below was a store that sold milk. An iron cow was the milk dispenser, and I watched, fascinated, as a boy dispensed milk from the mechanical animal whenever anyone wanted to purchase either a glassful or a pitcherful. The boy looked up at me a couple of times, and just as Ourania stepped onto the balcony, the boy winked at me. Teasing, my sister drew me indoors and scolded me for flirting. The next day we were to visit New York City. I could hardly wait. George led us to the *ontergroun*, the subway. We sat in this noisy train less than five minutes before it became so dark all around us that we saw only small red specks of light and little else. "What has happened, *Yeorgi*?" My brother laughed. "We are going through a tunnel, mother. We are below the East River right now."

"I don't see any water," Ourania whispered.

"Nor I," I answered. "Maybe we should not believe everything this brother tells us. I think he is a tease."

When we emerged from the *ontergroun,* we were amazed that my brother could tell where we were. George said this was New York City. It was not at all like the city of Athens, with signs that we could read and many trees and bright flowers growing between the buildings. Here, the letters were illegible, and the buildings reached to the sky, so that we could not see the sun. Hard pavement was everywhere, and more people were walking past us than I thought were in the whole world. Smoke and steam poured out of the roofs of the buildings and from the grates in the streets.

We wandered along the teeming sidewalks. We gaped at department store windows full of the most beautiful dresses and hats and shoes that we had ever seen, and we stopped to stare at the automobiles that drove up and down the wide avenues. We were exhausted by the time George took us to the train that would deliver us to the rest of our family in Ohio. Although we were sorry to say goodbye to George, we also were eager to be on our way.

At dinner time the next day, the conductor approached us and inspected the big tags we wore suspended from the top button of our jackets. George had printed each of our names in English, along with the name and address of our brother Anthony in Lancaster, Ohio, so that—like parcels being sent by mail—we would not be lost. The conductor said something to mother, which none of us could understand, and seeing our puzzled expressions, he pulled a round watch from his vest pocket and pointed to the numeral six. We nodded our heads, and told each other that he meant that we would be arriving in Lancaster at six o'clock. So we sat up straight and smoothed our hair and our dresses and clutched our bundles close to us as we waited patiently for the end of the trip. The next time the train came to a stop, a slim, light-haired young man came bounding down the aisle of the coach toward our seats. Mother's blue eyes lighted up as she exclaimed, "Who is this? I think he is my son *Panayiotis*!"

And surely it was *Panayiotis,* who was now called Peter, mother's third eldest son. His eyes were blue like hers and danced with laughter. He explained that he had met the train one stop before Lancaster, so that he could escort us the rest of the way. Ourania and I compared Peter to George, who had been quiet and serious. I did not remember Peter very well because he had left home when I was five.

When the train came to the next stop, we knew it was Lancaster, Ohio, because another young man, slightly heavier and more stately than Peter, came aboard and held mother gently in his arms for a long time. He, mother told us after she had regained her composure, was our brother Anthony, her eldest living son, who had left Bordonia for America the year I was born. It was he who had invited mother and Leonidas and me to America for his wedding, but we had not come. Then, two years ago, Anthony had sent for my oldest sister Arista to come to Lancaster to help him in his candy store. She now was married and lived near Anthony and Viola.

From the train our brothers drove us to Anthony's house in Lancaster. It was a large, white house with a picket fence surrounding it. The roof of the spacious front porch was covered with a flowering purple vine. As we arrived, we saw a familiar figure running down the front walk. It was Arista, and there were more tears and hugs exchanged with our big sister. A table was set and we ate, but I was weary and did not notice much. I remembered Arista taking Ourania and me upstairs to a room with a white tub filled with hot, soapy water. After that, I remember putting on a long nightgown and falling into a large bed.

The next thing I knew was the sound of someone imitating my heavy breathing, and slowly I became aware of voices and laughter. It was around midnight. A light was shining near my face, and I sat up, realizing that I was not dreaming. Ourania was grinning at me; next to her stood a plump, pretty woman who had not been present on our arrival. But I knew at once that she was Viola, the girl Anthony had married.

That was my first meeting with my wonderful new sister. (In-laws were considered sisters, brothers, mothers, and fathers as much as those related to us by birth.) Viola was to have an important influence on my new life in America. We called her

Nifi. The word has several meanings. It denotes bride, or daughter-in-law, or a brother's wife. It was Viola's choice to work the late shift at their confectionery store, and she had just closed the store. She was a warm-hearted woman, and had insisted upon seeing me as soon as she got home, after she had greeted mother and Ourania, who had waited up for her.

The next morning I had to spend a few hours in bed, not because I was ill, but because I had no clothes to wear. The only clothing I had was the nightgown that Arista had given me the night before. She suggested that I wear it around the house for that day, but I did not feel right about this and stayed in bed. About mid-morning, the acrid smell of smoke reached my nose, and voices at the back of the house brought me to the window. At the far end of the property, Viola and Arista were standing by a bonfire which sent out the distinct odor of burning wool. A few minutes later, Ourania came in to see if I was awake, and in answer to my questions, she said that mother's as well as her clothing and mine were in that fire. Nifi was burning everything to destroy any vermin from *Caselgarri,* or the ship, or elsewhere in our travels. She added, "Nifi went out this morning and has just returned with new clothes for us!" I could hardly wait to try them on, and once I was dressed, I was thrilled by the soft fabrics that immediately transformed me into an American.

Mother did not like America very much. She was like a flower which, when cut, stands bright and healthy in its new environment for a short time, but soon begins to droop and wilt. She had spent her life in Bordonia running a busy household. In Anthony's and Nifi's house, she was happily occupied with cooking and washing, but that was not enough; she missed her home. No Greek-speaking people lived near us, so mother was deprived of the companionship and the language of her relatives and neighbors in the village, and she also missed her church. At that time, it took several hours to drive to the nearest Greek Orthodox Church in Columbus, Ohio, so we did not go often. Ourania and I loved Lancaster. We took long walks every day around the neighborhood and into town. In autumn, when the sidewalks were layered with crisp yellow and red maple leaves, we pretended that they were the gold that lined the streets of our new country. Our favorite treat was when Arista took us to the candy store and served us ice cream at a table as though we were customers.

It was difficult for us to communicate with Viola at first. She spoke a few words to mother in Greek that A. D. had taught her. We soon learned to call Anthony by his initials A. D.—which signified Anthony Demetrios—as did everyone who knew him. To Ourania, Arista, and me, Viola spoke English, acting out the meanings of words in pantomime, and she expected us to answer her in English. It did not take long for me to understand and speak the language a little.

There were moments of confusion, as happened in the kitchen once. Mother had taken charge of the cooking because Viola worked at the store in the afternoons until midnight. A confectionery store at that time sold not only chocolates and holiday specialties, but also sandwiches and ice cream. With movies a major form of entertainment, people always were ready for a snack or something sweet after the show, so the store was busy day and night. As often happens, kitchen helpers do not always return cooking utensils to their original storage place. One morning, Viola decided that she would make breakfast for everyone. She looked for the skillet to fry eggs, but when she couldn't find it, she asked mother, "Have you seen the skillet?" She attempted to describe the pan with a handle, motioning with her hand. In Greek, the word for dog is *skili,* and mother kept shrugging, wondering why Viola expected her to bring a dog into the kitchen. Ourania finally figured out what Viola was looking for, and it caused much merriment when the skillet was located, and we realized the similarity of sounds of these two words—so different in their meanings.

Mother was an undemanding person. One day in Lancaster, my sister and I were walking with her past a millinery shop when she stopped to stare at a hat decorated with flowers. We had never seen her interested in anything for herself. Each time she went to town, she walked past the milliner's to look at what she began to call her hat. But she refused all offers by Anthony and Nifi to buy it for her, insisting that she was content to look at it in the shop window.

Things began to change when my brother Theophanes, who was now called Theo—who lived in Youngstown, Ohio—came to visit. The brothers had decided among themselves that Theo would take Ourania back with him to work in his candy store. Because she was so dexterous, she had quickly learned chocolate dipping, and soon was better at it than any of the professionals. About a month after his visit, Theo returned and took mother to visit with him for a while and to be company for Ourania. I stayed with A. D. and Nifi in Lancaster.

The changes in our names were either nicknames bestowed by friends, or adaptations of the Greek by our family. Arista kept her name, but Ourania became Irene. I was renamed Helen. Soterios became Wilbur, and Stavros was Steve. George and Spiros did not change their names.

Although we missed each other, mother, Ourania, and I were in agreement with A. D.'s decisions. He then turned his attention to my education. Before long, I was working in the candy store and going to school. A. D. walked me to the elementary school one morning, introduced me to the principal, and left me there for the teachers to decide what to do with a girl of fourteen who knew no English. The principal was kind and asked me to write my name. Thanks to my brother's coaching, I had learned how and promptly produced a sample. The principal praised me and smiled, then asked me to follow him down the hall to a classroom. We entered a room full of little boys and girls. The principal introduced me to the teacher and then spoke briefly to the class. The gist of it was that I would be in their class—the first grade. The children snickered, and I tried to disappear into the wall behind me. I was thin and not very tall for my age, but I was an incongruous figure in a classroom of first-graders. When the principal left the room, the teacher extended her hand in a warm handshake, and I felt a little better—but not much. She had not shown me to my desk, and as I was about to ask her, she instructed the class to rise. Then, to my surprise, they sang a song to welcome me—a song I did not understand. When they sat down again, they clapped their hands in a manner of welcome.

During recess that first day, I sat on a bench away from the playground. As a teenager in an elementary school, I felt out of place. From then on, I took my books and found a quiet corner to study during recess. When the teachers noticed that I preferred to read rather than play on the swings and seesaws, and since I was progressing in my studies, they took turns staying after school with me, or eating lunch with me, and during recess, giving me further lessons in English. They started with basic words and expressions such as "this is the chair"; "this is a window"; "give me an apple"; give me a pencil"; and insisted that I repeat everything as they had said it. I will never forget how helpful those kind teachers were and how much they encouraged me to learn to read, write, and speak my new language.

With the preparation of my stern village school and the patient assistance of my new teachers, I rapidly progressed from first grade to the fifth grade. I was a working girl too, so as soon as the final bell rang, I headed dutifully to Louvis's Confectionery to work. I cleaned the candy display cases and arranged the trays of homemade chocolates, as A. D. had shown me, to look enticing. Working at the candy store and conversing with the customers improved my vocabulary, which pleased my brother. "English is the language of this land," he counseled Arista, her husband, and me. "It is rude to speak Greek among ourselves when our customers cannot understand Greek."

Viola was wonderful to our family. She was a bride of less than a year when we came to live in her home. While mother was with us, Viola spoke to her in whatever Greek words she had learned from her husband, and we loved her all the more for that. A. D. had arrived at Ellis Island penniless, virtually friendless, with no knowledge of English. He had the address of a candy manufacturer in Ohio who had come from Sparta, but decided not to seek this man until he had earned some money and could present himself properly. So, he worked in New York City for a year and a half, learned English, and saved enough money to purchase new clothes and a ticket to Ohio. He was impressed by the man's successful business and worked for him until he was ready to open a store of his own. Making candy appealed to him as a clean occupation whose success depended solely on his hard work.

In 1908, he left his employer and took a train to seek his fortune. When the train stopped in Lancaster, Ohio, he liked what he saw. It was a bustling small town serving the small farmers who cultivated the surrounding rich farmland. He purchased a confectionery store named The Alps on the main street and changed the name to his own, Louvis's Confectionery, and soon established himself as a good business man and property owner. In those years, immigrants were not readily accepted in rural America. However, A. D. had endeared himself to the residents of Lancaster by his agreeable personality, his business ethics, and his civic awareness. He became a sponsor of the Lancaster Children's Home, donating many pounds of homemade candy to the children each year, and was the founder (through the Rotary Club) of Camp Ro, the Boy Scout Camp. He was the first foreign-born member to be accepted by the exclusive Lancaster Golf and Country Club, where he was the club champion in 1926 and 1930. A. D.'s candy shop was the most popular place in town for ice cream sodas, sweets, and desserts. It was the meeting place—from the mayor to A. D.'s Boy Scout troop—for snacks and for purchasing gifts of chocolates for special occasions.

A. D. was not only a philanthropist in his adopted land, but when he returned to Greece in 1921, he effected improvements in Bordonia. Recalling the drudgery of carrying water from *Ayiannis*, the deep spring, which was a long walk from our house, he arranged to have a system of pipes conduct the fresh spring water from *Ayiannis* to the village and to the door of our home. He purchased a larger house in a more convenient location in the village for Leonidas, who had remained in Greece to care for our parents. A. D. had photographs taken of the village and the family home; upon his return to Ohio, he had some of the pictures enlarged with the landscape of Mount Taigetus in the background with snow on its majestic the peaks. One of the Boy Scouts in his troop, an art student, E. D. Matheny, painted the landscape in oil and presented it to him. Another friend, Raymond E. Eifert, portrayed in watercolor billowing clouds over the village with Mount Taigetus in the background.

Viola told the story of how A. D. had asked her to marry him, but she had remained cool to his advances. One day, however, he hired a horse-drawn carriage (the equivalent of a chauffeur-driven limousine) and, carrying a three-pound box of his homemade chocolates, appeared at her father's farm. He impressed her so much "with his gentlemanly ways" that she accepted his proposal of marriage that same day.

About a year later, in 1916, my mother could no longer endure being away from her home in Greece, so she decided to leave Ourania and me with our brothers, and return home with a woman she knew who was returning to Sparta. By this time, I could speak English, and had a few friends my own age, so I was happy to stay in Lancaster. My mother, who had returned from Youngstown, asked Viola to promise that she would watch over me as though I were her own child. Mother went back to Bordonia with many gifts from her sons in America for their father and Leonidas, as well as several trunks full of clothes and household items. She would be traveling in second-class, not third-class, this time. As she was about to leave, A. D. and Viola presented her with the flowered hat mother had admired in the milliner's shop. She reported that she had worn it on the train and the ship and all the way back to the village.

I lived with A. D. and Viola until I was nineteen. I worked in the candy store, attending to the display cases and selling candy, and doing anything else I could do to help. Arista and her husband worked at the store, according to where my brother assigned each of us. In May 1917, A. D. decided that I did not need any more elementary school education, so he enrolled me in a local business school to learn bookkeeping. I never liked working with numbers, so after a semester, my brother let me drop the course.

A. D. took a personal interest in all aspects of his business, even going so far as to supervise the window displays. Eventually, he turned over to me the task of displaying his confections attractively in the front windows. It was pleasant work. Draping yards of satin or velvet cloth in the background, I then placed a beautiful crystal or silver dish on a lace doily and selected only a few specialty chocolates to display on each dish. Another piece of fine crystal might be placed on a pedestal overflowing with slices of colorful nougats to entice customers to come inside and try our candy.

Receiving payment for my work was new to me, and I do not recall the amount my brother paid me. But Viola encouraged thrifty habits, and I saved all the money I could. One day, I took most of my savings and purchased a mandolin. The instrument came with lessons, and soon I was meeting friends on my day off for impromptu concerts. Myrtle, Corinne, Opal, and I, with other girls, would hike to a meadow outside of town, each with her mandolin or another instrument. Sometimes we walked to a small village or hitchhiked a ride on a farmer's cart, singing as we rode. At our destination, we settled down on an attractive, grassy area, gossiped, and sang to the accompaniment of our instruments. The countryside was unspoiled and peaceful, and most of the farmers were known to us. We were appropriately dressed at all times—in our long-sleeved middy blouses and matching middy bloomers, which covered our ankles. The look was completed with a ribbon or bandanna in our hair, worn across our foreheads and tied in back.

In the heat of summer, we went swimming at Buckeye Lake. Our woolen bathing suits had short sleeves and pantaloons that covered our knees. We wore ruffled cotton swim caps, pulled low over our foreheads to protect our long tresses from the lake water. Staying overnight with Viola's parents, the Shorts, in their farmhouse in the country always was a treat. My impressions of the place began with the aroma of bacon and coffee and a big country breakfast. I spent the day exploring the farm, large and spread out, with its mechanized equipment—so different from our farms in Greece. My interest in their way of life pleased Viola's parents, and although they sometimes teased me about my broken English, they could never do enough for me. I was fortunate to have spent the first five years of my life as an American in their daughter's home. A tall, buxom woman, Viola was stylish and handsome. She also was strict with me in matters of personal grooming and housekeeping. This discipline stood me in good stead for the rest of my life. In our close relationship at home and in the store there never was a cross or impatient word on her part. While A. D. exerted his strong influence at work, Viola's even temperament ensured harmony at home.

CHAPTER 9

Dreams Come True

Gnothi sauton.
Know thyself.
— CHILON OF SPARTA, 570 BC

My idyllic life in Lancaster came to an end when two of my brothers sent for me. Soterios, who had escorted mother, Ourania, and me to Sparta on the first leg of our journey to America, returned to the United States after serving as a volunteer in the Greek army. With our brother Peter he opened an ice cream parlor in Ridgewood, New Jersey.

In the early 1900s, the ice cream parlor–candy store was the place to take a girl on a date, or buy a gift of homemade chocolates, or have lunch. The chocolate-dipped candy, the ice cream served in sodas and sundaes, and the chocolate, vanilla, and fresh fruit syrups were all made by the owner. Grilled cheese sandwiches were the most popular lunch with a slice of cheddar cheese between two slices of buttered white bread, toasted on a flat, buttered, pancake grill. One family-owned confectionery store in Louisville, Kentucky, featured grilled olive and cream cheese on raisin bread—Spanish olives chopped and mixed with cream cheese. Candy stores were located downtown, on a main street, and their large display windows faced the sidewalk. Entering the store, customers passed a cabinet with a glass front and shelves of freshly made chocolate-dipped nuts, caramels and creams, and took their seats on high, round, spinning stools in front of a marble counter, or chose to sit on the scroll-back chairs placed around small café tables.

As each of my brothers arrived in the United States, he was invited to Lancaster, Ohio to live with and work for A.D, who was a strict taskmaster. He insisted that his foreign employees learn English and that they observe his high standards of cleanliness, serving the public, and producing quality candy and ice cream. His guidance on how to conduct a business served them well because, in time and by mutual agreement, each brother eventually left Lancaster and moved to another city to make his own way.

One day, A. D. reported that he had received news from Peter and Soterios in New Jersey. They were doing so well in their candy store in Ridgewood that they were planning to purchase a building and open a second ice cream parlor in nearby Rutherford. Two months later, they wrote that the new store was so popular that customers were waiting in line to be served. It was difficult for the two men alone to handle the cash register and the production of enough ice cream and candy to satisfy the demand. They asked A. D. to send me to New Jersey to help them. They were living in a rental apartment, they wrote, but they would soon be moving into their own rooms above the candy store. I would be quite comfortable since there were three bedrooms, one of which would be mine. I had been happy in Lancaster. But as much as I loved my family and friends, I was now nineteen and it was time I had a home of my own. Other than a few innocent flirtations that neither I nor A. D. took seriously I had not met anyone I wanted as my life's partner. So, I was excited to make the change and experience new adventures. One of the main attractions luring me to my brothers in New Jersey was the proximity of Manhattan, the glamorous megalopolis just across the Hudson River from Rutherford.

Once again, I said goodbye to friends and relatives, this time in Ohio, and took the train to Ridgewood to the apartment of my two bachelor brothers, Peter and Soterios. It was customary at the time, and an economic necessity, for a young woman to live with her brothers. She was expected to cook and keep house for them as well as help in their business. Many girls from poor villages in Europe lived as I did without parents, chaperoned by their brothers or other close relatives. In the absence of parents, girls respected the authority of our male relatives, who, in turn, protected them and kept a watchful eye out for good marriage prospects. My two brothers had contrasting personalities. Soterios was strict and business-like, observing all proprieties; Peter, on the other hand, was more impulsive and fun-loving; however both were shrewd and hard-working businessmen, like A. D.

Our candy kitchen buzzed all day with the chocolate dippers chattering, the copper kettles bubbling with caramel or chocolate, and the porter washing down our marble work space. In summer, the ice cream machine in the back room worked almost constantly, churning the rich cream, eggs, sugar, fresh fruit, and flavored syrups as the mixture congealed into creamy, frozen desserts. People came for a dish of ice cream and to socialize at the ice cream parlor.

And then the ice cream soda arrived. During Prohibition, which outlawed alcoholic beverages, Americans sought ways to slake their thirst. Confectioners had discovered a simple machine that produced carbonated water or seltzer. They began to add flavored syrups to a tall glass of water that fizzed and topped it with a scoop of ice cream. In no time, the most popular order was for one chocolate ice cream soda for two, with two straws— and the soda fountain became the rage.

The apartment my brothers were renting above the store in Ridgewood consisted of living room, dining room, kitchen, bathroom, and three bedrooms. Taking care of it and two grown men might seem difficult, but I did not find it so, thanks to Viola's example and my own desire to be useful. I organized my mornings so that the house was cleaned, swept, and dusted before I went downstairs to help in the candy store at lunch time—one of our busiest times.

The automobile, the movies, and the soda fountain came of age together during the first half of the twentieth century. Young couples—with chaperones or in groups—drove in their new Model-T Fords to the latest entertainment, the talking pictures, and after the show, it was stylish to take a date or meet friends at an ice cream parlor. Ice cream was a delicacy. One scoop was served in a silver, stemmed dish and eaten with a small demitasse spoon.

When our new store in Rutherford and the apartment upstairs were ready, my brothers gave me the choice of staying either with Peter in Ridgewood or with Soterios in Rutherford. It was a difficult decision because I liked both of them, and did not want to hurt the feelings of either one. I am not certain, even now, why I chose my strict brother Soterios unless it was because I knew instinctively that his more disciplined household would be a better match for my personality. In another era, I might have chosen Peter, who owned a convertible, and occasionally said to me, "Take my car. Go out and find yourself a man!"

At any rate, Soterios and I moved into the apartment above the store in Rutherford. Across the street was the office of Dr. Williams, MD. Years later, I learned that he was the famous American poet and novelist, William Carlos Williams, who was for many years in private practice in Rutherford even as he was writing his celebrated novels and poetry. Ours was the only confectionery store in this commuter town, and I like to think that perhaps Dr. Williams sampled our ice cream and confections although I do not remember seeing him. From the moment we opened our doors, we were busy. People streamed in all day long; fortunately, we were young and energetic and enjoyed the constant activity.

When we could afford to hire more help, my brother gave me one day off a week. He would give me money to spend on a train ride into Manhattan for the day. With a friend I attended matinees of the Ziegfeld Follies or performances of Al Jolson or Eddie Cantor. Afterwards, we ate dinner at the best Greek restaurant in New York City at the time. It was formal and "European," with white tablecloths and fresh flowers on each table; young women alone were shown every courtesy. Sometimes, if we went to an evening performance that lasted later than usual (10:30 was late for me), my brother would be waiting at the door, worried. But I always found the way back to Rutherford on the commuter train.

I took over my favorite job of keeping the store windows and the display cases clean and attractive; I also served as cashier at the candy counter, and brought in trays of fresh candy, as needed, and refilled the tall, shapely candy jars with rainbow-hued hard candies; On the other side of the store was the soda fountain with marble counter and swivel stools; in the rear were several café tables and chairs—their seats of walnut wood, and their backs and legs made of coiled metal.

If we were short of waitresses, I put on an apron and stepped in, but it was rare that people did not show up for work because jobs were appreciated. I also did some of the bookkeeping; Soterios thought that six months in a business school had prepared me for this duty. I did well in keeping the accounts, but always was nervous working with figures. The worst error I made was writing an order for an entire barrel of select pecan halves instead of a 20-pound bag. When the barrel arrived, Soterios was annoyed, but he made the best of it by cooking up large batches of pecan brittle. With a little promotion on my part, such as stocking the window with silver compotes overflowing with pecan brittle, and reminding our customers—as they paid their bill—that the pecan brittle had been made that day, we were able to sell out.

They say that when you are around sweets, you lose your appetite for them. But I loved eating both the candy and the ice cream. Some days, I would have a sandwich and a dish of ice cream for lunch and for supper. In fact, it still is a favorite meal. Although Soterios appeared stern, he was quite innovative and had a streak of romance that I had not detected. One day, he decided to bring something new to the business. He placed several tables and chairs in a corner in the back of the store and surrounded them with tall potted palms that reached almost to the ceiling; This reminded him, he claimed, of the main square in Sparta, where he had spent some time as a boy, and he had loved the palm trees and watching people gathered there to enjoy food and drink. It was 1921, a time of land speculation in Florida; owning property had reached fever pitch, and the Sunshine State and its palm trees and beaches were in the news. So, we dubbed this corner the "Florida Room." It became very popular. Young couples came for ice cream and stayed so late that my brother often had to shoo them out at closing time.

Since business was doing well, Soterios added two more stories to the building, so that he could rent out space. We moved our living quarters to the upper floors, and I enjoyed choosing the furniture for my room, which I did with a set of what was called French Provincial. After we had been in Rutherford for two years, and my brother was over thirty and owner of a thriving business, he decided that it was time for him to marry. Soterios felt he could be happy only with a young woman of a similar background who had the values of his mother and sisters. Because he trusted mother's judgment, he wrote her, asking her to find the right girl for him. Mother's letter did not take long to arrive. "I have chosen a girl for you, Soterios," she wrote. "She is from a good family and is lovely—with dark hair and brown eyes. Her mother died when she was young, but her father and stepmother saw to it that she was brought up properly, and she is an accomplished young woman." A photograph was enclosed. Mother concluded her letter with, "Her name is Barbara." My brother approved of what he saw in the photo and of what mother had written, so he wrote back requesting that Barbara come to New Jersey. Her father gave Soterios his consent. He knew our family and that my brothers were industrious and honorable young men. He arranged to travel with Barbara to New Jersey to meet Soterios.

We were quite excited. Peter visited us daily to learn if there was news of the *nifi*. A. D. and Viola wrote from Ohio to say that they were glad that Soterios was bringing a bride from Greece and were eager to learn more about her. I was perhaps the happiest of all—even more than Soterios, who had moments of doubt.

Having his wife move in with us was to my advantage; I still would have my own room, my job, and my trips into the City—and I would have help with housework and a sister to share confidences as well as chores.

On the day that Barbara's ship was to dock in Manhattan, Soterios should have been the one to meet his intended bride and her father. However, unnerved at the prospect, he made some excuse that he was unable to leave the store that day and asked me to go in his place. I waited at the pier for some time after the ship docked, but did not see anyone who fit the description of Barbara and her father. At last, I asked a woman who seemed to have some authority why our relatives had not landed. She informed me that the newly arrived immigrants had to be processed at Ellis Island, and we could not see them until the next day. I regretted not having had the opportunity to meet *nifi* before the rest of the family.

When I returned home alone, my brother met me with a questioning look in his eyes. I decided to have some fun with him and told him that—although they could not leave Ellis Island—I had briefly met Barbara and her father. "She looks like she would be a good worker, and probably will make you a good wife," I told him, "but be prepared—she is not exactly like her picture."

My brother turned pale. "What do you mean?"

"Well, wait until you see her."

"How is she different from the picture?" he demanded.

"Don't worry, her nose isn't that big that you would notice right away. And you will not mind that she is on the plump side. I mean the very plump side. But she seems quite sweet." I could not go on, fearing that I would burst out laughing from his look of dismay. He muttered something. From his appearance the next morning, he had not slept. But he valiantly set out for Ellis Island to greet this less attractive girl and her father. It was my turn to wait to see what Barbara really was like. That day, Soterios took Barbara and her father to a hotel in Manhattan; the next day, he brought them to Rutherford to meet Peter and me. Soterios shook his head when he saw me, indicating his annoyance about my deception, but he could not suppress a smile when he presented his bride-to-be. Barbara was petite and very pretty—not at all as I had described her to my brother. She charmed us immediately with her lively personality.

Couples had no trouble falling in love even with a chaperone accompanying them. Barbara's father went everywhere with them, including the Florida Room. But Barbara was resourceful, and played tricks to evade him, while the rest of us in the store joined in to further the deception on the kindly gentleman. Acquiring a wife by correspondence was not the "cut and dried" affair it might seem. My brother and Barbara, with her father's approval, agreed that since they did not know each other, they would not rush into marriage, but rather would spend the next four months becoming better acquainted. By the end of that time, they were very much in love.

Since I too was of marriageable age, and because my brother's fiancée was a guest in our home and could not work in the store, she took me under her wing to polish my country manners. In Sparta, as the eldest of five daughters Barbara was accomplished in needlecraft, cooking, and housekeeping. In these, and in other ways, she proved to be both a good friend and a good teacher. When we had visitors in the afternoon, we usually served a sweet pastry or candied fruit, a tiny glass of *mastiha* liqueur, and a tall glass of ice water. Barbara taught me the art of serving. She pretended to be a guest and I, the hostess, and she coached me on proper presentation and timing: How the liqueur and water glasses had to be crystal clear, and that it was unacceptable to have drops of water skittering about on the serving tray. How to gauge the right moment, after the guests had arrived, to serve the candied grapefruit peel and cherry preserves. Barbara cautioned me not to offer a guest a tray bending over at the waist, but rather to bend my knees. I was not to hold the tray too high near the guest's chin, but instead near, but not on, the lap.

One day, my brother called me downstairs to help him in the store. It was earlier in the day than usual. I had a supply of attractive half-aprons that I kept laundered and pressed, and I tied one around my waist and hurried down to see why I was being summoned. Two young men had stopped by, and I was introduced to them and served them ice cream and coffee. Later that evening, my brother asked me if I had liked the younger of the two. I told him that I could not tell whether I liked him or not, but the fact that his teeth were not cared for prevented me from considering him any further as a prospective husband. Of course, there were other such visitors dropping by our store, either unattached men or their relatives, who were there to look over the unmarried sister. I, too, had my eyes open for the man who would some day be my husband, but I was not seriously attracted to anyone I had met.

Before Barbara arrived, Peter moved to the confectionery store he had purchased in Summit, New Jersey. A cousin, Tom, had become his partner. Tom was recently married, and he and his wife Frances became close friends. Frances was a beautiful girl with dark brown eyes, and before her children were born, often was my companion on my day off. One of her favorite anecdotes was about a trip to Manhattan, when she noticed two young men staring at us. She said to me, "What if they try to flirt with us? I'm a married woman and can't flirt, and as your chaperone, I can't let you flirt with them either."

I replied, "I'll wink at the good-looking one with my right eye, and at his friend with my left eye, and each of us will have an escort.

A few months before Barbara arrived from Greece, Soterios and I took a two-day vacation and traveled by train to Washington, DC, to visit a friend of his. When he served in the Greek army in 1915, he had met another volunteer who was born in Arcadia; they became friendly and made plans to visit each other after they returned to the United States. I could hardly wait to see the capital of our nation, and was surprised and pleased to find it was cleaner and prettier than Manhattan. Soterios and I walked around the downtown area until it was time to meet his friend Steve. He was a partner in a restaurant and was not free until after their busy lunch hour. Steve picked us up in his automobile and drove us to see the monuments and public buildings.

I was impressed by the white marble buildings surrounded by formal lawns, flowers, and clipped hedges, and I was amazed at all the steps leading to the lofty, domed Capitol. My favorite monument was the stately Lincoln Memorial— so like the Parthenon in my homeland.

After our tour, Steve took us to his home to meet his wife Bertha and their two young children, Helen and Andy. They made us feel welcome and I remembered little Helen, with big brown eyes, rocking back and forth in a little chair, unconcerned about the talkative company from New Jersey. Steve had arranged for us to have dinner at a restaurant, The Busy Bee, which had just opened; it belonged to the three Bacas brothers, cousins of Steve from his village in Greece. As Steve drove us through Rock Creek Park, he described the new enterprise and spoke about his relatives. I did not listen attentively to his description of the Bacas brothers because I was taken with the natural beauty of the park, reminiscent of the rocky terrain of Bordonia. When we arrived at the restaurant, I came to attention when a handsome young man with warm brown eyes and dark, neatly combed hair greeted us cordially. Steve introduced him as Basilios Bacas. "Just call me Bill." He smiled and shook hands with Soterios and me, and then asked his cousin about his wife Bertha and their children.

Bertha had been a waitress at the restaurant where the Bacas brothers and their cousins worked after their arrival in Washington. When Steve announced that he intended to marry Bertha, the family was disappointed at first because she was not Greek. However, they came to love her when they saw how much she cared for Steve. Bill was godfather to Andrew, their first son. We chatted with Bill as he led us to a large table and then returned to the cash register. Another young man with laughing blue eyes and fair hair (who resembled Bill) approached us and was introduced as Bill's older brother, Angelos. I do not remember much about what I ate that night because Bill sat with us for a while, and I decided that he was not only the most handsome man I had ever met but also the nicest.

When it was time for us to leave, Bill walked with us to the entrance. "I hope I'll see you both again soon." He looked at me and not at my brother as he said this. Soterios explained that we were leaving in the morning, and that probably we would not see him again unless he came to New Jersey. At that, Bill reached behind the cigar counter and handed me a calendar with a picture of the Capitol. "A souvenir from Washington," he said. The names "The Busy Bee" and "Bacas Bros." with the address below were printed on it. I carried it home and placed it in a drawer with other keepsakes, where I looked at it often. But I did not see Bill again that year. Soterios was scheduled to meet Barbara after that, and then it would be time for their wedding.

Steve and Bertha traveled from Washington to Barbara's and Soterios's wedding, but none of Steve's cousins could leave their businesses. The bride and I spent the day before the wedding preparing the bridal dinner. Barbara was a talented cook and presented the dishes attractively. As often happened at that time, the wedding took place not in our church, but in the living room of our apartment above the candy store in Rutherford; Greek Orthodox churches were found mainly in large cities and were not easily accessible to many parishioners. The reception supper was held in our dining room—quite effortlessly thanks to the bride's organizational skills; Barbara served appetizers and drinks immediately following the ceremony in the living room, while some of the men arranged chairs and food in the adjacent dining room.

It was summer, and I was almost twenty-two. Diligent in my work, carefree, and happy, I did not worry about my future. As a girl with six older, caring brothers, I enjoyed my sense of security. My brothers, beginning with A. D. were like parents to me—protective and concerned—while at the same time expecting me to do my part and work for a living.

One morning, I was cleaning a display case when three young men walked in. I recognized two of them and my heart skipped a beat. It was Bill Bacas and his cousin Steve. I attempted to greet them with some semblance of calm, as they introduced me to the third man, their cousin Chris. I showed them to a booth near the back of the store where we customarily seated our friends, so that Soterios could sit and talk with them. As soon as they noticed the visitors, Soterios and Barbara approached and shook hands, and Soterios sat down with them. From the day I had met Bill, almost two years before, I had harbored the romantic notion that we would meet again. No one else had impressed me as much as this dark-eyed Arcadian. And here he was! I hardly dared hope that he had come to New Jersey to visit me. But for what reason was he here? However, I was not to be rewarded with a romantic motive. My heart sank when Steve said that they had come on business that day and were leaving in the morning for a few days' vacation in Atlantic City.

My quick-thinking sister-in-law Barbara—knowing about the calendar that Bill had given me and liking what she saw of him—invited the three men to dinner at our home that evening. They accepted readily. Barbara hustled me upstairs as soon as they left, and she and I spent the rest of the day preparing what was then unusual—bite-sized hors d'oeuvres made with cubes of cheese, and some with ham, wrapped in pastry morsels to bake at the last minute and serve hot. She decided against serving the usual company meal of braised beef with tomato sauce or baked chicken. Instead, we made a large rib roast which we garnished with a border of duchesse potatoes. To the green salad she added anchovies and Kalamata olives. When all was ready, we showered and put on our prettiest dresses, prepared to receive our visitors.

That evening after the guests had arrived, Barbara thrust a tray of the hot appetizers into my hands and steered me toward the living room. "Helen made these," she declared unabashed, as she followed me. I started to protest but seeing the look in her eyes, I lowered mine and accepted the compliments. The glances of approval from Bill and his cousins during dinner made me blush because Barbara would say during a pause in the conversation, "This is one of Helen's specialties. Aren't I lucky to have such a talented sister?" She was a resourceful and charming hostess and, as I look back on that night, I realize that her next step had been planned even before she issued the invitation to the visitors as they sat, unsuspecting, in our candy store. Leaving the cups and saucers on the table after coffee, she took some records out of the cabinet and placed them near the Victrola. Soterios wound up the record player. We all joined hands and danced a round of Greek folk dances.

Since we were "modern," we had the latest American dance records too, and we put on some fox trots and waltzes. Barbara and I danced with each of the men a little, and then she cleverly maneuvered her husband into talking to Steve, while she kept Chris busy chatting, and saw to it that I was left alone or danced with Bill more than with the others. Bill and I had the opportunity to talk alone several times that evening. Whatever it is that brings two people together began to affect both of us that night. Bill's eyes sent exciting messages to mine every time they met, and he later admitted that he had been smitten that evening, but had not remembered much about my visit to his store in Washington. Avoiding sentiment, he would tell our children, "I was mainly attracted to your mother because she spoke good English, danced well, and if she had cooked that night, she was a great cook, or she would learn how from the other one."

Bill and I were seated away from the others when he turned to me and quietly asked, "May I write to you, if your brother approves?" His question sent my heart racing, so that I could not speak for a moment. "Yes, I think it would be all right," I answered demurely." I was very happy at this turn of events, and I thought my brother would be too because he had met Bill's family and had seen that Bill had a successful business. Nevertheless, out of respect for Soterios, I would have to ask his permission. This was the first step in Bill's courtship, and my head was spinning with happiness. His every word, look, and gesture were imprinted on my mind, and for several days I relived each moment that we had spent together. When a postcard arrived from Atlantic City, I had something tangible from him to hold close to my heart. More letters followed after his return to Washington, and I responded to each of them.

Thus, having declared himself my suitor, Bill was not permitted—according to the unwritten rules of courtship—to trifle with my affections for a protracted length of time. He would have to propose marriage within the year, or my brother would have to urge me to end the correspondence. One day, a letter from Bill arrived—but it was addressed to Soterios. My brother kept it hidden from me, not knowing that I had already looked in the mailbox. The next day, Bill wrote to tell me that he had written to my brother, and he had stated that he loved me and wanted to marry me if I felt the same about him.

"What did Bill's letter say?" I confronted Soterios since he had not mentioned receiving it.

He refused to show me the letter. "Bill is not the man for you," he answered, to my amazement. I struggled to understand why Soterios would oppose Bill's suit and begged him to provide reasons. He ignored my pleas. I could not believe that Soterios could feel this way about the man I loved, who had declared his love for me, and who wanted to marry me. Bill had his own business and was well able to provide for a wife.

"The subject is closed, Eleni," Soterios firmly put an end to my questioning. Tears started to fall. But, when my brother left the room, I stopped feeling sorry for myself. I fumed as the door closed behind him. How could he do this to me? What reasons could he have? It was my life, not his! I did not fret for long. Reaching for pen and paper, I wrote a letter to A. D. in Ohio, complaining that Soterios would not tell me why he opposed Bill's proposal—a man I loved with all my heart, who was so handsome, owned a restaurant, and wanted to marry me. I would marry Bill tomorrow if A. D. would approve it.

As soon as he received my letter, A. D. told me later, he took a train from Lancaster to Washington. I was touched that he had believed in me enough to take action based on my pathetic appeal. A. D. knew that Soterios would agree with his decision, and he went to Washington to see for himself what type of man

Bill was. In later years, Bill described the encounter: "I was at the cash when this good-looking man walked into the restaurant. He saw that I was busy and waited until I was free. I suspected that he was one of your brothers because he had that same look about him as Peter and Soterios. Then, he stepped up and introduced himself. 'I am Andonis Demetrios Louvis from Lancaster, Ohio.' We talked for a little while, he had something to eat, and then he asked, 'Do you expect a dowry from us—Helen's brothers? If so, how much do you want?'

'Well, I'll tell you, A. D. We came to America to improve ourselves and to leave customs like that behind us. I have my own business, thank the good Lord, and I bought a house on Pennsylvania Avenue. I make enough money to support a wife. So, why should I ask for anything from Eleni's brothers?' He smiled and we shook hands.

'That's all I wanted to know, brother Bill,' A. D. said and clapped me on the back. 'Our sister is a girl we are proud of . . .' Then he said many other nice things." Here my husband stopped the story as though it would turn my head, after so many years, to hear words of praise from one of my brothers.

Bill and A. D. telephoned Soterios to inform him about their agreement. The next day Bill—with his brother Aris and wife Mabel and A. D.—drove to Rutherford from Washington to announce their decision. Soterios had no further objections to our engagement. He, Barbara, and Peter welcomed Bill into our family.

Before the betrothal ceremony, A. D. called Bill and me into a room and questioned us. "Are you willing to live with Bill for the rest of your life? Are you certain that you love him?" In attempting to impress upon me the seriousness of the commitment I was making, A. D. made me more nervous than ever, but Bill took my hand in his, and together we assured my brother that we were certain of our love for each other.

We had very little time to prepare for an engagement party. But with Barbara's organizing the cooking, baking, and cleaning, our apartment was ready in no time. At the betrothal ceremony, Bill and I vowed before the priest that we were ready for marriage to one another, and the priest blessed the rings that affirmed our commitment. Gold wedding bands were placed on the third finger of the right hand and worn from that day on.

Bill, with Aris and Mabel, stayed for two days, so that we could go shopping. Bill wished to follow the custom that dictates that the fiancé buys his future bride's trousseau—dress, shoes, hat, gloves, handbag, and anything else she desires—an action similar to buying an engagement ring to seal the union. I dressed in my best, happy to be going shopping in Manhattan for new clothes with my fiancé. Soterios stopped me before Bill arrived and demanded to know where we were going. When I told him, my brother sternly forbade me to accept any gifts from my future husband. "Is there anything your brothers have not purchased for you, Helen? What is it you need?"

My brothers were proud men, and I did not want to go against their wishes. Nevertheless, I was very disappointed. I had wanted to show off the things that Bill gave me, but since my brother refused to let me accept anything, I had to obey him—that time. When Bill arrived to take me into Manhattan, I did not let my brother's injunction stop me from enjoying the excursion. Bill's younger brother Aris and his wife Mabel came with us. That weekend was our first meeting, and we became close friends from that day. Mabel and I walked down Fifth Avenue and stopped in front of one of the exclusive department stores. "We are going to buy you a dress and shoes and anything else you want, Eleni," Bill began. He always preferred calling me Eleni over Helen. "It is the bride's day to choose whatever she wants."

My heart leaped with joy, but I had to answer, "Thank you just the same, but I don't need a thing."

Bill looked at me questioningly, but when I kept insisting, he responded, "All right, then; maybe you don't need anything. We'll just find something that you will enjoy." We continued down the famous street, Mabel and I admiring everything in the shop windows. When Bill caught Mabel and me lingering longer than usual in front of a millinery shop, he took us by the arm and led us inside the store. "Aris and I are buying each of you a hat," he announced. We tried on the milliner's entire stock and when we had made our final decisions, Mabel and I chose two beautiful, and identical, hats. They were covered with flowers and fruits that nearly concealed our faces, but we thought they were very becoming. They also were very expensive. This was the gift that I was able to show off to my friends as I boasted that my fiancé had given it to me when we went shopping on Fifth Avenue.

Our next stop was in front of a jewelry store. "Now," Bill said, "We will follow American custom and buy an engagement ring."

But I had to refuse this too. "You are my diamond, Bill. I do not need a ring." This pleased him very much, so we walked past the jewelry store. As I came to know my husband better, I realized that he disliked showy ornaments. His proudest possessions were his Packard automobile, and a large, comfortable home in which to raise our family. Nothing could dampen our spirits that day. Mabel and I felt quite festive in our new hats and having lunch with Bill and Aris in New York City. We returned to Rutherford in time for Bill and his relatives to start their return trip to Washington while it was still daylight; I was sorry to see them leave.

Soterios did not smile as I showed off my new hat, but he did not openly object to it. Perhaps it was symbolic of our marriage that, contrary to custom in which the bride chooses the wedding date, in our case, Bill made that decision. He told me he wanted to be married on June 1, a date he felt was lucky for him. I did not mind, and a week before June, I stopped working at the candy store, which had been my life for the past three and a half years; I had to prepare for the wedding and for my subsequent move to Washington. Bill's cousin Bessie was married on May 3, a month before our wedding, and Soterios, Barbara, and I were invited. Bill met our train at Union Station in Washington. He drove us to the Willard Hotel, where our rooms overlooked the Treasury Department and the White House grounds. The hotel fell into disrepair after World War II. Years later, it was renovated, and one of my grandnieces, the namesake and grand-daughter of Barbara, held her wedding reception at the Willard Hotel's Crystal Room in 1991.

As a guest at Bessie's wedding in 1924, I fell in love with Washington all over again. Bill had reserved an imposing suite, which was large and beautifully furnished, and even had a grand piano. While we were there, he took us to the nicest res-taurants, and I was impressed by the attention showered on me and my brother and sister-in-law. In an orange lace ankle-length dress, I attended Bessie's wedding and met Bill's relatives and friends. On the day after the wedding, we were invited to Aris's and Mabel's home for dinner. The men played cards at the din-ing room table after it was cleared, and the women gathered in the living room to talk. During the conversation, I said that I loved ballet. Throughout the years the story changed and my sisters-in-law, Mabel and Doula, maintained that I had told them that I <u>was</u> a ballet dancer! We listened to records on the Victrola for a while, and then the girls (we were all in our early twenties) asked me to perform one of my dances. When I could no longer refuse, I stood up and danced to "Tales of the Vienna Woods," swaying to the music, like Isidora Duncan. For the ladies' eyes only, of course.

After returning home, letters from Bill arrived almost daily, and I wrote to him as often. Mabel's and Aris's daughter Elaine was two years old, and Bill was a doting uncle who mentioned her in most of his letters. 'When is Fish coming again?' he quoted her saying—fish was her word for *Nifi*. She was a darling child and in many ways was a role model for the cousins who followed.

Most of the florists in Manhattan were from Greece in those years, and their annual benefit, The Florists' Ball, was a spec-tacular affair. It was held in the most elegant hotel ballroom in Manhattan, which was decorated with exquisite floral displays. My brothers bought tickets for a table of ten each year, and that weekend, Bill drove from Washington to attend the Ball. He gave me the first corsage I had ever had, and we danced until the wee hours of the morning. On the weekends that Bill came to visit, we took drives around the rural back roads of New Jersey. Usually one of my brothers, either Soterios or George (who had by then married a girl from New York City and owned an ice cream parlor in Jamaica, Long Island) and his wife accompanied us to dinner and dancing, or to the theater. They served dual roles—both as chaperones and as friends. George's wife Margaret had a voice that still rings in my memory. She was from Great Britain, and if anyone said, "Margaret is English," she would draw herself up to her full height and correct them: "I am Brrritish—not English!"

On one of Bill's visits, we went to Wanamaker's to select my wedding dress. Wanamaker's Department Store was located on Tenth Street and Broadway in lower Manhattan, an imposing square edifice. At that time, it housed one of the great fashion centers of the city. As we entered the bridal department, I saw a beautiful sleeveless eggshell satin gown with lace at the neckline and hem and decided that it was the one for me. The salesgirl removed the dress from the mannequin; it fit as though it had been made for me. Little did I dream that day that this same gown would be worn by two other brides—my daughters Mimi and Athena—about a quarter of a century later. Decades later, in 2011, Stephanie, my first great-grandchild, and first to marry, was featured in a bride's magazine, *The Knot*, discussing the history of the dress.

My shopping spree began with Peter, who handed me his Wanamaker's charge card and told me to purchase whatever I needed for myself and for my household. Only another woman could truly appreciate the carefree hours I spent, armed with a credit card for the first time in my life, and with no reservations about using it. I purchased a pair of dressy shoes for $75, (expensive for that time), a few blouses, skirts, two dresses, and lingerie. I also bought full sets of linens, towels, and blankets for my new home; I had worked for my brothers without receiving a salary for the past three and a half years, and when I needed money I would ask them for it: the strict one would dole it out carefully, while the carefree one would be more generous. At this time, I knew that they wanted me to buy whatever I felt was necessary.

Our wedding was festive—typical of the lavish post-World War I 1920s. Bill hired a Pullman railroad car to transport his relatives and friends from Washington's Union Station to Newark's Pennsylvania Station on June 1, 1924. A. D. and Viola, and Arista and her two young daughters, Elaine and Magdalene, had arrived a day earlier. The rest of my family— Peter, George, and Martha—met at the home of Soterios and Barbara early in the morning. From there, we would proceed to the hotel in Newark where the wedding was to take place.

Several shiny, new automobiles were waiting at the curb. I entered the car Peter was to drive, and Bill and his family arrived to escort us. Peter and I stayed out of sight, so that the groom would not see me before the ceremony. As Bill took the wheel of his car, one of my brothers signaled to him that we were ready, and Bill drove off at the head of the procession of cars. Peter, the impulsive one, decided that the bride's car should lead the procession, so he pulled in front of Bill. I ducked down to hide, and it was probably just as well that I did not see the look on Bill's face. He explained later that he was not at all happy to have us precede him since he felt that the groom should have led the procession.

A. D. gave me away and the son of Bill's godfather came from Kansas to be *koumbaros*, Best Man. The Sacrament of Marriage was performed by Father Spyridakis, a priest at Newark's Saint Nicholas Church for many years. From the hall where the ceremony took place, we moved into the dining room. Seated at the bridal table in my lovely wedding gown I was very happy to look out at my brothers and my sister Arista, with her two little girls. She had made pretty dresses for Elaine and Magdalene, who served as my flower girls. Ourania had returned to

Greece a few years earlier, because my father had died, and the family decided that in addition to Leonidas and his family, one of mother's daughters should be with her as well. So, sadly, neither my mother, nor Ourania, nor Leonidas were with us, and I missed them very much. Brothers Theo and Spiros were unable to come from Ohio, and brother Steve had moved to California. Bill's three brothers—Angelos, Aris, and John—attended our wedding. Two of them were married, but only Aris's wife, Mabel was at the wedding. Doula, Angelos's wife, had just given birth to her first child, Homer. My sister-in-law Viola confided a few years later that she was concerned after meeting some of Bill's relatives. "I told A. D.—look at those snooty relatives of Bill. I was afraid you'd be unhappy with those people. You were a simple country girl, and I didn't see how you would fit in."

Viola was referring to Bill's Uncle Andrew and Aunt Fofo. When Soterios had denied Bill's proposal, he later admitted that he had heard about Uncle Andrew and his flamboyant wife, and believed that they were typical of Bill's family, and would make me unhappy. Fofo came to the wedding in a satin gown with feathers and holding a lorgnette; her husband looked regal in spats and a diamond stick-pin. The couple owned a fashionable restaurant in downtown Washington where Angelos, and later Bill, had worked when they arrived in America. Andrew was a first cousin of their mother, and they respected him for his success and his grand style. The brothers, however, were a practical lot, and while they respected Uncle Andrew, they maintained a different life style. Luxuries came only after debts were paid for their father's medical bills in Greece, support of their family there, and their sisters' dowries when they married.

Bill and I danced with each other and with our guests at the wedding reception until our feet hurt. My shoes were too tight, and I was tired by the time we said good-bye to our guests. Still in our wedding clothes, and feeling conspicuous, Bill drove us to a nearby hotel. The next day, we drove from Newark to Atlantic City, a trip of several hours; Bill had made reservations at the

Traymore Hotel on the Boardwalk. With its twin golden domes, beautiful gardens, and a lobby that was all marble and gilt, the Traymore was one of the most beautiful hotels of the day. Our suite had twin beds, which produced amused comments from Mabel and Doula, when I told them about it later. They found even more to tease us about when I told them that, since it was early afternoon when we arrived, Bill and I donned bathing suits and went for a swim. I loved my wonderful new husband all the more for his desire to please me and to show me something of this lovely summer resort, Atlantic City.

Angelos and Bill, proprietors,
Washington, D. C., 1920.

Harralambos Bacas, father
of the Bacas Brothers,
Athens, Greece, 1907.

The Bacas Brothers: Aris, Bill, Angelos, John. Washington,
DC, 1915.

A photograph of Bill; sent to
Eleni during their courtship,
1923.

A photograph of Eleni sent to Bill;
she is holding the photo he had
sent her, 1923.

Formal wedding portrait of Bill
and Elaine, Newark, NJ, June
1, 1924.

Bill and Elaine [Eleni's name changed to Elaine when she married] and their children (on right) with brothers' and cousin's families, and uncle, Easter, 1935.

Elaine (left) with friend, 1919.

Mt. Vernon. Mimi, Solon and cousin Maggie in foreground, 1930.

Bill and Elaine with Soterios and Barbara, and the children of both
couples, Sparta, Greece, 1937.

CHAPTER 10

The New Family

Yia tin hoo-hoo-vaya, to pio
omorfo paidi einai to diko tis.
To the owl, the most beautiful
child is her own.

— GREEK PROVERB

W hen I arrived in Washington as a bride, our house was furnished and waiting for me. Bill had purchased a row house on Pennsylvania Avenue, and had supplied it with the necessary tables, chairs, beds and appliances—a stove, a Frigidaire—anything the well-stocked house required. This included linens, kitchen and dining room tableware, as well as mops, brooms, and other cleaning essentials. I moved in with my clothing and the new purchases from my brother's charge card. Row houses were three-story brick edifices with a common wall with a neighbor on each side, except for those at either end of the block. On the street level, above the basement, were the living areas, and on the second and third floors, the bedrooms and one bathroom. The third floor was occupied by Bill's youngest brother John and his cousin Chris.

On the first morning after our honeymoon, I was alone and had no doubt of how I would spend my day. Bill had prepared a list. At first I thought it was a grocery list, but when I read it, I was surprised to see:

Make bed
Wash breakfast dishes
Dust all furniture with dust cloth
Dust floors with dust mop
Doula will walk over to accompany you to
the Navy Yard for dinner.

Doula was one of my two sisters-in-law who lived in one of the apartments above the restaurant.

I knew that Bill had seen through Barbara's maneuvers to mislead him into thinking I was an accomplished cook, and I was aware that he loved me in spite of my lack of domestic skills. I too had observed his need to lead an organized, well-managed personal life, as he did with his business. I loved my new husband with all my heart and had faith that we would be happy in spite of each other's differences.

By noon, I had made the bed, washed the breakfast dishes, swept and dusted, and was ready for my sister-in-law's arrival. It was almost a mile to the family-owned restaurant, "Bacas Bros. Visible Lunch," at the corner of 8th and M Streets, SE, across from the main gate of the U. S. Navy Yard. Our husbands had automobiles, but these were used only by the men, mainly for business and for family outings. Doula, Mabel, and I used the efficient public transportation system—street cars and buses—to shop and to visit friends.

The lunchroom was open for breakfast and lunch—not dinner. It was a cafeteria-style restaurant with a menu of cooked meats and poultry, vegetables, and sandwiches, as well as salads and desserts. All foods were prepared in the restaurant kitchen. Hot meats and vegetables were kept hot on the steam table, and cold foods were displayed on ice. A glass partition separated the customers from the food items. A customer took a tray and indicated to the server, who stood behind the steam table, which items he wanted. He received the food on a plate, which he placed on his tray, then paid the cashier at the end of the line. Both the restaurant and the two spacious apartments above it were called "The Navy Yard" by the family because of the location.

On this first day after my honeymoon, Doula and I were going to have dinner with the family. For the rest of the time that Bill and I lived in Southeast, I was never to cook dinner in the kitchen of my new home. Instead, the three married brothers—partners in business—made virtual partners of their wives. We women cooked and served dinner in the larger apartment above the restaurant. Although the brothers were in the food business, they preferred to end the day sitting down to a home-cooked meal. Every night, we ate together, including our youngest brother John and our cousin Chris—and any other unmarried cousins who were working for the brothers at the time. We often seated fifteen. Each woman cooked two days a week. Since dinner was cooked and served in Mabel's larger apartment, and Doula's apartment was adjacent, and because they were more experienced than I, Mabel and Doula cooked on alternate Sundays.

When my turn came, I was very nervous because I had never prepared meals for so many. When I lived with my brothers in New Jersey, we had been satisfied with grilled cheese sandwiches, ice cream, and other snacks from our confectionery store, and occasional dinners out—until Barbara came into our lives. Now, I had to learn how to prepare roasted meats and chicken, vegetables, salads, and desserts to serve fifteen hungry people. Mabel and Doula were the best friends a girl could have at this a time. I learned so much by observing their methods, and they stood by to help me whenever I needed them. Because our husbands provided food for the public, they were informed critics, and quite specific about what they liked and what they did not like. Hot foods had to be served hot, and cold foods, cold, and everything had to taste good. When the family was called in for dinner, everyone, including the cook, was expected to be seated and not to get up again until the meal was over. At first, this was hard for me since I had not learned how to keep all dishes at the proper temperature and serve them at the same time. Eventually I became as competent as Mabel and Doula at taking off my apron and bringing out the salad before the meat and the vegetables, and sitting next to my husband, and having everything ready on time.

Not only was the temperature of the food important, but the meats were to be well done; each leaf of the green salad had to be crisp yet coated with olive oil and vinegar; and the *horta*, edible greens, were to retain their fresh green color, yet properly cooked. Our husbands, forthright men that they were, were not shy about commenting on our culinary efforts. The *nifi* who prepared an especially succulent lamb roast or the "best apple pie" would receive praises from the entire group. On the rare occasions when I was the recipient of a compliment, it warmed me to the tips of my toes!

After the initial uneasiness had passed, cooking dinner for a large group became a routine part of daily life. On my two assigned days, I planned the menu, purchased the groceries, and cooked the meal. My sisters-in-law sometimes advised me if I had to prepare a vegetable or a food I was unfamiliar with, but they were mainly occupied with other household chores and their children. We had the added advantage that we could request that the restaurant downstairs send us fresh fruits, vegetables, and meats. But we had to plan ahead, so as not to interfere with their busy lunch hours.

Early on my cooking day, I arrived at Mabel's apartment. Asking my sisters many questions at first, I would prepare the meal. Doula, with her sense of humor, and Mabel, with her repertoire of recipes and her experience growing up on an Ohio farm, were patient with me. Soon I was able to prepare and serve a full-course dinner that drew favorable comments. Our meals consisted of meat or poultry, a vegetable, a starch, and a salad; they concluded with dessert. Our agreement was that the cook never did the dishes, and that the two women who were not cooking that day took over after dinner.

We were expected to vary the menu and serve something different each day. Good-naturedly, the men would openly discuss which *nifi* had baked the best pie or cake. Sometimes my new husband would side with his brothers in criticizing something I had baked, and I had to hide my irritation. Even more annoying were the times when I baked a pie that I thought was my best, only to hear one of the men comment, "This is good, but nobody can make an apple pie like Mabel!" Sometimes Angelos asked, "Who fixed the spinach tonight? There was sand in it." If Doula answered that she had been the cook, her husband would have no qualms about repeating his dissatisfaction. "Awful!"

Nor would it stop there. Bill might add, "Doula, you should always rinse spinach three, or even four, times, until there is no more sand." He would lift his palms upward, to demonstrate. I leave it to the psychologists to determine why we did not become a group of jealous, squabbling men and women. But we did not. In fact, all of the brothers and their wives remained loyal and loving friends for the rest of our lives.

In April of the following year, I gave birth to our first child, a son Solon. Bill was ecstatic. Two of his brothers, Aris and Angelos, had young sons, and their enthusiasm for the preservation of the male line was boundless as they reiterated an old world aphorism: "Only a man can have sons." In spite of such statements, their feelings ran as deep for the little girls who soon came along, with Aris and Mabel's daughter Elaine leading the way. In time, when Homer (Doula and Angelos's son) had four beautiful daughters, the old saw became a family joke because Homer was treated like a king. While I carried my children—the word "pregnant" was not spoken in polite company at the time— Bill took me for a drive every day after work to enjoy the natural parks that enhance the Capital. After parking the car, we walked among fragrant, blossoming plants; in winter, we took in the fresh air along the paths of the Potomac River. My husband believed that I would have an easier delivery if I spent part of every day of my pregnancy walking. A favorite stroll was behind the Capitol, along the paths in the gardens located there. Bill also believed that I should look only at beautiful objects— whether natural or man-made—so that our children would be born handsome and with a healthy outlook. Both of his theories proved to be right for me because I did have easy deliveries, and all of our children were beautiful.

The naming of children can pose problems in some cultures. When our son was born, Mabel and Aris already had used the paternal parents' names of Elaine and Harralambos, Harry, according to tradition. The other brothers agreed it would be impractical to have a number of children living in the same city all named either Harry Bacas or Elaine Bacas. So, we took names from Greek literature and some notable figures who had made an impression on us. Mabel and Aris chose Philip and Richard for their younger sons—the first after the father of Alexander the Great; the second, after Richard Byrd, a Virginian, who had accomplished the feat of being the first man to fly over the North Pole in November 1928, shortly after Richard's birth in October. Babies were usually baptized and named a few months after birth.

Doula and Angelos named their boys after the epic poet Homer and the philosopher Aristotle, and their daughter Helen, a translation of Eleni. Bill and I chose the names Solon, the noted lawgiver of Athens, and Byron because of the English poet Lord Byron's love and support of Greece during its fight for independence in 1821. Our daughters were Demetra and Athena, the former, the goddess of agriculture, and the latter, the goddess of wisdom. Another Harry joined the growing family when our youngest brother John and his wife Doris had their first son; they also had Angelos and Thomas.

Solon was a good baby, and I nursed him until he was six months old and began to have crying spells. I tried what I could to settle him down, but nothing helped. I was reluctant to ask Dr. Repetti, our family doctor—who delivered the babies, performed surgery, and gave advice and medical care—such a silly question as, "Why is my baby crying so much?" Desperate after a few days, I called him. He assumed that this was the first day of the crying; I did not correct his impression. His reply was that I should let the baby cry. There I was—faced with the same dilemma. The next day the subject discussed by Angelo Patri in the Family Section of our daily newspaper, *The Washington Star,* was about nursing mothers whose milk supply was not adequate for their babies. Angelo Patri was a syndicated columnist and an influential teacher in New York City. My sisters-in-law and I daily discussed his advice to parents. I realized that hunger pains were the most likely cause of Solon's discomfort, and called our doctor, explaining my suspicions. He solved the problem by immediately prescribing an infant formula.

As a youth in his village of Isari, Bill had been bitten by a vicious sheep dog in his left arm and his left hip. The wounds were deep and had never been properly cared for. Spending long hours on his feet in the restaurant aggravated a latent infection in the bone and caused him severe pain. As the pain increased, Dr. Repetti referred Bill to Johns Hopkins Hospital in Baltimore, Maryland, for diagnosis and subsequent surgery in order to save his leg.

It was three months before my husband was able to return home; this seemed like an eternity to me. He, too, was upset at leaving his young family and his work, but with prayers, the help of the Lord, and of our loving family, he returned home healed. I don't think I could have survived those months without the continual love and support of Bill's family. Brother Angelos left work at the Navy Yard after lunch every day, and drove me and baby Solon to Baltimore where we visited Bill for a few hours; then Angelos drove us back home. After his release from the hospital, Bill had to stay off his feet for several more weeks. Little Solon was crawling and he and his father were able to enjoy one another's company during Bill's recuperation.

When Bill and I married there already were three infants in the family. Homer was barely a month old; Harry was one and a half, with hair that stood straight up because it was so fine and would not lie flat; his sister Elaine was a sweet, well-mannered little girl just over three, whose bachelor uncles doted on her.

Before I knew her, Elaine had worked her sweet magic in keeping the family together. Aris had met Mabel, a bright young girl from Canton, Ohio—when she worked for the Department of the Navy. They fell in love and in due time announced to the brothers that they planned to marry. Angelos and Bill opposed the marriage because they had chosen Aris as the brother who would attain a college education, and they were helping pay his tuition. Marriage before a college degree could be achieved, and to a girl who was not Greek, was not in their plans, so the couple eloped. This was not well received.

However, after a few months, given Mabel's unrivaled culinary skills and Elaine's birth, all was forgiven. Her uncles were soon reconciled with Aris and his bride, and looked for excuses to visit their enchanting niece and listen to her latest babblings. Perhaps inspired by the wedded bliss of his brother, in 1923, Angelos married Doula, a tall, dark-haired beauty from a village near Sparta, and Bill and I were married a year later.

At that time in the mid-1920s, 8th and M housed The Car Barn—a cavernous brick building that served as the end of the line for streetcars (electrified trolleys running on tracks) that traveled around Washington. This terminal was located across from us on 8th Street. Motormen in neat black uniforms with brass buttons and flat-topped, brimmed caps would pull down on the rod that connected the car with the electric cables suspended above it, and walk the car around in a U-turn for the return route. Their schedules regularly brought the motormen into our restaurant for a nourishing meal, along with the conductors (who took the tickets on the trolleys), who wore dark suits and a different type of cap.

It was a quiet residential neighborhood with small stores along the 8th Street side of our corner building. A low, wrought iron fence on the M Street side separated our yard from the commuters. After tending to my house in the morning, I walked Solon in his buggy to the Navy Yard in the afternoon to visit Mabel and Doula and to prepare dinner when it was my turn. We had privacy to sit under the maple trees in our yard with the babies bundled in their carriages, and the older ones playing in the sandbox, or riding tricycles on the sidewalk that connected the apartment entrance to the side street.

With the increase in automobile traffic, the street cars became a hazard when they stopped to discharge passengers in the center of the narrow streets of Washington. Eventually, most of the tracks were dug up and the streets paved. The Car Barn disappeared; those neatly dressed motormen and conductors went on to other jobs or retired. Bill and his brothers moved away to larger homes as they expanded their business to other locations

After Mabel and Aris purchased a home on P Street, along Pennsylvania Avenue and across Anacostia Bridge, Bill and I began to think about moving farther away from downtown. We had seen other neighborhoods we liked and began to look in earnest. We sold our house on Pennsylvania Avenue and rented one of the apartments at the Navy Yard for a year. We found the granite-faced house that we purchased on Alaska Avenue just in time for the birth of our second child. Our family expressed surprise at our purchasing a home so far from the center of the city and from the restaurant. However, the brothers were planning to buy another building on North Capitol Street, which Bill would manage and the commute would be easier from Alaska Avenue. Bill and I loved the area we had chosen and our spacious six-bedroom house. Mortgage payments were high, but we raised four children there and lived on Alaska Avenue for the next seventeen years.

In April, before we had moved into our new home, and the baby Mimi (the shortened form of the name Demetra) was barely five months old, Bill was again afflicted with severe pains in the leg that had undergone surgery, and he had to be hospitalized a second time. As a veteran, he was accepted at Walter Reed Hospital, which was near our new home; he had a second surgery on his hip and had to remain in the hospital for a month. During this time, our house was ready, and we decided that the best thing to do was for me and our two young children to move in. This time, it was much easier to visit Bill. Every day I took Mimi out in her carriage with Solon toddling along, and we walked the mile to Walter Reed Hospital, with Solon climbing into the buggy whenever he was tired.

Byron was born two and a half years later, in 1928, and Bill was very happy to have a second son. He was just as happy in January 1931, when curly-haired Athena came along to balance the brood. "We have two and two—two boys and two girls," Bill liked to say. The back yard had a latticed fence, six feet high, enclosing the children's play yard. Within were a sandbox made of concrete and a swimming pool, six-feet square, of the same material. It was two feet deep with a drain, and the children spent many hours in it in the summer, filling it every day with fresh water from the garden hose. On hot summer days, the four-year-olds played in the pool without bathing suits. However, one day, Solon slipped out and ran into the front yard and an elderly neighbor called to say that she was quite offended. Bathing suits were soon located for the youngest because a new house was built next door, and the neighbors could view the pool area from their second-floor windows.

When it was time for Athena to arrive, I had had my fill of hospitals and felt confident that I would have another easy birth. I told Dr. Repetti that I wished to deliver my fourth child at home, and he agreed. So, with a registered nurse and with Doula's mother Georgia (a dear friend the doctor knew and respected) to assist him, I had natural childbirth. With my first three children, I had been sedated, so it was interesting to be awake and witness the birth of one of my children. Bill had gone to visit a cousin who had opened a restaurant in Richmond, Virginia, and returned home the next day to find a newborn baby girl.

A stone retaining wall bordered my flower garden, which had been planted with an eye to colorful blooms throughout the growing season. In early May, forsythia, narcissus, and tulips bloomed; then, in quick succession, purple lilacs, bridal wreath spirea, and pink and red peonies arrived; later came the mounds of fragrant white, yellow, and pink roses. Deep red climbing roses on the south side of the grey granite house ascended its trellis almost to our bedroom. A southern magnolia tree on one side of the trellis produced glossy green leaves every year but there were no flowers. At last, buds appeared, followed by creamy white blossoms that were ten inches across. From that year, Bill looked out of our bedroom window in spring and asked, "Well, do you think we'll have any magnolias this year?" We did, and I would place a few of the large white blossoms in a vase on the piano where they would overpower the room with their strong fragrance. The year we moved—1946—the tree was covered with flowers.

Along the same side of the house grew a large *platanos*, sycamore tree, its trunk covered with white and brown bark, similar to our tree at the *Lefko* in Bordonia. My boys and their friends never tired of climbing the sturdy sycamore and urging their sisters to join them. They claimed that from the top of this tree, on a clear day, they could see the apex of the Washington Monument, which was more than ten miles away. When my observant neighbor across the street noticed these forays, she telephoned me in alarm to inform me that my children were stuck on the top branches of the sycamore tree. Little did she know that these climbs were an auspicious beginning for Solon, who joined the U. S. Army Air Corps in World War II.

This same neighbor called one day, quite concerned that our kitten was in a tree, and could not get down. We trooped over to the designated tree until Solon reminded us that we didn't have a cat at the time. The kitten climbed down of its own accord a few minutes later and walked away unharmed. Our house was on a corner lot with a low retaining wall made of the same granite that had been used on the exterior of the house. Within its boundaries our children played "All Around the Mulberry Bush" under our two mulberry trees while I tended my flower garden. In those days of natural gardening, pesticide sprays were not used to prevent the fine leaves of the pendant branches of the mulberry trees from being covered with hungry caterpillars. In spring, no one wanted to walk into dangling threads of wriggling larvae or to slip on their remains as they fell onto the lawn. They were not even silkworms that could produce useful fiber!

Bill was busier than ever. The restaurant on North Capitol Street was near Union Station, Washington's principal railroad terminal; it also was a block from the city's main United States Post Office (now the Postal Museum); and was across the street from the Government Printing Office. He named it, appropriately, "PO Visible Lunch." It was cafeteria style, like the Navy Yard—cold and hot foods offered from a glassed-in counter—thus the "Visible" portion of the name. Angelos bought a restaurant on 13th Street near F Street, where the downtown movie theaters featuring vaudeville shows—the Fox, the Capital, and the Earle—were located. Because it was not far from these popular entertainment centers, as well as the prestigious department stores—Woodward & Lothrop, Jeleff's, and Garfinkel's—he named it Central Café, a modern restaurant with waitresses to offer alternative service to customers who did not wish to stand in the cafeteria line. Aris and our youngest brother John managed the Navy Yard together until Aris opened Bacas Brothers Café at 2nd and B Streets near the Library of Congress and the Supreme Court, and not far from the Capitol.

Almost every Friday night, the four brothers met after dinner, taking turns at each other's homes—for the card game, *prefa*, which is similar to pinochle. Over drinks (alcoholic or not, according to the preference of each brother), they played cards in a room separate from the family; it was here that they discussed their business affairs.

Bill might address his older brother Angelos thus: "Boss, I checked on the building for sale on North Capitol Street. I think it would be good. A restaurant downstairs. Upstairs is a clean hotel, eight rooms, one bath. Men only. There are stores next door. Maybe we can buy those later. Shall we go into it?" Angelos would squint his blue eyes, look at his cards, chew on his cigar, then say, "I've got the *dama*, the queen!" And play out the hand. A few minutes later, he would respond, "Okay, if you and our bookkeeper think it's good." I can only guess about their conversations—because what they said in their card room was not often repeated to their wives, nor did they discuss their business affairs with anyone else, except their accountant, when necessary. After cards, the men joined the women—who had been knitting or crocheting and talking—for dessert and coffee. As always, the hostess brought out her homemade apple pie or lemon meringue pie. Occasionally, other relatives or friends were invited, but there was no business meeting, and the poker set was brought out to accommodate the larger group of men and women guests who enjoyed the game.

Bill kept the books for the brothers' partnerships and turned them over to the accountant at designated times. Learning lessons from his two long hospital stays, Bill imposed a rigid timetable on himself for work and for meals, and did not deviate from this regimen for the rest of his life. We always had breakfast at nine o'clock. Then he made the forty-minute drive to the restaurant on North Capitol Street, arriving in time to oversee the cash register during the busy lunch hour. No matter where our children were playing at the time, no matter who was visiting us in our later years as retirees, dinner was always at five o'clock.

My husband believed in an annual vacation, and while the children were young, we would rent an apartment for two weeks in Atlantic City, New Jersey, where we had spent our honeymoon. Bathers walked many yards along the sandy beach at Atlantic City toward the ocean, before reaching the gentle spume of spent ocean waves, which tended to break farther out. Children could sit down in the shallow water, confident that the big waves would not overwhelm them, and dig their holes and build their sand castles with the salty Atlantic caressing them. Those who preferred to do so ventured deeper into the ocean, where they encountered the high waves and swam beside them, or dove into the mountainous surf farther out. At this time when woolen bathing suits modestly covered men, women, and children, everyone who vacationed at the shore changed for dinner. Girls wore dresses and white patent leather shoes; boys wore ties, shirts, long pants, and shiny shoes. Ladies wore pretty summer frocks and high heels to promenade on The Boardwalk with their husbands, who looked dapper in white linen suits and straw hats.

One year we decided to change our destination and vacation in Ocean City, New Jersey. We had not made reservations, because it was not quite as popular a resort as Atlantic City. "We'll be there early in the afternoon," my husband predicted, "so we can look around and take our pick of apartments."

It had been raining very hard all day from the time we left Washington, but we thought that this was just a local summer storm, and that the sun would be shining at the Jersey shore. As we approached our destination, however, the radio announcers warned of downed telephone poles and wires, and widespread flooding in the Ocean City area. Bill was a determined man, and he had decided that we were going to Ocean City. He would take his family there—no matter what! The heavy rains stayed with us all day, making driving hazardous, so that it was dark by the time we reached New Jersey. We were hungry, but at that time eating places along highways were not common, as they are today, and there was no place to stop. I had brought some milk and crackers as snacks for the children and that was what we shared for dinner that day.

The rain kept drumming on the car windows; sometimes the wind was so strong that I feared that our car would be swept off the road. We strained our eyes, looking for a place to stop, or for somewhere to eat, but no buildings or cars could be seen. The announcements on the car radio were becoming more urgent: "Some bridges are down. Motorists are cautioned to drive carefully. Ocean City is flooded." Bill drove on, while I tried to remain calm in front of the children and not distract my husband, who could barely see through the windshield in the blinding rain.

Bill tried to reassure me about the flooding in Ocean City. "They're only saying that to keep people off the streets. It can't be that bad." A littler farther on, however, we came upon a dismal sight. A car just ahead of us had stopped. As we craned our necks to understand the reason, we saw that two cars ahead were up to their windows in water. The drivers had kept on driving right into deep water, and now they were stuck. Fortunately Bill, who was a careful driver—but usually did not hesitate to pass slower drivers—had not attempted to do so this time, or we would have been in the same predicament. The storm had not abated; in fact, it seemed to be picking up force. Bill carefully backed up, saying, "It's time we found a farmhouse or barn or someplace to stay tonight to get out of this storm."

He turned off the highway, drove down a country road, and pulled into the driveway of the first house we came to that had a light in a window. I was chosen to ring the doorbell and ask for help. A grey-haired woman cautiously opened the door. In those days, when there were few motels, it was not preposterous to ask, as I did, if she had room for us to stay overnight. The lady listened politely, as I explained that we would have to spend the night in the car with our four young children if we found no other refuge. She studied me, and then our car, and asked me to wait a moment, while she called her husband. He came to the door and immediately signaled to my husband and the children to come in out of the storm. The woman provided us with towels—we were soaked from the brief run from the car to their wide porch—and we dried ourselves right there in the hallway of the old Victorian house.

We learned that our host, Mr. Babcock, was the Postmaster of the town of Berlin. His wife made hot cocoa and sandwiches, but our two youngest children had fallen asleep before she could offer them anything to eat. Mrs. Babcock and I made beds with clean sheets, and the six of us soon moved into three of the bedrooms. The wind blew fiercely all night long, and I thought that, at any minute, the house would collapse around us. Every window and door shook as the wind shrieked through the cracks. Mr. and Mrs. Babcock assured us that it was sturdy, even though it was built of wood. The next morning our Good Samaritans fixed breakfast for us, and showed us their garden. Surprisingly, it was filled with flowers and showed little damage.

The day was sunny and bright with little wind, but most of the roads were still flooded. We gave up on our plans to go to Ocean City, which the news on the radio confirmed was in bad shape, and proceeded instead to Atlantic City. We stayed at a hotel for a week, and the children enjoyed their fancy vacation, eating out every night, as much as my husband and I did. Grateful for their kindness and hospitality, we exchanged gifts and remained in close correspondence with the Babcocks for many years after that.

In 1937, we decided to take the trip we had talked about for years. We were going to Greece! We would be gone for six months—from March until September. We wrote to our families in Bordonia, Sparta, Isari, and Athens, and arranged to stay with each one for a part of our visit. They were overjoyed, as were we, and Bill made plans with his partners and brothers for running the restaurant in his absence. Our cousin Chris and his family agreed to move into our house, since they were in smaller quarters at the time, and we were happy to have them there, rather than leaving our house empty for all that time. Bill ordered a steamer trunk and a wardrobe trunk to be delivered to the house, with our name printed on each. These would hold clothing for all of us that would be needed for the five-day shipboard crossing. Other boxes were shipped directly to Barbara and Soterios's house in Sparta with clothing we would need while in Greece, and with gifts and necessities we thought our families there might find useful. We paid for tickets, obtained our passports, and finished our packing.

So, twenty-two years after having left Bordonia, I returned for the first time, with my husband and four children. For nearly six months, we toured our native land, renewing relationships with both of our families. Ourania, who had never married, had moved into the old family homestead, preferring to live by herself. Leonidas and his family lived in the larger home, which A. D. had bought for him and our mother years earlier. Soterios and Barbara had built a home in Sparta about eight years earlier and had moved back to Greece from New Jersey with their four children. Bill's two sisters and their families, in their village of Isari, were as welcoming as though we had known each other forever. Unfortunately, our plans to return to Greece for an annual summer vacation did not materialize. Relatives informed us of the guns and other weapons prudent householders were stockpiling in the event of war. The situation in Europe was tense and they believed that a major war was imminent. Hitler had marched, unopposed, into the Rhineland. We returned home in September 1937—and our lives were changed forever.

Epilogue

L ife changed forever for Elaine and Bill when they returned from their sojourn in Greece in 1937, not only because of the threat of war, but also because of their personal tragedy. Their eight-year-old son Byron became ill a few days before they embarked for the United States. Bill could not leave Byron in the hospital in Greece with Elaine in attendance, nor did any-one, in the 1930s, consider hiring an airplane to fly Byron across the ocean. So, Bill and Elaine kept to their schedule, hoping for the best, and sailed home. When the ship's physician diagnosed the sickness as malaria, Byron was quarantined during the five days of the passage. Cables sent from shipboard to Bill's family in Washington made it possible for Dr. Repetti, their family phy-sician, to meet the ship when it docked in New York harbor with an ambulance. Byron and his parents were rushed to Children's Hospital in Washington, DC, where spinal meningitis was diag-nosed. The science of medicine had not advanced enough in 1937 to successfully manage this condition, and Byron died two weeks later.

No one knows how we live through such a shock and loss. Elaine and Bill had the support of their brothers and their wives, but they had to resume their own lives with their other three children. They did. In 1946, due to increasing pain in Bill's hip, and his reluctance to have additional surgery, he decided to retire to Hollywood, Florida, where Aris and Mabel were spending the winter months. Bill benefited from the warm climate and a less hectic social life.

Their homes were seven miles apart and Elaine and Mabel joined The Hollywood Garden Club where each received blue ribbons in local and state competitions. Their conversation ranged from the use of palm fronds and sea oats in dried flower arrangements, to the cultivation of orchids and papayas. Mabel had one word—perseverance—to answer the question of how to squeeze the most juice out of small calamondin oranges to supply Aris's specialty—calamondin sours! Aris was the only golfer of the four Bacas brothers, and he continued to play golf almost daily until his death at age 94.

Elaine did not see her parents again after her mother's departure from Lancaster, Ohio, in 1916. She returned to Bordonia and Sparta twice to visit Ourania and Leonidas, as well as Barbara and Soterios and their families. Three of Soterios's children lived in the United States and they, Elaine and Bill's children, and those of her brother Peter and sister Arista visited one another and celebrated weddings and christenings in many states: Florida, Indiana, Kentucky, Maryland, Massachusetts, New Jersey, Ohio, North Carolina, South Carolina, Virginia, Seattle, New York City, and Washington, DC.

Bill and Elaine's children continued close warm relationships with their Bacas cousins, with visits or celebrations in Florida, Illinois, Indiana, Kentucky, Maryland, Massachusetts, Minnesota, Mississippi, New Jersey, North Carolina, South Carolina, Virginia, and Washington, DC.

Bill died in 1980 at the age of 88. Elaine was 97 when she died in 1998. When her sister Ourania, who lived in Bordonia, was told that Elaine had died, she said, "If my sister is gone, there no longer is any reason for me to live." She died one week later. She had claimed for years that their births had been inaccurately recorded, and that, in fact, she was 102, and that Elaine was 100. Their lives had been so different, yet the Fates had blessed each of them with a long and healthy life.

Whereas Elaine had married, had children, traveled widely, used canned and frozen foods, and had the latest conveniences in her home, Ourania had chosen a simple, back-to-nature existence. After her parents died, she moved out of Leonidas's larger house into the original family home, where she fueled her fireplace with brushwood. Leonidas had married and had two children. Ourania remained single; she rarely left the village, ate fresh produce from her kitchen garden and from local fruit trees, raised a donkey and a goat each year, and harvested her own olives. She had learned English during her years spent in Ohio, and was able still to communicate with visitors from the United States. When she was 90, she broke a wrist and a relative took her to Sparta to a nursing home, but independent spirit that she was, as soon as she felt strong enough, she took a bus back to her own house, where she lived the rest of her life.

Afterword

The history of Greece flows from Mount Olympus, over rocky hillsides carpeted with lavender and citrine daisies, past ancient gods, heroes, and thinkers, through the Byzantine Empire, to a tormented, 400-year subjugation by the Ottoman Turks. Shaking off this unendurable bondage, the Greek Uprising of 1821 renewed the spirit of this proud nation. As it struggled to its feet, however, the patriotic fervor that had spurred the courageous fight for independence could not produce the experienced economists and statesmen needed to prevent a devastating depression. Eleni Louvis's *My White Clouds* begins soon after this economic catastrophe, when hundreds of able-bodied men surged onto ships, leaving their starving homeland for The New World.

Faster ships and blighted grapevines were two of the major reasons for this emigration. Before the 1850s, transatlantic travel was reserved for the wealthy, and passengers endured several grueling weeks on the open sea. The arrival of steamships that disembarked from Liverpool, England, and arrived in New York City in only ten days transformed the industry, and it was not long before steerage class, affordable even by the poor, was introduced. Scores of young men who had toiled for years for enough drachmas could now afford passage. They filled the dank, dark areas near the ships' engine rooms to follow their dreams.

Southern Greece, the Peloponnesus, provided its share of men to the exodus. The destruction, in 1862, of the vineyards of France by the *phylloxera*, a type of beetle, was a leading cause.

The closest, cheapest replacement for the stricken French wine producers were the black currants grown in this region. Greek farmers rejoiced at their new prosperity, and many destroyed their wine-producing grapevines to make room for the fast-growing, hardy plant that produced the profitable black currant.

Within the next two decades, however, in the late 1870s, the French had succeeded in planting vines resistant to the scourge and no longer were dependent on currants from Greece. Without warning, the French government levied heavy tariffs on the importation of Greek currants, sending the stunned farmers into bankruptcy. This overwhelmed southern Greece, forcing many impoverished young men to set sail for America.

Most of Eleni's brothers had left Bordonia by the age of nine, either to work at menial jobs in Sparta or to set sail for America. The following accounts are in the words of Eleni's husband Bill and one of her brothers, Peter.

Bill Bacas, Eleni's Husband

In *My White Clouds* Eleni Louvis recounted how she had met Bill when he was a young man. Bill, my father, told occasional stories about his life as a boy, but I could not picture it. How did he grow up in a remote village, leave home, go to a place where everything was written in an alphabet that differed from the Greek, and become an American?

Numerous relatives and acquaintances from Greece had followed similar paths, but each story was unique. Whether they arrived at Ellis Island from sophisticated Attica and Asia Minor, or the craggy Peloponnesus, or northern Salonika, or the cosmopolitan islands of Andros, Santorini, or Cyprus, they spoke the same language, worshipped in the same church, and inhabited the early twentieth century in the United States in his or her own fashion.

When I presented a list of questions to my father, his response was, "Why do you want to bring up the past?" Yet as an honest, practical man, he felt obligated to reveal both his youthful achievements and his transgressions. He did—as many as he felt were appropriate—in the following response to my inquiries that he wrote down in 1953.

Bill Bacas
(1892–1980)

Kathe embodio yia to kalo.
Look upon every obstacle as good.
                    — SOLON, 600 BC

Our village is not far from the ruins of ancient Lykosoura, described by the second-century traveler Pausanias as the oldest capital of Greece. It was here that Lykaios, the son of the King of ancient Arkadia, established the Lykaion Games that predated the Panathenaic Games (566 BC) in Athens. Attesting to the antiquity of the area, legend had it that a sacred deer, weakened by old age, lived in Lykosoura when Pausanias visited. A collar around its neck had the inscription: "I was a fawn when captured at the time Agamemnon left for Troy." When one is a boy, legends are not questioned.

I was born in 1892 in the village of Isari, located on the northeastern slope of Mount Tetragion in the state of Arcadia. Visitors to Isari must find their way from the valley through the town of Megalopolis and up a winding road until they see a few terra cotta roofs rising above them. As the travelers continue on the crumbling asphalt road, they soon pass the first of the white-washed houses, and in a few minutes, negotiate another curve of the hillside that positions them above these first homes and leads into the courtyard of the Church of Saint Nicholas, the heart of the village. Formerly a threshing floor, paved with flat stones, this area has been expanded and remains the only level space in the town. It serves as the central square on market days and as a stage for dancing during festivals and weddings. Across from the square are two *caffenia,* coffee shops, which in their heyday served as taverns and general stores as well. The rooms above the *caffenia* are the administrative offices for both Isari and for the *demos,* the county, of which Isari is a part. The police department, which consists of one or perhaps two officers of the law, also is located here.

My grandparents lived through the war of Greek independence from the Ottomans (1821–1829.) By the time my father, Harralambos, was born, Greece was struggling with the problems of a developing nation. An inexperienced, newly-formed central government tried to lead the country forward as it simultaneously coped with fiercely opinionated guerilla captains, who had been heroic leaders, and with the machinations of the powerful leaders of Britain, France, Germany, and Russia.

My parents had nine children—six boys and three girls—but one of the girls and two of the boys did not survive childhood. When I was six, our household included six children, our father's mother, whom we called *yiayia*, grandmother, and our father's youngest brother Louis, who was nineteen. Louis married that year and moved into a small house near ours; a year and a half later he and his wife had a little girl, *Vasiliki*, Bessie.

Yiayia Eleni was a wonderful person. She took over our care and care of the house when mother and father left at dawn to work in the wheat fields or the cornfields. For breakfast, she prepared *trahanas*, a dried pasta mixture cooked as a porridge that resembled oatmeal. Sometimes she made omelets for lunch or cheese and home-baked black bread. *Yiayia* always had dinner ready in the evening when my parents returned; sometimes this was a savory vegetable stew of seasonal squash, tomatoes, eggplant, beans, and onions or *trahanas*. This staple pasta was served in many ways—cooked with tomatoes or other vegetables, or with cheese. We knew the day was special if we had a small portion of chicken or ham or macaroni and *mizithra*, a white goat cheese, grated over it. There always was plenty of sauce in these dishes, so that we could dunk pieces of dark bread into our bowls and fill up on the sauce.

Yiayia always wore a black *fostanee,* the traditional ankle-length skirt over several underskirts, according to the season, worn with a long-sleeved, high-necked sweater, and a black *mantili* covering her hair. For special occasions, she dressed in a *yelekaki,* an embroidered vest of black velvet, and a silk *mantili*. When she grew older she could not walk very far; nevertheless, she refused to use a cane. I had already left the village when she died in her late seventies.

Our grandmother was the best babysitter a child could have. She entranced us for hours with her stories about ancient Greek heroes and princes and princesses from exotic lands. Among my favorite stories were those about *Pithecanthropus*, a creature who lived in the jungles of Africa with the apes. *Pithecanthropus* means "ape-man" in Greek. *Yiayia* described how he was protected by the monkeys, how he killed man-eating snakes, how he swung from one tree to another on vines. She also described how *Pithecanthropus* had saved a beautiful girl from men who were exploiting the resources of the jungle, and that he eventually married the girl he had saved.

Years later in America, when I first read about Tarzan in the "funny papers"—as comic strips were called then—I was surprised at the similarity to my grandmother's stories. Edgar Rice Burroughs, the creator of Tarzan, published his first story, "Tarzan of the Apes" in 1912, twelve years after I had heard my grandmother's tales. In 1891, the Dutch physician, Dr. Eugene Dubois, discovered the fossil remains of the first prehistoric man whom he designated *Pithecanthropus erectus*, an ape-like creature who walked upright—also known as Java Man. Excitement over this discovery of a prehistoric man living with the apes in the jungles of Java was worldwide and certainly could have spread to our village.

The school I attended was about 100 yards from our house—if we slid down a steep hill behind our house. It was in this schoolyard that my brothers and I played "kick the stone," tag, and other games requiring level ground. Sometimes we played in the *plateia,* the village square, but space there was limited and we were chased away when our shouts disturbed the discussions of the men seated at the *caffenia.* Growing along one wall of the school were bushes called *koumaries,* which in the hot, dry climate bore sweet berries that looked like large strawberries. We ate the berries, and played in the dusty area between the bushes where little snakes nested. They were as thin as pencils and about twelve inches long. We would hold races with them, as we teased and prodded them with small sticks.

Another game was *voli,* marbles. This was played with a sharp-edged stone, which we hurled against the opponent's pile of stones to scatter and capture one of his smooth pebbles.

In the 1880s, a wealthy man named *Siyiros* donated funds to have new public schools built in every village in Greece. His philanthropic deed was similar in scope to Andrew Carnegie's establishment in the 1920s of free public libraries throughout the United States.

Our old school then became Isari's town hall and the magistrate's court for the 14 other hamlets in the *demos* of Lykosoura.

Once, when I was eight, my family was attending a festival at an *aloni,* a threshing floor on a hillside near another village. Mother decided that we needed another blanket to sit on while we ate, and sent me home to get one. It was a long walk in the hot sun, and by the time I got to the cool cellar where the trunk with the blankets was stored, I sat down and rested. Across from the trunk were three barrels of wine. They were marked 800, 500, and 200, but I did not know what these figures represented. I was very thirsty from my walk, and rather than go out again to the nearest village fountain, some distance away, I placed my mouth under the faucet of the 200 keg, and drank some of the semisweet wine. It was the one we boys like best. Before I knew it, I had drunk more than I could handle, and curled up and fell asleep on the floor of the wine cellar. Mother became alarmed at my long absence, and the search party was quite relieved to find me at home, sleeping peacefully.

The elementary school had six grades, which were roughly the equivalent of first grade through eighth grade in the United

States. After graduation from the village school, we were eligible to enter the *gymnasio*, the high school, for four years. It was located in the town of *Andritsena*, but neither I nor any of my brothers, nor countless other youths of that era who had left home to find work went beyond the third grade.

Small chapels, called *erimoklisia* can be found in every hamlet in Greece. There were twelve in the vicinity of Isari alone. Two were dedicated to Saint Nicholas, and two services were held—one in the spring and the other in the fall. Our main village church was also dedicated to *Ayios Nikolas*, and on December 6, the traditional date of his birth, a service was held there.

At night, there was nothing to do but talk for awhile or go to bed. Story-telling and narrative folk songs were favorite forms of entertainment. More people could tell stories than could sing, so we heard many wondrous tales. Stories of supernatural events that had occurred close to home were the spookiest, and captured our imaginations, and upset the entire village for weeks.

Once a farmer, coming home late, saw a shadowy figure sitting on a wall near the freshwater spring next to the isolated chapel of Saint Nicholas, and called out "*yiasou!*" in greeting. The figure neither turned around nor spoke. The man dashed home and breathlessly told his wife that he had seen Saint Nicholas himself, with a cane in his hand, seated near the chapel. His wife passed the news on to her neighbors; by the next day, everybody in town was talking about the apparition. It soon was established that Saint Nicholas did not use a cane, and that the farmer had not seen the saint, but rather the devil. A few nights later, another farmer came home later than usual; passing the Saint Nicholas spring, he too saw a figure exactly as had been described by his neighbor. Without a doubt, it was the devil himself. He had bushy eyebrows, a goatee, and large, pointed ears.

The village went crazy with fear; and for almost a week no one ventured out at night unless they had to, and then, only in a group and carrying guns. "We don't know how to defend ourselves from the devil, but we'll use the weapons we have," they would reply upon being asked about the effectiveness of a hunting weapon on the devil. A month passed, and one night, four farmers were returning from their fields, having joined together to take the route past the chapel. They approached the spring carefully; the man in the lead stopped short and cried, "There he is!" Seated on the wall, just as the first two men had reported, was the devil himself! "Shoot him! Don't dally!" Before the shooter could stop shivering from fright to take aim, the apparition spoke, "Hello there, fellows!"

Upon closer examination, and to their embarrassment, the "devil" was an elderly hermit who periodically migrated to the area. He had not answered the farmers who had greeted him weeks earlier because his back had been turned to them, and he was hard of hearing, especially near the spring, whose waters splashed noisily. What lent a sinister aspect to his appearance were the shadows of tree branches that hung over the old man and ignited the imaginations of the onlookers

During the wheat harvest in August, before my eighth birthday, which was on November 28 (Saint Katherine's Day), tragedy struck our family. Father was in the army fighting the Turks on our northern borders. The last sheaves of wheat were lying on the *aloni,* threshing stones, and my mother, my older sister Tasia, and our young aunt (Uncle Louis' wife), had ridden to the farm, all on horseback, to bring in the wheat sheaves before the rain, which was threatening in the distance, began to fall. They were about an hour by horseback from the village. Our baby cousin Bessie was six months old; her mother had left her in the care of our grandmother, who also was watching me and the other young children. The men and older boys were out in the fields, building a stone wall. These stone structures crisscrossed the hilly terrain of the Peloponnesus; and while their main purpose was to mark boundaries, they also prevented the soil from washing down into the gullies during heavy rainstorms.

The women at the threshing floor had hitched their three horses to a pole in the center of the *aloni,* and the animals were slowly walking around it, stomping on the sheaves. When the dark clouds rolled in, and the storm was upon them, the women piled the wheat into a heap, so that only the topmost sheaves would get wet. By then, the women were soaked, and with loud thunder crashing overhead, they herded the horses together, and ran to a nearby tree for temporary protection from the rain.

At home, I remember standing on the porch with my little brothers and sister and my grandmother, watching the rain drench the valley below. A brilliant flash of lightning lit the sky and a sudden boom of thunder startled us. My grandmother exclaimed, "*Theh, mou!* My Lord! Something terrible is going to happen to someone in our family!" Two hours later, the limp body of my young aunt was carried home; she had struck by lightning. The force of the lightning bolt had knocked my mother and sister onto the soft earth near the horses, but my aunt had fallen onto the stone threshing floor. The bolt had struck her forehead; it was as though a bullet had made a hole; her body was unmarked otherwise. Her death was very sad for all of us, and left Uncle Louis inconsolable. Their baby Bessie, was like another sister to us.

I left home at the age of nine. Before that, I had explored with my brothers and cousins all of the byways in our neighborhood. A few times, we hiked over the hills to the site of ancient Lykosoura which we were told had been the capital of ancient Greece and the site of athletic games (similar to the Olympics) of long ago. The ancient sacred precinct had been deserted for as long as anyone could remember, and to us this overgrown field with broken pieces of statues and columns looked like a dump. When we had played there as boys it was before the archaeologists had come to admire and collect the pieces of ancient statuary and sculpture to be displayed and preserved in the small museum of Lykosoura. (They took the more valuable items to the National Archaeological Museum in Athens.) These pieces were not the treasures they should have been to us, as we chased one another around the old amphitheater, and played hide and seek behind toppled temples.

Territorial disputes between Greece and Turkey had been renewed; this was the reason my father had joined the Greek army. When his term of service was up, in 1898, he and some of his relatives boarded a steamship sailing to America to improve the family's fortunes. In 1886 George Westinghouse had founded the company that bore his name, and the men from our village went to work at the Westinghouse plant in East Liberty, Pennsylvania. Father worked there for two years but his lungs were affected by inhaling zinc particles, and he had to return home.

In 1902, he attempted to journey overseas once more. This time he joined his cousins, Andrew and Nick Dracos, in Washington, DC. They operated a hat cleaning business, a profitable establishment. The solvents used—naphtha or carbon tetrachloride—were cheap and useful, but the fumes were disastrous for my father's already weakened lungs, and he had to return home—a sick man. On his return, he called for his two eldest sons, Angelos, who was 13 and me (I was ten) to his side and explained that he no longer would be able to work, and that he would have to depend on the two of us to support the family. This meant that we had to go to Athens and send whatever we earned back home. Our household included our parents, paternal grandmother, two sisters, two younger brothers, and Uncle Louis' daughter, Bessie, who was now four. Before we left home, my dear mother cautioned us to be mindful of three things: keep ourselves from bad women; be honest and sincere; and be good Christians. My grandmother counseled that a good reputation is better than all the money in the world. Well, their advice came in very handy in later years.

In Athens, we worked long hours, sweeping floors, doing odd jobs—anything honorable— to make a living for ourselves and the family we had left behind. Really, Athens was like a dream that passed me without my realizing it. When I think back on those days, it is as though they had happened to someone else—and not to me.

I was frightened and deeply troubled at having to leave my family to work in this big city. Fortunately, I had my brother for company, and we remained close friends—and with our younger brothers as well—for the rest of our lives. A relative found us a room with two cots just behind the Metropoleos Cathedral. We went to work for the Apostolakos Hadzithopoulos general store and coffee shop. We started out sweeping the store; after a while, we were given more responsibility: to sell water that was stored in a large barrel in the store. Glasses were rinsed in the water trough on the street and used for the next customer. Each boy was on duty at the barrel for several hours each day.

We gave all the money—that is, the tips we were given—to the owners; out of this money they paid us. It was not much, but when I look back, I believe that we had been fairly paid and had not been exploited. Times were hard for everyone, and these people, Apostolakos and Hadzithopoulos were working to make a living and, at the same time, were providing work for us.

The Byzantine Emperor Theodosius had banned the ancient Olympic Games in 308 AD because athletic and artistic competitions had degenerated into contests to win gold rather than to be honored for high achievement with a laurel wreath. Legendary Olympia fell into ruin, and earthquakes and floods soon submerged memories of the historic precinct. In 1826, nearly fifteen centuries later, the ancient sites of Olympia were slowly uncovered through archaeological excavations. With a resurgence of interest in the ancient world, Greece reinstated the competitions and built a new Olympic Stadium in Athens in 1896 for the revival of the Olympic Games that year. This stadium is considered one of the best in the world; it is built entirely of white marble, including the seating, columns, and walkways.

In 1904, with the 100th anniversary of the Louisiana Purchase promising to be an international attraction, the committee decided to hold the Olympic Games in St. Louis, Missouri. Greece, not wanting four years to pass without the Olympics, now that they had been reinstated, decided to hold the Panhellenic Games in the Athens Stadium. Celebrities and wealthy, beautifully dressed people traveled from the far corners of the earth. For seven days, I worked at the Athens Stadium, selling *loukoumi*, Turkish paste, and water for the equivalent of 25 cents. As I moved around the stadium selling my wares, I was able to watch some of the contests and was thrilled by the track-and-field events. Among the dignitaries who came that year, the most impressive was King Edward of England, a short man with a full beard. He was the first reigning monarch of Great Britain to visit Greece, so it was a splendid occasion, and Athens was in its glory that year.

In 1905, when I was twelve, my brother Angelos and I brought our father, who was by now very ill, to the best hospital in Greece, Evangelismos in Athens, to see if there was a cure. The doctors said there was not much that could be done, but prescribed medication to relieve his symptoms. Father returned to the village, where he died a year later. Angelos and I had to borrow from moneylenders to pay father's hospital bills and the doctors. We were twelve and sixteen years old, and it took us nine years, throughout our teens and young adulthood, to pay our creditors the enormous sums of interest they had charged. However, we considered this debt a sacred trust, and so my brothers and I honored our vow and paid it off.

My father's death was one of the saddest moments of my life. I can remember crying for the first time since I had left home three years earlier. Angelos and I could not even return to the village for the funeral; we owed so much money for father's medical care that we could not afford to leave our jobs for even one day. I had always looked up to my father with admiration and respect, and his death was a great loss to me and our family.

Our younger brother Aristomenes became so upset at father's death (and even more so at mother's weeping) that he begged her to let him join Angelos and me in Athens to help the family. He was only eight years old, so mother refused. However, when he turned nine, he was so insistent that she sent Angelos word that Aris was on his way to Athens to join us. Aris was a bright, energetic boy, and was so excited to be on a train for the first time that he did not want to miss a thing, so he spent the trip running up and down the corridor—which runs alongside the compartments—looking out of the windows. Then, he found out that he could see even more by dashing from one side of the train to the other. Each compartment had a door with a window, and opened onto the station platform. The doors were locked while the train was in motion. Aris ran from this window to the window in the corridor—back and forth. Just after the train stopped at Leontari, and started up again, Aris raced from the corridor into the compartment to look out of the window. He landed against it with all his might. The door must have been left unlatched, because it opened instantly, and he fell down a terrifyingly steep hillside. Someone must have see what happened, and pulled the emergency cord; the train came to a screeching halt. Aris was bloodied head to toe because where he had fallen was so rocky. It was a miracle, witnesses claimed, that he was still alive. In later years, he marveled at his narrow escape. He was not allowed to continue his journey to Athens, and was put on a train home to mother. Mother blamed herself that she had let her young son travel alone to nearly fall to his death. But my brother was not to be restrained for long. As soon as he had healed, Aris once again left home for Athens. Angelos and I had worked for the two partners, Apostolakos & Hadzithopoulos for a year; and now our younger brother joined us.

A few months later, we decided that Angelos would go to America. We were not making enough money to help the family; we could not even pay the principal of our father's medical ills. The cheapest passage was on a steamship to Canada; Angelos made the journey with Uncle Louis on a freighter that took two and a half months to reach Montreal. By the time they arrived Uncle Louis had contracted an eye infection and was not allowed to enter Canada. He was sent back to Greece and did not come to America for another three years. A week after landing in Montreal, Angelos arrived in Washington, DC, where our Uncle Andrew owned The Dairy Lunch, a popular lunchroom for white collar businessmen. In 1907, the year that Angelos left for America, I was 13 and Aris was 10.

Meanwhile, Aris and I kept our eyes open for better work opportunities in Athens; we found jobs with the Sardis Carpet Shop. When someone bought a carpet, the drivers of the small, horse-drawn wagon had to have a helper to hold the tape to measure the room and—depending on the size of the carpet—to carry the carpet. The younger boys also swept the floors, and all of us shined shoes. Each of us was assigned a shoeshine stand on a different corner of downtown Athens. We were kept busy at that trade until one of the owners of the carpet shop needed an errand boy and summoned one of the eight or nine boys they employed. If it was very heavy work—like moving a piano—the owners had to do it themselves, with the help of the bigger boys, who were 15 or older. We had to be called upon three or four times a day to stay in the employ of the carpet shop. Next, we joined a band of young boys who worked for the Argyrakos Brothers, who owned department stores and sold fabric by the yard. Eight boys worked for them. Four of us slept in one partner's house, and the other four slept in the other partner's house—four to a room. We were there only to sleep in a spare back room. I don't recall whether we slept on mats or on the floor; we were always so tired that we fell asleep immediately. Our young lives were miserable, but we persisted, knowing that we were helping our family survive.

The partners' wives saw to it that every Saturday we took baths in a tub with soap and water and changed into clean clothing. Our clothes were handed down from one boy to another. On days that we made extra money from tips, we took hot showers in the public baths for ten *lepta*, about one penny. As with the carpet shop, each boy had to have three or four jobs a day to survive. Extra money was used to buy food, since we were hungry all the time, so there was very little money to send home. Boys who worked in Athens were called *rogiasmena*, which means rogues.

Breakfast consisted of a piece of bread in the morning and maybe some watery oatmeal. We never had milk to drink unless we were given a tip before lunchtime. Then, we could slip away to a milk bar and have milk and *loukoumathes*, round puffs of fried dough with honey and cinnamon or anything that we could eat fast, so that our bosses did not catch us eating. If we made no tips by lunchtime, we went hungry. For dinner, one of the partners' wives cooked us bean soup and bread; once in a while, they made lamb stew or fish stew.

In 1907, Prince George of Greece married Marie Bonaparte of France, one of the richest women in Europe. Her maternal grandfather had been a waiter who went on to found Monte Carlo's gambling resort. Her paternal great-grandfather was Napoleon's brother, Lucien. Prince George was very handsome. Well, I helped move their luggage—many boxes and gifts from a ship filled with their possessions, including dozens of steamer trunks. We were 15 boys and men who took that stuff from Piraeus (the port of Athens) in trucks to their mansion on the outskirts of Athens. It took us a full day.

We also worked for milliners. In those days no one went out without a hat. Women's hats were made in small factories run by women who had 15 to 25 girls working long hours. These shops usually were on the second and third floors of commercial buildings. When customers sent word, the milliner took 10 to 20 hats to their homes, so the clients could try them on in comfort. This was the chance that all milliners took—hoping to sell one or more hats.

As a carrier, I accompanied the owner of the hat shop. If she made a sale, she gave me the equivalent of fifty cents or one dollar, depending on how long the visit had taken. Sometimes, it took four to five hours for a woman to decide on a hat. In those days, one dollar was the equivalent of about five *drachmas*.

We did not have much time off, but once in a while, a group of boys took the train to Phaleron Bay to go swimming and play on the beach, which consisted of small white pebbles—smooth like marbles. One holiday that we always had off was *kathari deutera*, Clean Monday, the first day of Lent, which was celebrated by family outings. Since the Acropolis was a plateau, and not the popular tourist attraction it is now, we would form teams against other boys and play war games—*petropolemos*, which consisted of throwing rocks at each other—or *sphentones,* a violent game using slingshots—two strips of elastic with the wider part in the middle to hold the stone. We country boys would fight the "city slickers" for hours until one group started to run to the city. As far as I can remember, we country boys won every time. I have a scar on my forehead from one of these contests.

I was 15 when Angelos wrote to me inviting me to join him in America. This had always been my dream—that someday I would live in America. After direct steamship service from Athens to New York City was established in 1902, emigration to America increased rapidly. Posters with departure dates and offers of jobs with high wages were everywhere. All of us had memorized the fare—200 *drachmas*—190 *drachmas* for passage and 10 *drachmas* for insurance; this would be about forty dollars today (1953). The insurance covered our return passage, if we were refused entry at Ellis Island. I went home to Isari for a few days to say goodbye to my mother, my youngest brother John, and my sisters Tasia and Olga.

With other young men, I journeyed to the port at Patras to take the steamship, *Argentina* to New York. I was almost 16, but not very tall. There, a heartless inspector shook his head when I stood under a stick that measured my height. "Too short," he declared, and denied me and one of my companions passage. Later, I learned that too many young boys were leaving Greece, and the government feared that if war came in a few years, no young men would be left to be called into military service. Unwilling to trust the youth's documents or his declaration of age, the inspectors had set up a measuring rod. If a boy was below the mark, he remained in Greece in reserve for the country's future armed forces.

Well, I wept buckets. I cried so hard I felt that I had aged five years in five minutes. The next morning, I returned home to Isari. My family was surprised to see me again. Having recovered from the shock of having been sent home, I refused to give up.

A few days later, I arrived in Athens, and with the help of an uncle, who was a magistrate there, the next day I was on the ship *Patris,* which was owned by Ethnicon, Inc. The ocean was kind of rough, and I could not keep any food in my stomach. The bunks were stacked three beds high in a large, airless room, and at night I lay in my bunk. During the day, I sat on the deck to keep from being too seasick. Someone announced that we were nearing the harbor of New York City; soon we heard that we would arrive that evening. The men who had gone before us had advised us to carry clean clothes, packed separately, so they would not become infested with fleas or other vermin from being in close quarters with so many people. Another fellow and I put on our clean clothes, and threw the old clothes into the ocean. Well, about eight that evening, it was announced that we would not disembark until the next morning.

So, instead of going back to the crowded cabin, my friend and I slept in a lifeboat covered with canvas. In the early morning, one of the guards found us; we must have been snoring. He ordered us back down to our cabin. We explained to him that we were wearing the only clean clothes that we had, so he left us alone.

Twelve days after leaving Piraeus, I saw the Statue of Liberty, the most wonderful sight of my life. Soon after our arrival, they took us to Ellis Island (or *Castlegarri* as it was called by many Greeks) for medical inspection. After a few hours, they put a tag on me that indicated I was to go to Washington, DC. I did not understand what they were saying as they pointed the way—to go downstairs, all alone. Tears came to my eyes because I thought they were sending me back to Greece. As I went down the stairs crying, someone asked me in a mix of Greek and English, "What'sthematter?" "They are sending me back." He answered, "My boy, you are going to Washington—not back to the boat."

A woman was selling a box lunch for 50 cents: two oranges, a sandwich, two bananas, some nuts, and cake. By the time I boarded the train for Washington, I had eaten everything in the box. I had been so hungry!

The next day, I arrived in Washington. It was June 1, 1909. I was 16—the happiest young man in the whole world—as I stepped off the train in Union Station for the first time. Since there was no one to meet me, I decided to walk around the area, hoping that I would find someone I knew. My uncle, Andrew Dracos' lunchroom was nearby, but I had no idea where. By chance, he was out on an errand and he saw me. He took me home to stay with him for a few days. In the narrow streets of Athens, I often hailed a brother or cousin as we passed each other,so it did not seem strange to me that I could run into a relative if I strolled around in the small southern town that was Washington, DC in 1909. Uncle Andrew took me to visit his brothers and other relatives, and then I boarded the train to Richmond, Virginia, to join Angelos.

For the next two years, Angelos and I ran a shoe shine stand; we hired other boys to work for us. We also sold chestnuts on the street. We bought large bags for one dollar each, and divided the contents, to make a profit of six dollars. We did anything we could do to make an honest living, but this kind of life did not appeal to me.

In 1911, we turned the shoeshine business over to our father's brother, Uncle Louis, and returned to Washington to work in the restaurants of relatives. Two years later, when a store came up for lease across from the Marine barracks in South East (as the area near the Navy Yard was called), Angelos and I opened our first lunchroom, The Model Lunch. Every morning at 9:01, the US Marine Band woke me up. For several years we worked 15-hour days to pay off our father's medical bills, and to provide our two sisters, Tasia and Olga, with proper dowries.

I attended night school to learn English, but after several classes, I gave it up. I had to travel a distance and transfer street cars three times to get to school. After working all day, I decided I would learn what I could on my own. Some of our restaurant customers would correct me whenever I made mistakes; at night, I read the newspapers and wrote down my own comments, using a Greek-English dictionary that I had bought in New York to translate. The marines from the barracks started to come to our place after playing in the band each morning; they teased me and played jokes on me. There were three troublemakers: an Irish-man, a German, and an Italian; at first I would get so mad that I wanted to put them out of the store. One of their jokes was to take a donut in one hand, and pretend to hit the table with it, so that it made a noise. With his other hand, the jokester knocked a spoon underneath the table at the same time and said, "Boy, this donut is really stale, Bill." Country boy that I was, it took me a while to catch on. But, after a while, we began to understand one another. I had started reading a history of the United States, so every morning I quoted to them from something that I had read. "Believe me, George Washington was some student," I said, and then tell them what I had learned from my reading the night before. We began to like each other, and I soon appreciated their sense of humor as I started to catch on to their jokes. We remained friends for many years.

When we opened The Model Lunch in Washington in 1913, I worked with Angelos. Then, after a few months, Aris came with our friend, George King, and we all worked hard together. Then, Uncle Louis came from Richmond, Virginia, and we had a fine team for a few years and we were a happy lot.

Since Angelos and I wanted our restaurant to succeed, and could not take time to go to school, we decided that Aris would be the educated brother. He graduated from Emerson Institute, and then enrolled at George Washington University to study electrical engineering.

After working so hard for four years, I noticed that Angelos was leaving the store in my hands more than ever, and that he was taking hours off to play pool and to participate in a bowling league. I got mad at him, and told him that if he did not work, I would quit. A few months later I did quit and left all of my inter-est in the business to him. I had only one hundred dollars with me. By this time, we had paid off our father's debts; and Tasia had married after we sent her a dowry. I finally was free of financial obligations and could go my own way.

I decided to go to Atlantic City for my first vacation. I had the time of my life—swimming during the day and dancing until

3 a.m. for six days. When I ran out of money, I went to work as a waiter, or whatever job was available, at night clubs for a few days. Then I took the train to Philadelphia. Someone had given me the name of a Greek who owned a restaurant there, so I applied for a job. Since I expressed myself more fluently in Greek than in English, I spoke to him in Greek. He lashed out at me in his broken English. "Dawn't spik to me in a foreign language, boy!" He practically booted me out of his place. I never forgot this experience. He had not given me a chance. I too believed that we should speak the tongue of the country that had given us so much, but he was talking to a young man down on his luck.

Childs Restaurant in Philadelphia hired me a few days later, and they liked me well enough that, after a week, they sent me— all expenses paid—to Norfolk, Virginia, where they had a busier restaurant. I was there two weeks when I received a telegram from Angelos and a second telegram from Uncle Dracos to return and take over The Busy Bee, their latest venture. So, after only three weeks of working for others I went back to Washington, where I owned and managed several restaurants with my brothers until I retired in 1945.

When the United States entered World War I in 1917, Angelos and I were drafted into the US Army. I was managing The Busy Bee and left my cousin, Steve Chumbris as manager. For two years, he had served as a volunteer from the US Army in Greece during its war with Turkey. He chose not to reenlist and remained a civilian. Our youngest brother John had arrived a year earlier and was now 17. He ran my store The Busy Bee with Steve while I was away, and Uncle Dracos and his wife Fofo ran The Model Lunch while Angelos was in the army.

While I was training at Fort Niagara, I invited Aris to come and spend a week at beautiful Lake Ontario and visit Niagara Falls. When his term at George Washington University was over he came to visit. It was June, and Aris was wearing a lightweight suit that was fine for Washington, but not for the cold weather that would greet him in upper New York State. Arriving by train, he took the streetcar to the Fort that was a few miles away, and happened to sit next to Fred, the bugler in our unit. Noticing that my brother was shivering with cold, he asked Aris where he was going, and when Aris told him he was visiting his brother Bill, Fred informed him that Bill was his best friend. He took off his coat, and gave it to Aris, and brought him directly to our camp. My brother had a fine time for a week. I saw that he got some warm clothes. When I was busy, the other soldiers took him out. A few weeks after he returned to Washington, he decided to defer his next semester of college and join the Marines, and he was sent to Paris Island, South Carolina, for training.

At the end of June 1918, my unit was due to return to camp in New Jersey. I had received a letter from Steve, who was managing my store, asking me to come to Washington to be his best man. He was planning to marry Bertha, one of our fine waitresses. When I asked my captain for leave, he told me, "We are at war. It is impossible. However, when we arrive in New Jersey, you may have a 48-hour leave." I telegraphed Steve and asked him to wait a week, or to choose someone else as my proxy, and I would pay the expenses. He replied that he and Bertha wanted no one else but me as their *koumbaros*, best man, and they would wait. A week later, I took my 48-hour leave and was at the wedding of two fine people.

By early 1919, my brothers and I had returned to Washington, and a year later, we opened a larger restaurant in a building we had bought across the street from the main gate of the Navy Yard.

Peter Louvis, Eleni's Brother
(1892–1979)

Anthropos agrammatos
xilo apelekito.
An illiterate person is like an
uncarved piece of wood.
— GREEK PROVERB

Peter Louvis relates incidents from his childhood in a village in Greece; as a boy of twelve trying to earn a living in New York City or Brighton Beach; and as a successful business owner in New Jersey. He was my uncle, one of the brothers of Eleni Louvis Bacas. On a visit to my home in Murray Hill, NJ, in April 1969, he recalled these events.

———

At our farm in the country, called the Lefko, my father set up a shelter where he served ouzo, a liquor flavored with anise, and other simple refreshments to travelers from Sparta who were passing through the area. On this property grew a large fig tree that bore white figs as big as oranges. My brothers and I could hardly wait for them to ripen.

As a boy of eight, while harvesting olives with mother, I asked her what we would be paid for our labor. Her reply: one tenth of what we had gathered. When I heard this, I refused to help any more; she had to agree that the sum was too little for bending over all day to pick up the olives that had fallen to the ground. So both of us quit. I turned to gathering olives from trees in remote areas. Even though they were abandoned trees, they were the property of others, and I had no right to these olives. One day I climbed up an olive tree bearing huge, choice olives. I had just filled the sack I was holding in my hands when below me appeared the furious owner. He was brandishing a machete—a sharp, curved knife used for pruning thick tree limbs—and he ordered me to get down at once. I was so frightened, I dropped the sack of olives; it fell on his head and knocked him down. I ran home as fast as I could, as he tried to extricate himself from the fall. Later, he was the man who lent my father the money to pay my fare on the ship that took me to America.

One day in school, the teacher was talking about God. I asked, "Have you ever seen Him?" The teacher was a relative, but this did not help me; without a word he slapped me so hard that I twirled around twice and then ran out of the room. As I dashed into the road, I ran into another relative, who when he learned from the other students what had happened, was instrumental in having the teacher removed from his position for striking me.

When I left home at age 12—as did many boys at the time—to sail to America, I thought that all bodies of water were like our river Eurotas. I thought you could look across the ocean and see the other side. On my arrival at the port of Patras on the Ionian Sea, I looked out at a vast plain without a mountain in sight, and commented to my companion how impressed I was by the vista of this beautiful valley.

"Valley, nothing," he said. "What you are looking at is water! This is the sea, and you and I will be on it, in a ship sailing to America." I was so panic-stricken at the sight of so much water that I turned around to return home. Despite my fears, I was persuaded to board the ship, and made it safely across the Atlantic Ocean, eager to find in New York City the streets that I had been told were lined with gold. I found gold—but not then, and not in New York's streets. It took me years of hard, sometimes unpleasant work, to achieve reasonable success and happiness—true gold in my estimation.

As soon as I arrived in New York, I went to work in a store, and when I was done, the manager offered to let me sleep in a room down the street until his shift was over. The pillow was soiled and I turned it over to sleep on the 'clean' side. When I did so, I saw in the dim, flickering light of the gas lamp a large black mass in the middle of the pillow which seemed to be liquid ink, since it moved when I disturbed it. When I looked more closely, I saw that the "ink" actually was a mass of bugs. I had never seen bedbugs before, but I had heard of them. I jumped out of the bed, ran out the back door, and did not work for that man again.

I walked down a street until I recognized the name on a tavern as belonging to someone who had been recommended to me. I told the owner my story, and the man said, "Go up these steps to the room in back." I did as I was told—quite weary by now—and found myself in a room where ten women of assorted ages and sizes, wearing very little clothing, were lounging. They were street walkers who walked up and down Broadway. The streets were thick with them. They started to tease me. When one of them sidled up to me, asking, "Where have you been all my life?" I retreated. As I ran down the stairs, the owner saw me, and asked what was the problem? I explained, and the man led me to an empty room, where I was able to sleep undisturbed.

During Prohibition, in the 1920s, when alcoholic beverages could not be legally imported or sold, I visited one of my brothers in Schenectady, NY. He had found work with a well-educated crook who imported whiskey from England, and then shipped it south to a crony. This illicit commerce made him very wealthy. One evening, he invited my brother and me, and some other workers to his fine house. I was a poor country boy, and careless, and sat on his sofa with my feet tucked up under me. When our host noticed this, he asked, "Is that any way to sit?" I was so embarrassed to have been called down in front of the others, that I got up and left. I had 53 cents in my pocket, and took a boat back to New York City; the fare was 50 cents. At midnight, passengers either rented a cabin or slept in a large dormitory with bunk beds provided with clean sheets. I preferred sitting in the fresh air on a deck chair, and spent several hours running from one side to the other side of the ship to avoid the stewards. They finally caught me and directed me to the dormitory room. I clung to the deck chair, repeating the word "good"and indicating that I wanted to stay on deck. This was not allowed, so I had to sleep in a bunk the rest of the night.

When I arrived in New York the next morning, I saw a trolley with a sign that I could not read. I did understand "three cents," which was all I had in my pocket. Using hand motions, I asked the motorman what the sign said. He read it to me: "Trolley to Brooklyn Bridge. Three cents." So, spending my last three pennies, I rode the trolley to Brooklyn Bridge. After getting off the trolley, I sat on the steps of a public building, trying to decide what to do. Across the street, I saw a large sign with a mug of frothing beer for five cents and free lunch. It was noon, and I was getting very hungry, so I decided to see if I could get something to eat. I went in, asked the proprietor for work, and attempted to explain that this was the only way I could earn enough for lunch. The owner was sympathetic and very kind to this young immigrant with rudimentary English. He insisted that I sit down, and served me soup, then roast beef, and anything else I wanted. After I had eaten, this kind person sent me off with good wishes.

Leaving the lunchroom, I walked down the street and decided to ask for a job in a small store. As soon as I walked in, the proprietor, who was Jewish, approached me, eager to sell me "a suit? some nice shoes?" thinking I was a customer. When I told him I was there to see if there was any work I could do, the man had me clean out his basement and paid me 50 cents. Then, he introduced me to the other shopkeepers on the block, and I cleared out old newspapers, cleaned, and did anything else that I was asked to do. I earned 17 dollars in one week, and proceeded down the next street, enjoying the feeling of my new prosperity.

I even took a job cleaning spittoons—large brass things that needed cleaning and polishing. It was a little repulsive, but I was

willing to do anything to support myself honestly. The propri-
etress of the bar liked me and asked me to stay on as a permanent
worker, but I declined and explored another street—looking for
something else to do. I stopped to admire the spotless display in
the window of a candy store. The chocolates were presented in
neat rows in crystal dishes and were arranged on velvet and
satin-covered trays. Standing in front of this store, I said aloud
in Greek, "*Ti na kano tora?*" ("Now, what shall I do?") Out of
nowhere, a robust man appeared at my elbow. He startled me
when he asked "*Tinous paithi eisai*?" ("Whose son are you?")

Without thinking, I answered, "*Tou patera mou. Poios allos
na eimai?*" ("My father's, whose do you think?") The man's
response took me by surprise. "I am looking for a boy to work
for me. I don't suppose you would be interested?"

"I'm your boy!" I replied immediately. I worked at his candy
store for many months. The man's wife was pleasant, and kept a
clean home with an extra room for me and with bathroom that I
could use.

Once, when I was working in a candy store in Connecticut,
a young fellow called me an SOB, so I hit him. The man called
the police, so I took off my apron and started to leave. As the
officers entered, they passed me, not recognizing me without my
apron, so I told them who I was. A trial was scheduled, but it was
postponed while the police checked to see whether I had a
record. I did not, so I appeared before a judge. My boss brought
in witnesses who testified as to what had happened. I admitted
that I had walloped the man because—without provocation—he
had called me a bad name. I said that I would do it again if I was
insulted again. The judge fined me one dollar and dismissed the
case.

I was very devout, and traveled miles out of my way to
attend the nearest Greek Orthodox Church in Manhattan on Sundays. I also attended lectures in New York whenever I learned
that they were free. One night, I heard a man speak, saying,
"There is no God." This shocked me. No one had ever suggested
such a thing before. Later on, I attended a lecture entitled, "God
Is Love." I decided to learn about every major religion, and went

to the Public Library on Forty-Second Street where I painstakingly read about Zarathustra, Judaism, Buddhism, Islam, and every other religious belief I could find.

This immense library became my schoolroom. I was impressed by Victor Hugo's "*Les Miserables,*" and I read every book the librarian suggested. I wrote down the words I did not know on slips of paper and gave them to her to translate for me.

One summer, I worked odd jobs at Brighton Beach. This was a vacation spot of the rich people from Flatbush (a very nice neighborhood in Brooklyn).The mother of Averell Harriman was one of the guests at the hotel where I worked. Her son later became the governor of New York and a presidential candidate for the Democratic party. Noticing that I always read in my spare time, Mrs. Harriman gave me some pacifist-anarchist literature. At the time the United States was fighting World War I. One pamphlct was titled "War, What for?" Its cover appealed to my pacifist sentiments because it showed the gruesome effects of war. I liked the pamphlet so much that I sent for copies and started giving them out to people I knew were in sympathy with me.

My job at Brighton Beach was selling water. That is, I was given a recipe: mix one quart of orange juice with five gallons of water and sell it as an orange drink. The owners made more money than the exclusive restaurant at the Pagoda Hotel across the way. When I first arrived in Brighton Beach, I had applied for a job at this restaurant, since the owner had come from my village, and he would know of my family and my background. He refused me, saying "What do you know? You don't know anything."

He was a large, sloppy man, a showy type, who wore diamond rings and a stickpin in his tie, and boasted about his possessions. I could not understand how a man like that could have a nice business. His restaurant was always busy; a satin rope was placed across the main entrance to indicate that only those with reservations could enter. Evidently, he and his wife were poor managers in one way or another, and eventually lost their business and their money. One day, a few years later, I received a shipment of cheese from my village; one head of cheese was to be delivered to the former owner of the restaurant. I was doing well in my own candy store at the time. I asked a customer who was a good friend to lend me his chauffeur for a few hours. The chauffeur drove my car; I delivered the cheese to the flat where the man now lived. He was so impressed by my apparent success that he called me a few day later to borrow money from me!

Working odd jobs at Brighton Beach and saving my money, I had amassed $1,000. From what I had seen, I could do just as well as anybody else by going into business for myself. So, I decided that either I was going to make money or I was going to live like a man I had met in Central Park. We had sat next to each other on a park bench and started talking. The man told me that there never was any need to worry about making a living. He was clean and well-dressed, and spoke as though he were well-educated. He then rose from the bench and said, "Let's get some breakfast." We headed for the subway, where the man held out his hat and rolled his eyes upwards to simulate a blind person. After a short time, he looked at the coins that had been tossed into his hat, and said, "Seventeen cents! Now we'll eat." So we walked to a bakery type delicatessen, where we bought bread, milk, and cheese, and took the food back to the park bench, and ate well. My companion wrapped the leftovers in a napkin and left it on the park bench. "For someone else who may be hungry," he said.

We talked some more. "How do you keep so clean," I asked him. "That, too, is easily solved," he replied. We walked down to the river where the structures of Columbia University had not yet reached. At that time, it was shaded by trees and fairly deserted. We bathed in the river and came out refreshed. In the evening, we again begged for money for our dinner, and then passed the time eating and talking. The man informed me that he went South in the winter, following the warm weather.

This man's story intrigued me because I had been disillusioned by the actions of one of my brothers, and a life with no ties, as a vagabond, appealed to me. I had enclosed a blank check in an envelope addressed to a man who was helping me with documents to become a citizen. I gave this check to my brother George to mail for me. George—assuming the man would fill in an amount that was more than I had expected—opened the envelope and wrote the check out to himself for $400! With this money, he and his wife opened their own business!

Later, I forgave George, since I had been partly in the wrong to offer a blank check to anyone. We were both looking for a business, and I asked him to be my partner in a candy store I wanted to lease in the town of Westwood, New Jersey, population 4,000. Although we each paid $1,000, I kept the lease in my name. The builder installed the best of everything: marble counter, soda fountain fixtures, overhead chandeliers. Because he trusted us to pay him on time, he sold us everything at cost, and we were able to open the newest, modern ice cream parlor in the area. The pure cream we used cost eight cents per gallon; it took one pint of cream to make a quart of ice cream, which sold for eighty cents a quart. The store was always busy. We made $5,000 in three months—$400 dollars a day, which was good money at that time. I began to notice that, as busy as we were, the bills were exceeding the money coming in. I suspected that George and his wife were helping themselves to our profits. One day, I overheard my sister-in-law Margaret whisper to George, who was at the cash register, "Look out, George. He's watching you!" I immediately fired her, and George decided that he too had to leave.

In my store, I spoke freely about my aversion to the war and became an outspoken conscientious objector. I continued to pass out the pamphlet, "War, What for?" to anyone who wanted one. One copy fell into the hands of a woman, who sent it to her nephew who was stationed at a training camp. Of all places to send it—an army camp! I had not realized the seriousness of my actions. With a war in progress, it was treasonous to publish and circulate anti-war materials. The pamphlet was brought to the attention of Army brass, who traced it back to me.

I had run out of copies and was unable to get more. One day, the mayor's son came in and asked me if I had more copies. He then said, "There are some men in dad's office who are quite interested in those pamphlets, Peter. They sent me to get a copy for them. They're from the FBI, and I think they are coming to see you."

When the FBI questioned me, I told them the truth: I believed—as did Mrs. Harriman—that war was evil. The agents wanted to search my store, but I knew enough to tell them that before they could do so, they needed a warrant. That night, I saw from my bedroom window that someone was smoking cigarettes in a deserted shack across the street that had been a realtor's office. I thought it was some poor guy who had had a spat with his wife. Later, I learned that it had been FBI agents, who were watching to see whether I threw out the pamphlets or was passing them out.

A few days later, a big meeting took place in the town auditorium where it was decided that everyone would boycott my store. Boycott! I had never heard this word. Well, for a couple of days, not even the alley cats would come in. But then people from neighboring towns kept patronizing my store—those who did not know about the boycott— so business remained steady. One Sunday, despite the boycott, the place was jammed. Some people came to ask me about buying it. When they offered me a good price, I sold it on the spot!

I then went to Ridgewood, which was about five miles from Westwood, and purchased a candy store that was for sale by two brothers. The owner of the local lumber yard came in one day and announced, "I know why you left Westwood! And I know why you're here! Don't you try any of your funny stuff, or we'll throw you out of town!" It wasn't long afterwards that I was asked to donate to the building fund for a new hospital. Not knowing what was expected of me, I decided this was a good cause and pledged $500. When the owner of the lumber yard learned about my contribution, he came to the store and told me how impressed he was by my generosity and apologized for what he had said earlier.

When I settled in Summit, New Jersey in 1923, customers came out of their way braving traffic and hard-to-find parking spaces for coffee ice cream sodas, and other specialties made at our soda fountain. Alcoholic beverages had been outlawed during Prohibition, and people were substituting the new carbonated drinks: soda water mixed with chocolate, vanilla and fruit syrups and freshly-churned ice cream. The ice cream parlor was a star of the Roarin' Twenties.

One of my good customers, Mrs. Purina, gave me literature promoting Wendell Willkie for President. Someone else gave me Franklin Delano Roosevelt pamphlets. I decided to give Mrs. Purina some of the socialist literature. She was furious! What she didn't say! I clammed up and didn't open my mouth. She was so hot under the collar. A couple of weeks later, I answered the phone. It was Mrs. Purina. "Mr. Peter, Mr. Herbert Hoover is coming to my home for dinner. For dessert, I want ice cream in the shape of roses. You are the only one who can do this."

The ice cream roses had to match the color of the blood-red roses from her garden that she was using as centerpieces. She brought me one of her roses as a sample. One of the most difficult colors to copy using food coloring was that particular red. I experimented with a variety of color mixes, but the ice cream did not match the color she wanted. At last, I came up with a solution. I coated the inside of each mold with a thin layer of raspberry ice, and then filled the molds with vanilla ice cream. When they were unmolded, they exactly matched the color of her roses.

Mrs. Purina bought 65 of these ice cream roses for 60 cents apiece. This was quite expensive, but I always gave good value. People in the 1920s who had money were willing to pay for luxuries such as quality ice cream and chocolates.

The People

Demetrios Louvis and Magdalene Louvis,

Parents of:	(Anglicized)
Andonis	A. D.
Spiros	Spiros
Yiannis	died on Albanian front
Georgios	George
Theophanes	Theo
Peter	Peter
Arista	Arista
Stavros	Steve
Soterios	Wilbur
Ourania	Irene
Eleni	Helen; Elaine
Leonidas	Leonidas

Despina Louvis
Yiannis Louvis

Sister of Magdalene, wife of
Demetrios' cousin

Parents of:

Eva
Sophia
Nikos
Stratis

Kyrios Andonis Zacharias	Chief of rural police
Kyria Amalia Zacharias	His wife
Parents of:	
Kostas	
Georgios	
Menis	
Paulos	
Theia Dina Arnopoulos	Sister of Andonis Zacharias
Kyrios Arnopoulos	Her husband

Neighbors and Friends

Theia Xenia	Elderly neighbor
Heracles	
Agamemnon	Her two sons
Kyria Stamata	Outspoken lady
Kyria Aliki	Told fortunes
Phillipas	Her grandson
Kyria Olga Hatzakos	Recently moved to Bordonia
Eugenia	Her daughter
Christos	Her son, a waiter in Alexandria
Elias Andamas	Shoemaker, widower
Demarchos Alexandros	Mayor; a leading citizen
Kyria Alexandros	His wife
Pater Georgios	Village priest
Presbytera	His wife
Thanasis Paladinos	Matchmaker
Pantelis Kanaris	Shepherd; flute-player
Telemachus	His lame son
Petros	His flirtatious son
Kyrios Danzos	Farmer
Roula	His daughter

Vasilakis	Owner of the olive press
Georgios	Mule driver
Kyrios Diogenes Hatzis	Rug merchant from Athens
Kyrios Dinos Rolas	Suitor from Egypt
Ibrahim	His servant

In America

George Louvis	Eleni's brother; meets mother and sisters at Ellis Island
Peter Louvis	Eleni's brother; meets them in Ohio
A. D. and Viola Louvis	Eleni's oldest brother and his wife (Lancaster, Ohio)
Arista and James Poulos	Eleni's older sister and husband (Lancaster, Ohio)
Soterios Louvis	Eleni's brother
Barbara Louvis	His wife
Anastasia Bacas	Marries John Roupas
Angelos Bacas	Oldest brother; marries Doula Metrakos
Olga Bacas	Marries Basilis Titsis
William Bacas	Bill; marries Eleni Louvis
Aris Bacas	Marries Mabel Clouser
John Bacas	Marries Isidora Sakellariades

Glossary

In the text of *My White Clouds*, words and idioms in Greek are italicized, with the English meaning provided after each. They are written phonetically as they would be pronounced by most Greek speakers. My sources were *The Oxford New Greek Dictionary*, Oxford University Press, 2008, and my parents.

Akou! — Listen!

Alithos Anesti! — Truly He Has Risen! (in response to Christos Anesti!)

aloni — stone threshing floor

ambeli — vineyard

anastasi — resurrection

antidoron — bread blessed by the priest and offered at the end of the service

Apayorevete! — It is forbidden!

apoyeumatino — afternoon nap

apothikes — storage places

arravones — engagement

bakaliaros — dried codfish or hake

baklava — layered pastry filled with nuts and honey

baoulo — trunk

berraka — lookout post

boukouvala — slices of bread dipped into warm olive oil

bouzouki — guitar-like instrument

caffenion — coffee shop

christopsomo — sweet bread served at Christmas

Christos Anesti! — Christ Has Risen!

diliterion — poison

demosios dromos — county road

despinis — Miss

dodekaimeron — Twelve Days of Christmas

dolmathes — stuffed grape leaves

eikosi — twenty

Ela! — Come here!

elaiotrivio — where olives are processed to make oil

ennea — nine

entaxi! — all right!

epitaphios — sacred representation during the Good Friday procession

erimoklisia — rural chapel

esperinos — vespers

exetasis — examination

exi — six

exo — exit, outside

exomologia — confession

fasolada — bean stew

fasolia nerovrasta — steamed beans

feta — white, semisoft cheese

floyera — flute-like instrument; also a pastry

fostanee — ankle-length skirt

fournos — oven

fourtalia — omelet with potatoes and sausage from Andros

frangosika — fruit of the cactus plant

gliko koutaliou — sweet preserves of fruit served on a spoon

gymnasion — secondary school

gymnasterion — school gym

gynaika — woman; wife

hayati — porch or balcony

heimoniatiko — winter room

hirino — ham preserved in olive oil, red wine, and spices

horta — boiled leafy greens

horostasio — level area for dancing

Hronia polla! — Live a long life! (Congratulations!)

kallikanzaros — goblin

Kalophayeto! — Bon appetit! (Enjoy your meal!)

karidies — walnut trees

kasela — storage chest

Katalavenis? — Do you understand?

kathiste — be seated

katifes — marigolds

katoyi — underground storage room

katsika — female goat

katsikaki — young goat; kid

kefalotiri — head cheese

kerasi — cherry

klarino — clarinet

kokoretsi — grilled organ meats

Komitis — Halley's Comet (long-haired star)

kopela — young lady

koulourakia — round or twisted butter cookies

koumbaros — godfather; best man

koumbara — godmother

kounellakia — bunny rabbits

kourambiethes — shortbread cookies topped with powdered sugar

koutsonilios — hopscotch

kreatopolion — meat market, butcher shop

kyria — Mrs., woman, lady

kyrios, kyrie — Mr., Sir, gentleman

lihnizoume — winnowing wheat

loukoumi — firm, jelled confection, also known as Turkish Paste

loukoumathes — honey puffs, similar to fritters

loutroveio — laundry house

mageritsa — egg-lemon soup with tripe and dill

mantili — kerchief to cover the hair

mastiha — anise-flavored liqueur

mati — The Evil Eye

Megali Paraskevi — Great and Holy Friday

Megalo Sabato — Great and Holy Saturday

meltemi — hot summer winds

mitera — mother

mizithra — an unsalted cheese

Musulmanos — Muslim

miroloyes — women mourners

nai — yes

nifi — bride; sister-in-law

ohi — no

oktapodi — octopus

oli mazi — all together

ortikia — tiny, preserved quails, a delicacy

Panayia — All Holy Virgin Mary

paparounes — poppies

papou, pappou — grandfather

Pascha — Easter

Pater, Papas — honorific title for a Greek Orthodox priest

paximathia — zwieback toast

pazari — bazaar, county market

peiratis — pirate

pente — five

peninta — fifty

pentovolo — game of jacks using five stones

Peraste! — Come in!

petropolemos — rock throwing competition

phlomos — anaesthetizing weed

plateia — village square

pontiki — mouse

pragmatefthes — peddler

protimaiou — first day of May

proxenitis — matchmaker

psaltis — chanter in church

psiloi — fleas

psomi — bread

raki — distilled liquor similar to a Turkish beverage of the same name

reekie — purple heather

retsina — resinated wine

sapouni — soap

sarakosti — forty days before Easter Sunday

saranta — forty

skili — dog

sphentones — slingshots

stragalia — chickpeas

Sto Onoma tou Theou! — In the Name of God!

syrtos — traditional Greek dance

taverna — tavern

telos pandon — anyway

tessera — four

Theos — God (not to be confused with Theo, a man's name)

Theia — Aunt

Theios — Uncle

thymari — thyme

trahana — pebble-sized pasta

trianta — thirty

trifylli — cloves

tsai — tea

tsamiko — traditional Greek dance

tsipouro — a strong liquor distilled from grape skins; also called raki

tourbani — turban

vasilopeta — sweetened yeast bread with a hidden coin, served on Saint Basil's Day

veeka — narrow-necked terra cotta jug to hold water

visinatha — beverage made from cherry preserves mixed in cold water

vlita — edible greens

voli — game of marbles

yaithouraki — donkey

yiayia — grandmother

Yiasou! — Hello! To Your Health! Goodbye!

yelekaki — embroidered vest

Zephyros — West Wind

Recipes

F resh, appetizing foods and the manner in which good cooks prepare them have always been an important expression of Greek
culture. The recipes that follow reflect a few of Eleni's family favor-
ites. She did not mention this in her story, but all who dined at Eleni's
table for over seventy years enjoyed wonderful meals.

Arni Psito (Roast Leg of Spring Lamb)

Avgolemono Soupa (Egg-Lemon Soup)

Fasolada (Green Beans in Sauce)

Giouvetsi (Vegetable Casserole)

Horta (Boiled Greens)

Koulourakia (Cookie Twists)

Loukoumathes (Honey Puffs)

Makaronada (Traditional Macaroni)

Milopita (Apple Pie)

Psari Plaki (Fish Baked in Sauce)

Spanakopita (Spinach Pie)

Arni Psito (*Roast Leg of Spring Lamb*)
Serves 8-10

Easter dinner at Bill and Elaine's included lamb with lemon potatoes, salad, vegetables, and strawberry shortcake.

One 7-pound to 8-pound leg	*2 tablespoons dried oregano*
of spring lamb	*1 tablespoon salt*
½ cup wine	*1 tablespoon pepper*
¼ cup olive oil	*3 lemons*
1 medium onion, chopped	*Fresh mint leaves*

1. Mix together the wine, olive oil, onion, and 1 tablespoon oregano and pour over the leg of lamb. Marinate overnight in the
   refrigerator, turning once.
2. Drain and save the marinade. Place the meat in a roasting pan
   that is 2 inches deep.
3. Rub salt, pepper, and the second tablespoon of oregano over the
   entire leg.
4. Squeeze the juice of two lemons over the meat; add ¼ cup water
   and any leftover marinade.
5. Cover loosely with foil.
6. Roast at 350°F, 30 minutes per pound, about 4 hours.
7. Baste occasionally; add water so the bottom of the pan is not
   crusty. The meat should be well done, but juicy, and falling
   from the bone.
8. Serve the roast lamb garnished with lemon slices and fresh mint
   leaves.

Avgolemono Soupa (Egg-Lemon Soup)
SERVES 4–6

Eleni made this with rice; now it often is made with orzo.

4 cups chicken broth
½ cup orzo
2 eggs
*½ cup lemon juice (about
2 lemons)*

*1 tablespoon flour mixed with
2 tablespoons cold water*
Salt and pepper to taste

1. Bring the broth to a boil in a 2-quart pot.
2. Add the orzo and lower heat to simmer for about 8 minutes. The orzo should be al dente.
3. In a 4-cup bowl, whisk together the eggs, the flour-and-water mixture, and the lemon juice.
4. Turn heat off, but do not remove the pot. Ladle about ½ cup of the very hot broth into the bowl of egg-lemon-flour, and quickly blend with a whisk or spoon; continue ladling and stirring the broth into the egg-lemon-flour until the mixture is hot. Avoid ladling in too much orzo.
5. Turn the heat to medium high, and begin ladling the heated egg-lemon mixture back into the large pot of broth and orzo, stirring constantly and gently.
6. Continue heating and stirring. As soon as the soup begins to bubble, remove it from the heat and stir occasionally as it cools. Add salt and pepper to taste.
7. The soup is best if allowed to stand 15 minutes before serving. Keep warm with a lid. If made ahead and refrigerated, the soup should be reheated but not brought to a boil.

Fasolada (*Green Beans in Sauce*)
SERVES 6

Whether they are green beans, fava, or lentils, *fasolia* add nitrogen to the soil and thrive among the rocks of the Peloponnesos. When cooked with onions, tomatoes, and herbs, *fasolia* are as delicious as they are nutritious.

2 pounds green beans	*¾ cup water*
1 medium onion	*1 tablespoon fresh mint*
2 tablespoons olive oil	*½ teaspoon dried oregano*
4-ounce can tomato sauce	*Salt and pepper*

1. Wash and remove strings from the beans, then cut into 2-inch pieces.
2. Dice the onion; chop the mint.
3. In a large saucepan, cook the onions in olive oil 5 minutes until limp.
4. Add tomato sauce and water and bring to a boil.
5. Add green beans, salt, pepper, mint, and oregano.
6. Turn heat to simmer, and cook until beans are done, about 20 minutes.

Giouvetsi (*Vegetable Casserole*)
SERVES 10-12

Eleni prepared this casserole of fresh vegetables every year for *Ayios Basilios*, Bill's nameday celebration on January 1. In some regions the name *giouvetsi* refers to a meat or pasta dish, but this was Eleni's method.

2 diced onions	*¼ cup olive oil*

Group I Vegetables
Wash, peel, remove strings if necessary, and cut into 1-inch pieces:

1 cup celery	*1 cup green beans*
1 cup carrots	*3 peeled potatoes*

Group II Vegetables
Wash, peel, and cut into 2-inch pieces:

1 eggplant	*½ cup chopped fresh mint*
3 onions	*1 tablespoon dried oregano*
3 small zucchini	*Salt and pepper to taste*
1 garlic clove, mashed	*¾ cup olive oil, as needed*
1 8-ounce can tomato puree mixed with ¼ cup water	

1. In a large skillet that will accommodate the ingredients in Group I, sauté the 2 diced onions in 2 tablespoons olive oil.
2. Cook and stir until onions are soft.
3. Add Group I vegetables and cook for 15 minutes, adding olive oil or water and stirring occasionally.
4. Coat the bottom of a 9 × 13 × 2 roasting pan with olive oil.
5. Arrange Group II vegetables in three layers.

6. Top each layer with ⅓ of the Group I vegetables, 2 tablespoons olive oil, 2 tablespoons tomato puree with water, salt, pepper, mint, and oregano.

7. Pour the remaining olive oil and tomato puree mixture over all; let stand for 30 minutes.

8. Bake at 350°F for one hour, or until the carrots are tender. After the first half hour in the oven, lift portions of the bottom layer with a spatula, so it does not brown too quickly.

9. Cover lightly with foil if the top begins to brown.

Horta (*Boiled Greens*)
SERVES 4–6

Those who yearn for a plate of *horta* may call ahead to order it at a good Greek restaurant. But while some often enjoy the dish at home, *horta* does not have admirers everywhere. Once, when Eleni's nine-year-old grandson Jim invited a friend to dinner, the friend responded, "I'd love to have some wonderful Greek food!" Jim's reply was, "How can you say that? Greek food is mainly weeds!"

2 pounds of greens such as dandelion greens, leafy endive, escarole, kale, beet greens, vlita
½ teaspoon salt

8 cups of water in a large pot
4 tablespoons olive oil
Juice of one lemon
Salt and pepper to taste

1. Cut off the tough and sandy stems; wash and rinse the greens several times to remove all sand and soil.
2. Drain the greens and drop into the pot of boiling water.
3. Add salt and stir.
4. Cook until the thickest stalks are fork-tender, from 10 to 20 minutes.
5. Drain; the water can be saved for use as stock.
6. Serve the greens well-done but still green, dressed with olive oil, lemon juice, and salt and pepper.

Koulourakia (*Cookie Twists*)
3 DOZEN COOKIES

Beloved *Yiayia* Lula, a close friend of Eleni, kept an 18-inch high glass jar full of *koulourakia* in her pantry in Louisville, Kentucky. She made the cookies small, so that her grandchildren could reach into the jar and take a few at a time.

¾ pound butter (3 sticks)

4 tablespoons shortening (Crisco)

1 cup sugar

½ cup unsweetened pineapple juice

1 teaspoon vanilla

2 tablespoons brandy

6–7 cups flour

3 teaspoons baking powder

1. Using a mixer or food processor, blend the butter, shortening, and sugar.
2. Carefully beat the liquids into the butter mixture.
3. Stir the baking powder into 6 cups of the flour.
4. Add the flour mixture to the butter mixture, gradually.
5. If the mixer begins to slow down, stop and mix by hand with a large wooden spoon.
6. The dough is ready when a small piece can be rolled out like a pencil and holds its shape.
7. Add up to 1 cup flour, if it is needed.
8. Take a piece of dough the size of a walnut and roll out into a 5-inch rod; bend it in the middle and twist right over left
9. Brush tops (see below) and bake at 350°F for 10–15 minutes until the tops are light brown.

Optional: For the traditional form, shape the pencil-sized dough into a ring and press the two ends, one over the other. Although considered an Easter cookie, *koulourakia* also can be served at Christmas as wreathes with small pieces of red and green citron pressed into the dough where the ends cross.

Before baking, for a shiny finish, brush the tops with an egg wash (a whole egg mixed with a teaspoon of water) and top with sesame seeds.

Loukoumathes (*Honey Puffs*)
ABOUT 3 DOZEN PUFFS

Barbara, Soterios's wife, passed this recipe on to her daughter, who sent scores of relatives and friends from her New Jersey home licking their fingers after being served a plate of these *loukoumathes* made by their *Theia* Kalliope.

About 6 cups of canola oil; follow deep-fryer directions

3 cups flour, sifted

2 packages dry yeast

¼ cup warm water, plus another ¼ cup

½ teaspoon salt

1 cup honey, warmed

ground cinnamon

1. Heat the oil according to the directions for the deep fryer. Dissolve and stir the yeast into ¼ cup of very warm water.
2. Add the yeast mixture to the flour and stir.
3. Mix in the salt and the remainder of the warm water to make a thin batter.
4. Let rise until bubbles form on top.
5. Drop one spoonful into the hot oil until it puffs up; if it browns too quickly, lower the heat.
6. Scrape spoon-sized pieces of dough into the oil, about four to six at a time, so they are not crowded and will cook evenly. They should be light golden, crisp outside, and soft inside.
7. Drain the puffs on paper towels; then arrange on a serving platter.
8. Spoon the warmed honey over them and dust with cinnamon.

Loukoumathes can be made several hours ahead without adding the honey, then reheated, dipped in warm honey, and sprinkled with cinnamon.

Makaronada (*Traditional Macaroni*)
SERVES 8

Visits to Eleni's brother Peter and his wife Eugenia in Summit, New Jersey, always featured platters of buttery *Makaronada*, and the best Chicken *Oreganato*—specialties that their children, Maggie and Anthony, continue to offer their guests.

1 pound macaroni (long spaghetti)
1 teaspoon salt
2 tablespoons olive oil

¼ pound butter
1 cup grated kefalotiri or parmesan cheese

1. Stir salt into a large pot of boiling water, add pasta, and cook for about 12 minutes; drain well.
2. Spread 2 tablespoons of the grated cheese over the bottom of a large serving platter.
3. Place half of the macaroni over the cheese. Drizzle half of the olive oil over the pasta and cover lightly with grated cheese.
4. Add the rest of the macaroni and drizzle with the rest of the olive oil.
5. Heat the butter until it foams, to a golden brown. Do not let it burn.
6. Cover the top layer with the grated cheese, and slowly pour the browned butter over all.

Milopita (*Apple Pie*)
SERVES 6–8

Pumpkin pies, lemon meringue pies, or apple pies were always the best when prepared by *Theia* Mabel, *Theia* Doula, *Theia* Doris, or mother. Bill's favorite was apple pie with "a little vanilla ice cream on top."

2 pie crusts, 9-inch rounds	*1 teaspoon cinnamon*
2 tablespoons butter	*½ teaspoon nutmeg*
7–8 apples	*1½ tablespoons minute tapioca*
¾ cup sugar	*2 tablespoons orange juice.*

1. Grease the bottom and sides of a 9-inch pie pan.
2. Fit one pie crust into the bottom of the pan.
3. Cut butter into small pieces and dot half over the pie crust.
4. Peel, core, and slice the apples into eighths and place in a large mixing bowl.
5. Toss and mix the apples, sugar, cinnamon, nutmeg, minute tapioca, and orange juice.
6. Fill the crust with the apple mixture.
7. Dot with the rest of the butter.
8. Cover with top crust; trim edges so there is a half-inch overlap; fold this around the moistened edges of the bottom crust, and crimp. Cut vents on the top crust.
9. Bake at 375°F for 45 minutes to 1 hour, or until juice bubbles through the vents and the top crust is light brown.

Psari Plaki (*Fish Baked in Sauce*)
SERVES 4

Fish was the usual fare on Fridays. For the children Eleni sauteed it because they liked that best. For company, though, she made fresh fish, *plaki*.

*2 pounds fish fillet, such as
flounder, cut into 4 pieces*

2 lemons

1 onion, diced

¼ cup olive oil

½ cup tomato sauce

¼ cup water

¼ cup carrots, diced

¼ cup celery, diced

1 clove of garlic, crushed

1 fresh tomato, sliced

1 teaspoon dried oregano

Sprigs of fresh dill and parsley

Salt and pepper

1. Preheat oven to 350°F.
2. Place the fish fillets in an attractive baking dish. Squeeze the juice of one lemon over all. Add salt and pepper, and set the fish aside.
3. In a large frying pan, heat the olive oil, add the onions, and sauté until soft, about 5 minutes. Mix in the carrots, celery, and garlic; then add the tomato sauce, water, and oregano; stir gently and simmer for 15 minutes, adding more water, if necessary.
4. Spoon the sauce over the fish and top with the tomato slices.
5. Bake for 30 to 40 minutes.
6. The sauce will reduce and the fish should be done. If too watery, spoon out some of the sauce and cook to thicken it in a saucepan. Garnish with lemon slices, dill, and parsley.

Spanakopita (*Spinach Pie*)
ONE 9 × 12 × 3 PAN SERVES 8–12

Whether served as an entrée or as an appetizer, spanakopita is a perennial favorite.

2 ten-ounce packages of
frozen spinach
1 medium onion
½ cup fresh parsley
¾ cup feta cheese
¼ cup grated parmesan
cheese

3 eggs
1 teaspoon dried oregano
Salt and pepper to taste
2 tablespoons butter melted
with 4 tablespoons olive oil
1 pound filo dough

1. Allow spinach to thaw and drain in a sieve while preparing the baking pan and the other ingredients.
2. Set oven at 350°F. Spray canola oil on the baking pan.
3. Chop the onion and cook in a frying pan with 1 tablespoon olive oil until soft, about 5 minutes.
4. Add the spinach and cook on medium until heated through, stirring occasionally.
5. Place the spinach in a mixing bowl.
6. Chop the parsley; cut the feta into small pieces, and beat the eggs.
7. Combine the parsley, feta, parmesan cheese, salt, pepper, and oregano with the eggs.
8. Fold the feta mixture into the spinach
9. Open the package of filo, and place the first piece on the bottom of the greased baking pan. Fold it in at the sides to fit the pan. Brush the filo lightly with the butter and oil mixture.
10. Follow with 6 more pieces of filo, brushing each one lightly with the oil mixture.
11. Spoon the spinach mixture on top of the last piece.

12. Top the spinach mixture with 7 more pieces of filo, each one brushed with oil. The last one should be neatly tucked under.

13. With a sharp knife, score the top layer of filo into serving sizes. Bake at 350°F for 35 to 45 minutes or until crisp and light brown.

Spanakopeta can be baked a day before serving. Store in a cool place, lightly covered. Reheat at 300°F for 15 to 30 minutes until the filling is hot and the top is crisp. The same filling can be used for triangle-shaped appetizers.

About the Author

D. G. Bacas is the daughter of Eleni Louvis Bacas, who tells her story in *My White Clouds*. The author was born and raised in Washington, DC, with her sister and two brothers. Ms. Bacas received her BA in Greek and English Literature at Radcliffe College. She has two children and five grandchildren and lives in Florida.

7287671R00162

Made in the USA
San Bernardino, CA
30 December 2013